God's PEOPLE?

ONE HUNDRED AND TEN CHARACTERS
IN THE STORY OF SCOTTISH RELIGION

ANDREW MONAGHAN

RADIO FORTH/MAX-AM

SAINT ANDREW PRESS
EDINBURGH

First published in 1991 by
SAINT ANDREW PRESS with RADIO FORTH/MAX-AM
121 George Street, Edinburgh EH2 4YN

ISBN 0 7152 0656 7

British Publication in Catalogue Data

A catalogue record for this book
is available from the British Library.

ISBN 0-7152-0656-7

This book is set in 11/12 pt Times

Cover design by Mark Blackadder

The details on the cover have been taken from the frieze of famous Scots by William Hole (1846-1917) which can be found along the four sides of the central hall of the National Portrait Gallery, Edinburgh.

Printed and Bound in Great Britain by
Athenaeum Press Ltd., Newcastle upon Tyne.

CONTENTS

	INTRODUCTION	vii
	ACKNOWLEDGMENTS	viii
	ILLUSTRATIONS	ix
1	NINIAN *Ninia the Bishop*	1
2	KENTIGERN *The Saint with most Dedications*	3
3	COLUMBA *'The Dove of the Church'*	6
4	BALDRED *The Hermit of the Bass Rock*	9
5	MARGARET *The Queen who changed Scots Psychology*	11
6	DAVID *'Ane Sair Sanct for the Crown'*	14
7	JOCELIN *The Monk who gave Glasgow a start*	17
8	ADAM *The Bible from Dryburgh*	20
9	WILLIAM MALVOISIN *What sort of Neighbour?*	23
10	DEVORGUILLA *From Balliol to Sweetheart*	26
11	BALDRED BISSET *Scotland's Defender*	28
12	JOHN DUNS SCOTUS *Dunce or Subtle Doctor?*	30
13	LAURENCE *Lindores makes its mark*	33
14	ROBERT HENRYSON *The Poet Teacher*	35
15	WILLIAM ELPHINSTONE *'Light from the North'*	37
16	ROBERT CARVER *Rogue Musician?*	39
17	PATRICK HAMILTON *Forerunner of the Scottish Reformation?*	41
18	GEORGE WISHART *Saint or 'Stiff-necked' Rabble-rouser?*	44
19	ELIZABETH ADAMSON *Woman behind the scenes*	47
20	MARY OF GUISE *Power and Piety*	49
21	JOHN KNOX *Reformation from Abroad*	52
22	MARION OGILVY *'Behind every successful man ...'*	55
23	JAMES HENRISOUN *The Visionary Merchant*	57
24	NINIAN WINZET *The Power of the Pen*	60
25	WILLIAM BROCAS AND JAMES YOUNG *Hammermen divided*	62
26	JOHN BLACK *Catholic preaching changes—too late!*	64
27	JAMES HAMILTON *Vacillator or Survivor?*	66
28	GEORGE GORDON *'Pope of the North'*	69

29 JOHN ERSKINE OF DUN
  The Reformer who spanned Four Generations 71

30 MARY, QUEEN OF SCOTS
  The Woman of Destiny becomes its Victim 73

31 ALEXANDER GORDON *A Curious Bishop* 76

32 REGENT MORTON *Rapacious Lord or Pious Reformer?* 78

33 JOHN CARSWELL *Reform goes Gaelic* 81

34 MAITLAND OF LETHINGTON
  Evil Genius by Nature as well as by Name? 84

35 LORD JAMES *'Blessed are those who die in the Lord'* 87

36 JOHN DURIE *Monk turned Rabble-rousing Reformer* 90

37 GILBERT KENNEDY
  Dithering on the Catholic-Protestant divide 92

38 ANDREW MELVILLE
  The True Architect of Scottish Presbyterianism 94

39 GEORGE BUCHANAN *Poet, Historian or Revolutionary?* 97

40 JOHN WELSH *Married to John Knox's Daughter* 100

41 JOHN OGILVIE *A Catholic Martyr* 102

42 SAMUEL RUTHERFORD
  Brilliant Bigot or Caring Pastor? 105

43 ROBERT LEIGHTON
  Saintly Bishop or Ecclesiastical Opportunist? 107

44 JAMES SHARP *Murdered on Magus Moor* 109

45 MARGARET LAUCHLINSON AND MARGARET WILSON
  Drowned for their Faith 111

46 ISOBEL YOUNG *Strangled and burned* 113

47 ANNE *God's Duchess?* 116

48 THOMAS NICHOLSON *Bishop 'in his Grand Climacteric'* 118

49 ROBERT BARCLAY *The Quaker Theologian* 121

50 EDWARD HICKHORNGILL
  'Now you see him, now you don't!' 123

51 WILLIAM CARSTARES *'Cardinal Carstares'* 125

52 ALEXANDER SHIELDS
  From the Bass Rock to Jamaica 127

53 EBENEZER ERSKINE *Man of the People?* 129

54 ROBERT KEITH *Factious Priest or Builder of Bridges?* 132

55 JAMES KIRKWOOD *A Moderate among Extremists* 134

56 THOMAS GILLESPIE *'God chooses the Weak'* 136
57 DUGALD BUCHANAN *The Gaelic Bard* 138
58 WILLIAM ROBERTSON *History teaches* 141
59 JOHN ERSKINE
    'Shall I go to War with my American Brethren?' 143
60 ALEXANDER CARLYLE
    'The Grandest Demigod I ever saw' 145
61 JOHN HOME *God or the Devil?* 147
62 JOHN WITHERSPOON *The American Connection* 149
63 ARCHIBALD McLEAN *From Glassite to Scotch Baptist* 151
64 ELSPETH BUCHAN *Woman of Revelation* 153
65 DAVID DALE *Christian Capitalist* 155
66 LADY GLENORCHY *Lady Bountiful?* 157
67 HENRY MONCRIEFF WELLWOOD
    'A Force to be reckoned with' 159
68 ROBERT BURNS *Saint or Sinner?* 161
69 THE HALDANE BROTHERS
    From the Deep Sea to Evangelism 164
70 GREVILLE EWING *Congregational Man of Peace* 166
71 JAMES HOGG *The Shepherd Sinner* 168
72 THOMAS McCRIE *Light from the 'Auld Lichts'* 170
73 ANDREW SCOTT
    Building for the Future or Exploiting the Poor? 172
74 JOHN PHILIP
    The Kirkcaldy Weaver who fought for the Blacks 174
75 JOHN LEE *In the Tradition of St Luke* 176
76 ANDREW THOMSON *Evangelical but Enlightened* 178
77 THOMAS CHALMERS *Together or Apart?* 180
78 CHRISTOPHER ANDERSON
    Charlotte Baptist Chapel and more 183
79 DONALD SAGE
    Man of the People in Sutherland 185
80 EDWARD IRVING *'The Spirit moves ... '* 187
81 THOMAS AND JANE CARLYLE
    Twin Pillars of the New Faith? 190
82 JOHN McLEOD CAMPBELL
    'Atonement and Assurance for all' 193

83 HUGH MILLER *The Mass Media hits the Kirk* 195
84 THOMAS GUTHRIE *Preacher of the Ragged School* 198
85 ALEXANDER DUFF *The First Kirk Missionary* 201
86 JAMES BEGG *Happy Homes for Working Men* 204
87 NORMAN MACLEOD *'Whole Salvation not Soul Salvation'* 206
88 DAVID LIVINGSTONE *' ... I presume'* 208
89 ALEXANDER PENROSE FORBES
    'Slumming it in Dundee' 211
90 JOHN TULLOCH *Moderately Depressed* 214
91 ROBERT RAINY *'Principal Rainy'* 216
92 MARGARET OLIPHANT *A Scots Victorian Feminist* 218
93 DONALD MACFARLANE *The Timid Giant* 220
94 LORD OVERTOUN
Capitalist Monster or Christian Gentleman? 223
95 WILLIAM ROBERTSON SMITH
    Intellectual Colossus who paid the price 225
96 MARY SLESSOR *The Red-haired Firebrand* 227
97 HENRY DRUMMOND *Free Kirker or Free Thinker?* 229
98 SIR GEORGE ADAM SMITH
    'The Historical Geographer of the Bible' 231
99 GEORGE JACKSON
    'For the Making of Good Men and Women' 233
100 MARGARET SINCLAIR *'The Scaffie's Daughter'* 236
101 ERIC LIDDELL *Running for God* 239
102 JOHN WHEATLEY *Irish—and what's worse, a Catholic!* 242
103 JAMES BARR
Home Rule, Pacifism and Socialism in the Kirk 245
104 JOHN WHITE *A Man of Contradictions* 247
105 ANDREW JOSEPH McDONALD
    'The Archbishop who relished a Fight' 250
106 WALTER MURRAY *The Kirk and Scottish Home Rule* 252
107 THOMAS TAYLOR *The Builder of 'a Scottish Lourdes'* 254
108 JOE HOLDSWORTH OLDHAM
    Christians together to change the World 257
109 THE BAILLIE BROTHERS *Brotherly Inspiration* 259
110 ARCHIE CRAIG
    'The Prophet is never appreciated in his own Country' 261

INTRODUCTION

THIS book is the natural sequel to *God's Scotland?* by Anne Pagan, the book of the radio series which revised a great many myths of Scottish church history, thanks to the help of Radio Forth and the history experts of the Scottish History Department, University of Edinburgh (and their colleagues throughout Scotland and abroad). *God's People?* is the book of yet another independent radio series originating this time in MAX-AM, and looking at 110 characters discerned more or less clearly from the long and often only partially glimpsed centuries of Scottish church history. The expertise is that of the Scottish History department of the University of Edinburgh in conjunction with their colleagues at New College. Professor Barrow, Dr Lynch and Professor Brown are particularly vital to this project and all the other experts who offered their help so generously. The choice of characters and the research is that of the history experts. I would like to express my thanks to all the contributors individually for their time and patience; and to Joan Oswald for her efficiency and hard work in conducting the radio interviews.

Acknowledgment is also due to Tom Steele at the radio station for his constant support, Anne Pagan for the inspiration of the original idea, Mhairi for help with typing and the professionals at Saint Andrew Press for making this book possible and ensuring it became an attractive and efficiently produced reality.

The more I learned about the characters in *God's People?*, and the more I struggled to capture a little of their rich diversity and individual bids to make some sense of this crazy world, the more I became convinced of how much we can and should learn from every one of them. I'm conscious I may have failed to do them justice, often just narrowly failed to make them come alive, but I hope the book will help in some way to give you at least a glimpse. Be encouraged to search further! The chapters include some sources for further study, and at least a beginning point to look a little deeper into the intriguing people we have touched upon.

ANDREW MONAGHAN, *Edinburgh 1991*

ACKNOWLEDGMENTS

BOTH the series on MAX-AM and this book were made possible by the research and generous co-operation of the following:

Dr John W M Bannerman, University of Edinburgh
Professor Geoffrey W S Barrow, University of Edinburgh
Dr David Bebbington, University of Stirling
Professor Stewart J Brown, New College
Dr Ian Campbell, University of Edinburgh
Professor Alex C Cheyne, former principal of New College
Dr Tristram Clarke, Scottish Record Office
Reverend Mark Dilworth, archivist of the Roman Catholic Church
Wendy Doran, Head of History, Trinity Academy, Edinburgh
Reverend Ian Dunlop, retired minister of the Church of Scotland
Dr John Durkan, University of Glasgow
Dr Richard Finlay, University of Edinburgh
Dr Julian Goodare, University of Edinburgh
Revd Roger Greaves, Methodist minister
Dr Christine Johnston, assistant archivist of the Roman Catholic
    Church
Mark Loughlin, University of Edinburgh
Dr Michael Lynch, University of Edinburgh
James McLeod, post-graduate student, New College
Professor John McQueen, School of Scottish Studies
Dr Rosalind K Marshall, National Portrait Gallery
Dr Donald Meek, University of Edinburgh
Dr Marcus Merriman, University of Lancaster
Dr Derek Murray, St Columba's Hospice
Hugh Piper, University of Glasgow
Dr Andrew C Ross, New College
George Rosie, journalist
Revd Ken Roxborough, Baptist minister
Norman Shead, head of History, Hutchieson's, Glasgow
John Simpson, University of Edinburgh

Revd (and Mrs) F J Stewart, retired minister of the Church of
    Scotland
Revd Rowan Strong, post-graduate student, New College
Ken Stewart, post-graduate student, New College
Dr Elizabeth Templeton, freelance theologian
Professor J B Torrance, New College
Professor Andrew Walls, New College

ILLUSTRATIONS

The illustrations in this book have taken from the following
sources. The publisher acknowledges the kind lending of such
material (where relevant) with thanks:

1
NINIAN
Ninia the Bishop

AT the time of writing, arguments still rage as to whether Ninia—or *Ninian* as he came to be known in the twelfth century—was at the height of his vigour around AD 400, 450, 500 or even 550. One previous argument now settled is whether Ninia came from the Celtic monastic or Roman diocesan tradition. It is now agreed that he was a bishop in charge of an area (a *diocese*) rather than a monastery. Nonetheless, the excavations at Whithorn are presently at an exciting stage, determining the date of monastic earth beds in the style of a monastery garden, and split tree-trunk coffins which parallel those in Armagh in Patrick's foundation. Most important will be the nature and dating of the rectangular buildings which clearly illustrate the British nature of the foundation.

The argument for the earlier date of 400 comes mainly from Bede's *Historia Ecclesiastica* (*c* 731) in which he presumably gives the local tradition as related by his friend Pechthelm, the Anglian Bishop of *Candida Casa* ('White House' in the Roman manner, perhaps lime-coloured stone) at Whithorn. A Latin poem later in the century gives more details. The wider historical context rules out the date of 550 and seems to favour a date of either 400 or 450. Archaeology may give a more definite answer, but meantime many of the arguments rest on place-names and analysis of handed-on stories.

Whatever the dates, the evidence of Bede, place-names and folk stories help us understand much more clearly the wider importance of Ninian. He seems to have been a local Wigtownshire man, born at the fringe of the Roman Empire which by his time had become officially Christian. He was sent to train for the priesthood somewhere on the continent: early records suggest Rome, for travel there was much more feasible than it had been 100 years before. He obviously also acquired some familiarity with St Martin of Tours. On his return, his appointment as bishop was to organise the official sort of Christian diocese in the south-west of

Scotland. He seems to have been the first person on record to have been sent to organise Christianity beyond the wall (Hadrian's).

The question of whether Ninian and his followers did convert some of the southern Picts was confused for some time by the discrediting of a vague statement by Patrick to Coroticus, and indications in later documents. Evidence from place-names is a much more sure foundation for a role with Picts and this evidence doubles Ninian's significance at a stroke. The key place-name is ECCLES, the word for 'a church in British' (ancient Welsh). Thus *Eccles* in Dumfriesshire and in Berwickshire; *Eaglesham* in Renfrewshire; and an *Eccles* at Stirling. All in all these indications are obvious right across the area up to the Antonine Wall and beyond in the east up to Aberdeen (there's no evidence in the north-west).

Another source of information used by scholars to attempt to flesh out the Ninian story is a very fascinating one concerning two characters, Niniau and Pebiau, with one living north of Bannockburn and the other south. Interestingly, they were wicked people who were transformed by God into oxen for their sins. We have to ask: is this transformation into oxen a satirical look at the discipline and hard work of the monastic life?

Some stories tend to describe Ninia's Whithorn as a monastic foundation. There is, for example, a story of the brothers which tells how they ran short of vegetables one day. Ninia went into the garden, planted some seeds and a crop grew in a few hours! How to interpret that sort of miracle is *intriguing*. Again too the stories point to a school at Whithorn. Indeed this would have been possible either with a monastic foundation or a bishop's establishment. One story tells of a naughty boy running away to Ireland in a tiny coracle (boat) by virtue of the bishop's staff (*crozier*) which he stole from Ninia and used as an oar. This too could be a powerful teaching story, but unlike biblical teaching stories, we have insufficient evidence as yet to allow for effective interpretation. Details apart, however, Ninia, or *Ninian*, awaits a fuller revelation!

Bede: *The History of the English Church* (Penguin).
Forbes: *Lives of S Ninian and S Kentigern* (1872).
MacQueen, J: 'Miracula', poem in *St Nynia* (Polygon: 1990).

2

KENTIGERN
The Saint with most Dedications

KENTIGERN or *Mungo* is the saint with most dedications in Scotland, but the one with fewest hard facts. Wells, farms and chapels are dedicated to him either in his proper name of Kentigern or his pet name in Brythonic (Welsh), *Mungo*, which may mean 'my very dear one'. He seems to have been active at the end of the sixth century: the very much later chronicle of his life has him dying in AD 612, but undermines the credibility of the date by claiming he lived for 180 years. For that we can at least substitute that he died as an old man.

Another common characteristic in the stories and memories of Kentigern is that he journeyed a great deal. The seven journeys to Rome at least, however, seem pure invention or an exercise in biblical 'completeness' with the symbolic number seven. The pattern of dedications throughout Scotland and down to North Wales would seem on the other hand to substantiate to some degree the message in the stories that he journeyed north to the Highlands and the Picts; and that he journeyed south to Cumberland (better evidence) and so to North Wales.

The major difficulty in assessing the stories about Kentigern rests in the commission by Jocelin, Bishop of Glasgow in the twelfth century, to a monk Jocelin of Furness to write a 'good life' of the saint he regarded as founding his Glasgow bishopric. The result of this has been described by Professor Kenneth Jackson as making Kentigern 'the cuckoo in the nest' among the Celtic saints, for he seems to be an amalgam of various saints, and even ancient deities, and also to have doubtful links with Columba (only an exchange of *croziers*), St Serf and David of Wales.

The connection with St Serf comes in Kentigern's richly embroidered fictional birth story. It begins with him being born to a prince and 'Saint Enoch', daughter of the King of Lothian, outside wedlock. Her father is said to have thrown the pregnant Enoch off Traprain Law and then, when she survived that, to have set her adrift in Aberlady Bay in a coracle. She was towed as far as the Isle of May and set adrift. The fish followed the coracle and miraculously it was directed to Culross where Enoch gave birth to Kentigern on the sands and St Serf (who wasn't alive at the time!) brought him up until he left to establish a monastery at Glasgow.

It's certain that Kentigern founded the monastery at Hoddam in Dumfriesshire but, despite the strength of the stories, not so certain that he, rather than a disciple, founded the great monastery at Govan: and further not so certain that his monastery was on the site of Glasgow cathedral as the stories maintain, instead of some distance away, in Govan proper. References to Melvin also occur in the area. An old story about a local king refusing to pay *tithes* has Kentigern cursing him and the River Clyde rising to lift his barns over to where Kentigern was: this could be an elaboration of the re-allocation of Kentigern's original foundation to where the cathedral now is. It is also the charter-myth of the Gorbals, the tithe-lands of the parish of Govan. All this is difficult to find evidence for, since excavations would have to take place under the present cathedral!

In the stories of King Rhyddech (the Generous), King of Strathclyde, and Kentigern, there are pointers to a connection of Kentigern with North Wales. It's most unlikely Kentigern met St David, as alleged, but it may well be that a pupil of Kentigern founded St Asaph's in North Wales. It's particularly interesting to note the parallels between the valley of Clwyd there and the valley of the Clyde at Govan. The Welsh language, we must remember, was the common link between Wales and Strathclyde right up to 1200.

The famous ring and salmon story on Glasgow's coat of arms is a common folk tale; so also is the robin story; again too is the rhyme:

> *This is the tree that never grew.*
> *This is the bird that never flew.*
> *This is the bell that never rang.*
> *This is the fish that never swam.*

—all reflecting the bringing together of St Serf stories and common fables. The keeping of Kentigern's death on the octave of the Epiphany, the Baptism of Christ in the Jordan, has interesting reflections in the story of Kentigern praying 150 psalms in the Molendinar at night, and in the story of him dying in the water of a hot bath with 600 of his disciples managing to get into what they saw as the holy waters before they cooled and lost their power. This last surely points to the baptisms Kentigern celebrated over what must have been a wide sphere of influence in the west of Scotland.

Forbes: *Lives of S Ninian and S Kentigern* (1872).

3

COLUMBA
'The Dove of the Church'

COLUMBA (*c* 518-597)—or *Colum Cille*, to give him his Gaelic name—means 'dove'. The dove of peace conjures up the peace of Celtic monastic life, the peace of the island of Iona and the modern day work for peace centred on Lord George MacLeod of Fuinary and the Iona community he founded. The Iona community, which opens out from the Church of Scotland to being an ecumenical organisation, stands at that meeting point of politics and Christianity which begins with Columba and continues down through the ages of Scottish church history.

Scotia was the name given by Latin writers to Ireland, and *Scoti*, the Scots, were the inhabitants of Ireland. Thus Columba was born as a Scot in Donegal as a member of the Royal family of

PEACEFUL SCENE on the SHORE of IONA

UI NEILL, the descendants of Neill, the most important people in Ireland in the sixth century. Had he remained a layman, he could have been king. A legend suggests that he was the cause of a bloody battle (*Cul Drehene*) and that either forced exile or self-imposed exile in self-recrimination brought him to Iona. Since this story was not mentioned by his biographer (Adomnan) and since coming to what we now know as Scotland is a fairly natural consequence of Columba's monastic life in Ireland, the legend may have to be discounted except perhaps as a reflection of Columba's reputation for being a peace-builder.

Columba had already founded one or two monastic communities in Ireland before coming across the sea in a *coracle*, a boat made of skins. This 'emigration' was part of a fairly general movement of Scots over to what we now know as Scotland, where of course they eventually took over from the native Picts. Columba came over to the court of the King of Dalriada in 563 and it was only after two years at the court that he founded the monastery of Iona thanks to the generosity of the king. Columba in turn

personally crowned Aidan King of Dalriada rather than other claimants and in so doing began a close political partnership which enabled Iona to become in due course the source of a great number of Scottish monasteries. It was also the place where kings came for advice; and where they were buried.

Columba's coming to Dalriada and then Iona is ascribed by Adomnan to the Celtic spiritual conviction that love of God was best proved by journeying out of your own area. This was, in the light of their being deeply attached to their kindred, the greatest sacrifice or penance the monk could do, and it led to the re-Christianisation of Europe by Celtic monks and here in Scotland to a dramatic expansion of Columba's influence in monasteries throughout the land. The only recorded mission in Columba's own time, however, concerns yet another spiritual and political journey: it was to King Bridei, or *Brude,* of the Picts at his stronghold at Inverness. The stories added on to this encounter underline its importance. We have a confrontation between Columba and the king's *magus,* or druid; and a story of his saving a servant at the crossing of the River Ness from a 'monster' which gave rise to the long saga of the Loch Ness monster. The political character of the visit is even clearer when we note that King Brude had defeated the Scots in battle not long before the visit. It's not clear whether Columba converted King Brude, because not even Adomnan claimed he did: what he achieved was his friendship and an honour which laid the foundations for his followers to build on.

When we ask what sort of man Columba was, Adomnan relates a real sensitivity and family feeling towards his monks. The two great strands of Egyptian monastic tradition came through Ireland to Iona. The early fourth century despair about the laxity of moral life in the Roman Empire led to both community and solitary foundations. In Iona we find the Celtic scatter of buildings: church, hospice, refectory, cells, scriptoria for the writing and decoration of manuscripts and agricultural buildings. Again in evidence from the Egyptian tradition is the intellectual and cultural strand. Adomnan portrays Columba on the day of his death copying a psalter and commissioning Baithene—who significantly was his successor to complete the psalter and thus carry on the tradition.

Columba has always been regarded as one of the triumvirate of great Celtic Church saints. Patrick was, however, in the Roman tradition and was only adopted by the Celtic Church. Bridget may only have been a Christianisation of the Celtic goddess of fire. Columba, however, emerges unchallenged as the most important churchman of the sixth century in the whole British Isles.

Anderson, A O and M O: *Adomnan's Life of Columba* (Nelson: 1961).
Menzies, G: *Who are the Scots?* (BBC Publications: 1976).

4

BALDRED

The Hermit of the Bass Rock

BALDRED of the Bass Rock is a mysterious figure from the eighth century who seems to have been slightly later than the great church historian, Bede. He seems to have been born in what is now East Lothian at a time when the traditions and organisation of the Celtic and Roman traditions had been brought together. His early experience of monastic life probably would have been at Coldingham or Melrose before moving to live as a hermit on the Bass Rock.

The BASS ROCK

It was an age when the contemplative 'retreat from the world' in religious life was regarded with awe and veneration by the ordinary people. Thus it's not surprising to find Baldred acclaimed as a saint by the people (originally the only way saints could be recognised in the church). He is connected specially with the churches at Tynningham in East Lothian and Preston in Berwickshire. Presumably people would, as in the legends, journey to his hermitage in search of cures. Be that as it may, the folk memory of his sanctity was so clear in the Middle Ages that many Scots were christened Baldred (chapter 11 outlines the life of the most important of his namesakes). By the fifteenth century, Baldred appears in Bishop William Elphinstone's list of Scottish saints in the *Aberdeen Breviary*.

To understand how an East Lothian man ends up a hermit on the Bass Rock, we need to go back to the very origins of monasticism in Egypt. There were always two strands: the communal and the eremitical, that of the lonely hermit. The *communal* tended to stress the coming together of monks to provide a place of caring and hospitality, to reflect Christ's love not just to one another but to all who took refuge in the place dedicated to the ordered life of work, study, worship and individual prayer. The *eremitical* was meant to be a sign to the world of the transitory nature of this world's goods. In Egypt the extremes of asceticism led to such strange phenomena as Simon Stylites, for example, who prayed on top of a pillar in the desert: people flocked to draw inspiration from his witness.

These two strands of Egyptian monastic life were quite effectively transferred to Celtic monasticism via the Church in Gaul. Celtic monasteries often combined the two elements with little individual hermit cells within the surrounding *vallum* of the monastery (the spiritual enclosure). That strand of Celtic monasticism came in turn to Scotland where a collection of beehive style buildings in the Firth of Lorne still show the pattern. Iona too would have had such cells, and with Aidan's establishment of Lindisfarne the Celtic tradition began to interact once again with the European and Roman monastic tradition coming from the south. Melrose—*Old Melrose*—and Coldingham were founded on the pattern of Iona and so the Bass Rock was situated in a well established monastic tradition.

The old abbot, Boisoil, so inspired Cuthbert at Melrose with the vision of the inner life that after the turmoil of enthusiastically enforcing the changes agreed at the Synod of Whitby, he withdrew to St Cuthbert's Isle, and then on to the more remote Farne Islands where he erected a cell with such high walls that he could only see the sky and ocean. In fact religious obedience brought Cuthbert back as Bishop of Lindisfarne, but the dramatic character of his witness must have lived on to inspire characters like Baldred.

One last reflection is necessary on the sort of hermit life which manifested itself in the Celtic tradition. The hermit very often settled in a place of great natural beauty: in line with the Celtic sensitivity to seeing the greatness and beauty of God in nature. The wild mysterious backdrop of the Bass Rock is an intriguing symbol of Baldred's contradictory witness both in retreat from the world and immersion in its beauty. A desert experience, yes, but one with more traces of resurrection hope than its stark Egyptian origins.

McKinlay, J M: *Church Dedications in Scotland* (Edinburgh: 1915).

5
MARGARET
The Queen who changed Scots Psychology

MARGARET, Queen of Scotland (*c*1040-1093), changed the way the Scottish nation thought of itself; she also changed the image that the church was concerned to maintain within the Scottish nation at that time. That is perhaps why she has been accused by her critics of 'Englishing' Scotland and of destroying the ancient Celtic Church in favour of the foreign Roman Church.

As with all myths in history, there are reasons why they develop. Margaret was born in Hungary, but her father, Edward, was a member of the West Saxon royal house. Cnut—or more popularly *Canute*—was, as the Danish King of England, responsible for sending Edward and his brother into exile with a pretty clear hope that they wouldn't survive the journey and continue to be a threat to his throne. They went to Sweden, then to Kiev, and finally to Hungary where the king, Andrew, was engaged in a major campaign to make the country Christian. There Edward married a member of the German imperial house and Margaret of our story was one of his three children. Their home would have reflected the country's intense Christian faith, a faith with all the enthusiasm characterising new beginnings.

When Edward the Confessor was dying, it was intended that Margaret's father would succeed his cousin, but he died leaving his son Edgar, and daughters Christina and Margaret. In turn, it was intended that Edgar would succeed, but when it came to the bit, in 1066, Harold of Wessex seized the throne, surprisingly taking no action against Edgar. When William the Conqueror took over that same year after the Norman Conquest, the position of Edgar became impossible. He fled with Christina and Margaret to the north of England where resistance was initially strong; but when it crumbled they sailed north and are reputed to have landed on the Fife coast in the midst of a dangerous storm.

Malcolm III of Scotland—Malcolm Canmore—seems to have

fallen in love with Margaret almost at first sight. It wasn't in any sense, however, the traditional story of 'Beauty and the Beast': Malcolm was a forceful and competent King of Scotland who had years of culture behind him at the court of Edward the Confessor in England. But his first wife had just died and he decided Margaret was a perfect choice as his new queen. Her life had prepared her admirably for the role.

Once married, Margaret had six sons and two daughters, all of whom quite remarkably survived into adult life. Three of her sons, particularly David, committed themselves to make practical realities of the very clear vision Margaret had for Scotland in both secular matters and the church. She knew what she wanted and as the court moved from place to place—for sanitary and provisioning reasons apart from anything else—her influence spread far and wide.

Margaret was a complex character with a love of rich dresses and jewellry; her insistence on this led the courtiers, it is said, to a major new influx of continental merchants to the Scottish scene. On the other hand, she was deeply pious, making herself available to ordinary people with their problems; and showing her concern for the vast numbers of poor people in Scotland by caring for some of them with her own hands every day. This was balanced by quiet times of prayer in the little cave hidden beneath a pedestrian precinct in present-day Dunfermline, and in St Margaret's chapel in Edinburgh castle. The ferry at Queensferry—which was only outdated by the Forth Road Bridge—was also named after her for ensuring that the poor people on pilgrimage to St Andrews could cross without charge.

On coming to Scotland, Margaret was shocked by the lack of diocesan organisation and territorial jurisdiction with the bishops. The claim that she destroyed the Celtic Church is based on her harangues of the old bishops to establish church discipline with regard to the observance of the Sabbath and children going to communion too early. Again too she had to ask Archbishop Lanfranc of Canterbury for the monks she needed to realise her ambition of establishing a Benedictine monastery like those she had admired on the continent as centres both of prayer and caring.

Her idea, however, was for a Scottish foundation at Dunfermline. The priory was designed to be, and did in fact later become, an independent abbey. As for the remaining representatives of Celtic monasticism—the *Culdees*—respect for them is clearly recorded. And similarly she is said to have taken the devastated Iona monastic situation to her heart. It had been devastated by Norse raids but the kings of Scotland were still buried there: she committed herself to its renewal. Had she lived a further ten years, her achievements would have been clearer. As it is, we can best glimpse her uniqueness in the work of her sons. The judgment which saw her declared a saint as early as 1251 by Innocent IV was not unreasonable.

Anderson, A: 'Life of Margaret' in *Early Sources of Scottish History*.
Duncan, A: *Edinburgh History of Scotland* (Market Press), volume 1.

CHANCEL ARCH of ST MARGARET'S CHAPEL,
EDINBURGH CASTLE

6

DAVID

'Ane Sair Sanct for the Crown'

STANDING by the grave of David (*c*1080-1153), James I suggested David emptied the coffers of the crown by his generosity to the church: 'ane sair sanct for the crown.' David was incredibly generous to the church, carrying into practicalities the ideals of

his mother Margaret, Queen of Scotland, but any assessment of his value to the crown would have also to take into account the fact that he reorganised Scotland into the feudal system, bringing in Normans, Flemings, English and Bretons to hold land as feudal lords. It would also have to consider the cost to Scotland of David's loyalty to the pledge he made with the great barons of England to maintain the right of his niece Matilda to the Scottish crown, for this led to one successful war in England and then the disastrous defeat at the Battle of the Standard near Northallerton in 1138.

DAVID I

As the youngest son of Malcolm III (Canmore) and Margaret, no one envisaged David as ending up on the throne. It came about first of all because his brother Edgar, who became king in 1097, never married and died in 1106. Edgar was then succeeded by Alexander I who died childless, leaving a wife, in 1124.

David was accepted by most as the natural successor. It's true that during his reign he had, like most Scottish kings, to face rebellions, revolts and dynastic challenges, but most accepted him. His enormously attractive personality and a respect for his competence enabled him to do things others wouldn't have managed, especially when this involved outsiders coming in.

What made David different was the fact that he was the youngest son of Margaret and grew up with her when she was at the peak of her power. Also, as very much the youngest son, he was sent at his mother's death in 1093 (with his sister Matilda who married Henry I of England in 1100) to the English court. There and on the estates of Normandy he developed a wide clear vision of a quite different way of life from what he had seen in Scotland. This was followed up by marriage to Matilda, widow of the Norman Earl of Northampton, with whom he had a deeply happy and faithful family life (quite unlike his patron Henry I, who had a succession of illegitimate children). The final chapter in a life which unexpectedly prepared him to be king came during his brother Alexander's reign, when he administered southern Scotland and part of Cumbria as earl.

When David became king in 1124, his first priority was to ensure that the Scottish bishops should be organised into proper territorial units of jurisdiction. Norway had always appointed a bishop in Orkney and a bishop of the western isles. To this David added or consolidated ten *bishoprics,* dividing Scotland into ten areas of pastoral administration with ten bishops. He wanted the Pope to make St Andrews an archbishopric to ensure Scotland's church independence against the claims of York and Canterbury in England, particularly York. The Pope was even working on a seventh century Roman map which pictured Britain as one country full of Anglo-Saxons. David sorted that out, but England still managed to block the archbishopric. Nevertheless, St Andrews was confirmed as the leading Scottish See, with Glasgow second.

The second achievement of David in church life was a massive increase of parish churches to serve the needs of ordinary people. His ideal was that a parish should be formed by a day's walk in any direction. The old round towers and wood and wattle buildings had to give way to the sort of buildings David saw on the continent. All of these ideals required money: David transformed the situation by imposing a system of *teinds* (tithes), so that in the biblical pattern, everyone who bred animals, who fished, undertook commerce and similar activities had to pay ten per cent of their profits to the church to support a local priest and parish. This gave a remarkable degree of independence to the local bishop and priests from the landowners and led to scores, even hundreds of new parishes. It was that independent source of income that James I envied.

Lastly, the church had to thank David for the practical achievement of Margaret's desire for the new reformed-style monks and nuns to come in as centres of prayer, preaching, learning and caring. David's first priority was to strengthen Dunfermline with help from Canterbury, but with its erection to Abbey status ensuring its independence. Its variety is impressive: Benedictines and Cluniac Benedictines; Cistercians (Melrose, Newcastle, Kinloss, Coupar Angus and Culross) and Tironensians from Tiron near Chartres; Augustinian canons (Jedburgh) and Premonstratensians (Dryburgh).

When we think of religious houses, and parishes to a lesser extent, being the welfare state of the day, David can certainly be seen as a 'gude sanct' for the people.

Barrow, G: *Kingship and Unity* (Edinburgh University Press: 1989).
Duncan, A: *Edinburgh History of Scotland* (Market Press), volume 1.

7
JOCELIN
The Monk who gave Glasgow a start

JOCELIN of Glasgow was a monk from the Cistercian abbey at Melrose who became Bishop of Glasgow in 1174. During his time he had Glasgow made a burgh by King William. In that sense he gave Glasgow a start on its commercial journey, but from the little we can glean of his life he gave Glasgow a new start also as a focus of religious faith by the strength of his own faith and energy.

Jocelin's origins are obscure. From the date of his death in 1199, we can only deduce a date of birth to the 1130s. He had two brothers and a nephew that are known about. One brother had land in Lanarkshire and is on record as giving a grant of Dunsyre church to Kelso Abbey. From that, and from the fact that Jocelin offered himself as a monk to Melrose Abbey, stems the presumption that he was a Scot himself.

That aside, Jocelin appears in the life of Waltheof of Melrose, where he is noted organising the opening of Waltheof's tomb and finding the body incorrupt. Another reference to him is in a letter written by '*R*' (*Ralph*, the abbot of Melrose when Jocelin died) in which there are the usual stock phrases about a pious person. Beneath the rhetoric, however, the facts speak for themselves. He seems to have come at an early age to offer himself as a novice at Melrose in the time of Waltheof. He soon appeared as extremely able and quickly rose to become prior. In 1170 he was elected abbot and in 1174 he became Bishop of Glasgow.

The significance of what Jocelin did for Glasgow is difficult to assess. We can only guess at there having been a small village community downhill from the cathedral above the flood-water level and near the ford of the river. As well as gaining for it the status of burgh from King William, Jocelin also got a grant from the king to hold a market every Thursday, and to organise a week-long fair to begin each year on the feast of St Peter and Paul with the aim of being an international gathering. We have no idea how successful all this was, but it was bound to bring in money for the burgh and thus for the cathedral.

This financial aspect became more critical with the tragedy of fire at the cathedral, probably in the 1180s. Jocelin created a fraternity to raise money for the rebuilding and was able to dedicate at least the East End with the altar in 1197. What was it like? We don't know. The cathedral had to be rebuilt in the thirteenth century, but in the lower church there is a little corner which does not fit—so it is reasonably assumed to be a bit of the old cathedral.

One of the major problems in learning about Glasgow's past is the fact that Archbishop Beaton took the records with him to France in 1560. Fortunately the University of Glasgow got transcripts in the eighteenth century of many of the charters, for the originals disappeared during the French Revolution. Another source emerged, the *Red Book*, which is kept by the Archdiocese of Glasgow today, but that is as much as we have.

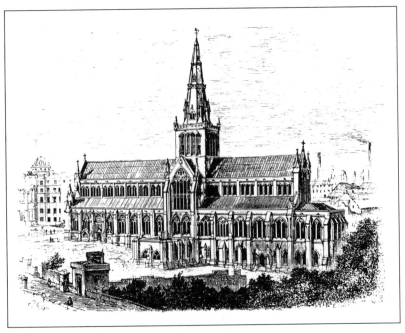

GLASGOW CATHEDRAL from the SOUTH-EAST,
as it LOOKED in the NINETEENTH CENTURY

From the 25 or 27 of Jocelin's charters we learn that he was a capable administrator, dealing efficiently with the Bruce family over churches in Annandale and a local nobleman over a church in East Kilbride. He may well have been the one who established the office of 'official' to act in place of the bishop. That is not surprising in view of the large area of the diocese, from Loch Lomond in the north right across the Borders region to Galloway and to Roxburgh. Jocelin rode around his diocese on horseback and is even on record visiting Melrose as late as 1199.

Jocelin's importance is seen by the fact that he was sent on behalf of King William to get the excommunication lifted which resulted from a dispute over the appointment of a bishop: he returned with a golden rose. Then in 1176 he went to England to negotiate on behalf of William with the King of England at the Council of Northampton. There he vigorously defended the independence of the Scottish Church from the claims of York (which was trying to balance with Canterbury by achieving more *Suffragan Sees*, the associated bishoprics which gave an archbishop greater status). Here he put forward the claim that Glasgow was the *filia specialis* (special daughter) of the Roman Church. This direct link with Papal authority meant there was no Archbishop in Scotland until 1472, but that its defensive role against English claims was in Papal Bulls from this point on.

Jocelin was the product of the Cistercian reform at a time when Bernard was still alive to ensure its continuing austerity. He is said to have taken that austere and simple spiritual life into his life as bishop, but his wider vision is clear by his commissioning of Jocelin of Furness to give the See a history all the way back to Kentigern. The monk had made his mark.

The Red Book of Glasgow (Roman Catholic Archives, Glasgow).
Duncan, A M: *Edinburgh History of Scotland* (Market Press), volume 1.

8

ADAM

The Bible from Dryburgh

ONE of the questions about twelfth century Scotland is whether
all the money poured by St Margaret's son David into founding
monasteries was a total waste of the wealth of the Scottish kingdom. Adam of Dryburgh (*c*1150-*c*1210) is a very powerful argument to show the value of a very constructive revolution of
religious values taking place in the twelfth century. Long before
the Scottish reformers of the sixteenth century we find in Adam
a real love of the Bible and a broad-based scholarship to make
full use of that biblical familiarity.

All we know of Adam's early days was that he was born in
Berwickshire just before the Abbey of Dryburgh was founded.
His father was a small landowner, but certainly not a noble. Adam
was of average size, 'stout enough' for his height and came across
as pleasant and cheerful. Even in advanced years, he combined a
good head of white hair with striking looks: he inspired respect.

Beginning as a novice in Dryburgh, he went on to be ordained
as a priest of the Canons Regular of Premontre who had been
founded by St Norbert. In the whole movement in which religious orders were vibrant and took over the clerical scene, Dryburgh had been founded by a noble. Adam was part of that vision,
convinced that secular priests were incapable of reforming themselves without regular priests showing the way by example. The
impression given is that he *did* live up to all he stood for. He was
so convinced of the value of community that it made him extremely impartial with secular canons, who were in many ways similar
to his own order but who all too often ended up living at court.

Two factors help us to know a great deal about Adam. One is
the collection of his works—80 sermons!—which was published
in Paris in 1518. These writings derive mainly from the period
when he was Abbot at Dryburgh (1184). Second, in 1188 he decided to dedicate the rest of his life to the austere, reformed life of the

Carthusian order. That took him to the only Carthusian house in Britain, down in Somerset, and so a lot of information about him survived; whereas the Scottish material disappeared in the massive destruction which took place over the years.

From these sources, we see Adam as a deeply spiritual man, devoted to Latin theoreticians and the classical authors like Ovid, Horace and Juvenal, but also familiar with the works of the Fathers, especially St Augustine. The Bible, however, was central: he used it in the customary way of the time, according to the school of St Victor in Paris where another Scot, Richard of St Victor, was prior. He clearly owed a great deal to him and to the great scholar, Hugh of St Victor, and had visited the mother house of Premontre in France. The Bible was thus for him the story of great men who often came to a tragic end. He used allegory, extracts, moral, mystical and spiritual meaning far beyond the

DRYBURGH ABBEY

21

literal, revealing something in the Bible for everyone: 'it's a river in which the lamb may wade and the elephant may safely swim.'

One of the great challenges about Adam of Dryburgh is to see him in the context of the whole country at the time. In terms of Scottish nationalism, he is a somewhat ambivalent character. In 1174 William the Lion had given an oath of allegiance to the King of England as part of the Treaty of Falaise. The Scottish clergy were deeply apprehensive that they might be subject to the English bishops. Adam would not share that sort of worry. With reference probably to Gaelic- and English- speaking Scots, he said: 'we are in the land of the English and in the realm of Scotland.' And when giving the genealogy of Scottish kings, he chose to start with Queen Margaret and then, 'trace things back through English ancestry to Adam and Eve.'

In other ways he was closely linked with monastic life throughout Scotland. He addresses one of his books to Walter Prior of the less strict 'black' Augustinian canons at St Andrews. Most of all, however, we find a deep friendship with the neighbouring John, Benedictine Abbot of Kelso. He was suspicious of the 'modern' dialectic logic (Aristotle's method of explaining faith) and remained instead safely in the Augustinian tradition, even paraphrasing Gregory the Great who stated that contemplation was central to faith. Adam was more rounded even though he eventually became a Carthusian contemplature. Reading Aristotle was for him no contradiction to reading the Bible: both helped him to search for and live the 'good life.'

Adam of Dryburgh: *Works* (Paris: 1518).
Bulloch, J: *Adam of Dryburgh* (London: 1958).

9

WILLIAM MALVOISIN
What sort of Neighbour?

WILLIAM Malvoisin arrives on the scene of Scottish history as Bishop of St Andrews in 1202 after having been Bishop of Glasgow for two or three years previously. His origins are just north of Paris on the Seine, but apart from that we know little of his earlier days. He was, however, trained in both Roman and *canon* (church) law and this expertise was to mark his time as Bishop of St Andrews right up to his death in 1238. He was an energetic organiser of the church, and indeed a reformer: neither of which is a recipe for popularity—hence the play on his name 'bad neighbour.' One significant example can be found on the edge of a contemporary manuscript written by the incumbent of a church at Melrose which was subject to St Andrews. It read: 'Getting on fine till this Bishop Malvoisin came along, a bad neighbour in every way.' Whether Malvoisin was a 'bad neighbour' or not depended very much on one's perspective. Many of his contemporaries praised him highly for raising the church's profile. This was very much his aim, but his tool of the law for this purpose was very much a double-edged sword.

In his time, Malvoisin made himself an awkward neighbour for the English See of York which was trying to balance Canterbury's range of *Suffragan Sees* by taking over the Scottish bishoprics. To do this he got the Papacy to confirm Scotland's position as an autonomous church directly answerable to the Pope. This was a fairly unique position. Each bishop had to go to Rome for confirmation of his appointment and was often consecrated there. In one sense it was a centralising move and attractive to the Papacy as such, but in Scotland's position it was the guarantee of the separateness it needed. For practical decision-making, there had to be a regular council of bishops with a 'conservator of privileges' in charge of the council. This was normally to be the St Andrews bishop and certainly was so during Malvoisin's time of office. With that, and with his term as Chancellor from 1199-1201, Malvoisin had real power within Scotland.

Malvoisin used that power to shake up both secular and religious clergy in Scotland. Religious clergy had enjoyed in the previous century a certain mystical respect for their rigorous lives and the reputation for holiness which had gone before them. Malvoisin would be concerned to see that they were kept in their place and that they lived up to the rule of their founders. They would have the independence enshrined in canon law, but with him would have to take heed of the local bishop, no matter how powerful or wealthy they might be. Discipline and order were the virtues of the day. In all of this, William Malvoisin was typical of those in church authority at the time.

It was the age of powerful and effective Popes. First there was Innocent III, arguably the greatest Pope of all time, and Honorius III. There had been important councils from 1170 onwards, coming to a climax in the vitally important IV Lateran council which began in 1214 but had its public sessions in 1215. Malvoisin was there and was to come back to Scotland determined to put its legislation into effect.

The IV Lateran council was to the Middle Ages what the II Vatican council was to the Roman Catholic Church in the present century. It was the greatest gathering of the Middle Ages (412 bishops, 800 abbots and priors and representatives of all the states) and it consolidated a process of thinking which led up to that point and became effective afterwards. The council dealt with the Holy Land, but what was critical for Scotland were the 70 canons (or laws) designed to reform the whole life of the church. The first laws are about what is to be believed and then the bulk of the legislation reviewed the life of the church, denouncing the weakness and wickedness within the church and providing punishment for the obstinate. The legislated minimum of the sacrament of Confession once a year, and communion once a year (in the Easter period), was laid down.

The final section went on to set up the structures to ensure the law was obeyed at every level: Pope, bishop, priest, religious and lay person. Malvoisin was the ideal person by training and temperament to bring this structure to Scotland and to ensure that the code of canon law as finally concluded in 1234 would discipline and order Scottish church life. It had great benefits in the short term but it has to be said that it ultimately brought that destruction of the spirit of the law in favour of the letter, which has been a problem for Christianity from the Pharisees to the present day.

Malvoisin, however, would not have been a bad neighbour in all this, but he would have made sure that everything was done by the book!

Watt, D E R: *A Biographical Dictionary of Scottish Graduates to 1410* (Oxford University Press: 1977).

Duncan, A: *Edinburgh History of Scotland* (Market Press), volume 1.

10

DEVORGUILLA

From Balliol to Sweetheart

THOSE who see God's people only in terms of men have reduced Devorguilla to a footnote in Balliol history. She married John, the grandson of Bernard who had succeeded the Norman Guido and built the great fortress of Barnard Castle in the north of England. In her own right, however, she was by far the most famous Scotswoman of the thirteenth century. Subsequent historians spoke highly and warmly of her contribution to Scottish history. Andrew Winton, for example, wrote of her in the early fifteenth century: 'a better lady were there nane in all the isle of mair Britaine.'

Devorguilla (*c*1209-1289) was the daughter of Alan, Lord of Galloway and Margaret, daughter of David, Earl of Huntingdon, who in turn was brother of William the Lion. This gave the royal connection which, quite unexpectedly in terms of all her expectations, resulted in her son John Balliol becoming King of Scotland and later still his son Edward.

Their short reigns were surrounded by tragedy, whereas Devorguilla had a much happier life with no real inkling of what would happen after her death. Her elder sisters died without leaving offspring and so she became in her own right after her father's death, Lady of Galloway. In this, Scots law was different from English and French law. When she married John Balliol the elder, with his estates in his own right in Northumberland and Durham, he became Lord of Galloway by courtesy of her, and so the title passed in due course to their son. The death of the Earl of Huntingdon in 1219 had meant his estates being divided into three, but even one third meant vast estates throughout Scotland and northern England for Devorguilla: Inverurie, Inverbervie, Dundee, Longforgan, Lindores (where Balliol founded the abbey) all appear along with properties in the south, such as the lordship of Wigtown and Kirkcudbright which brought a great number of administrative functions.

Devorguilla was acutely aware of and sensitive to her position and responsibilities. She was deeply pious and committed to works of caring which bettered the lot of the poor. In addition she was famous for her pious foundations. In Dundee, where her part of the legacy from Huntingdon contained the important parts of the city around the castle, she founded the Greyfriars (Franciscan friars).

Her husband, John, had always been sensitive to the needs of Scottish students at universities in England, particularly Oxford, but had done nothing about it. After his death, she gathered money together and founded a house for lodging students at Oxford which became in time one of Oxford's earliest colleges, Balliol (fourteenth century). At this stage there were no universities in Scotland and so Scottish students went to Oxford, or occasionally Cambridge, Paris, Bologna and other European universities. Her foundation became the centre for Scottish students, provided they were—in the absence of war at that particular time—able to go there. Significantly the actual charter of foundation is sealed at Buttle near Galloway.

One last story illustrates the fact that Devorguilla was a woman of her age in tune with the romantic gestures which characterised European life at that time, and yet a woman of real religious commitment. She arranged that when she died there should be a religious foundation for Cistercians near her place of death. This came to be known as *Douce Coeur,* or Sweetheart Abbey, because she ordered her heart to be embalmed and put above the body of her husband in the tomb.

Devorguilla was not a politician in the sense of power struggles, but she was exceptionally aware of her inherited position and used it for others. Her personal qualities thoroughly merit her a place in the story of God's people in Scotland.

Paravicini, F: *History of Balliol College.*
Historic Buildings and Monuments: *History of Sweetheart Abbey* (HMSO).

11

BALDRED BISSET
Scotland's Defender

BALDRED Bisset is best known for defending Scotland's right to independence from Edward I at the Papal court; but as a canon (church) lawyer, he is one of the many Scots of this time who gave witness to the quality of Scottish church life by gaining an international reputation in their own field of knowledge. Personal details are scant: all we can say is that he was alive in 1312 after a very long life so he may have been born in the 1240s or 50s.

We know little of his family origins except that he came from a laird's family somewhere near Stirling. The name witnesses to the Anglo-Norman derivatives of the family, but it is clear that they were well integrated into Scottish life from about the twelfth century. The name Baldred is after Baldred of the Bass Rock, a clear witness to the family seeing themselves very much as Scottish.

Baldred was trained in canon law at the University of Bologna, the best law school in Europe. He must have been very able, for as well as pastoral work at Kinghorn, he was appointed Official of the Diocese of St Andrews, the most important diocese in Scotland. To be Official meant to be president of the bishop's court for hearing church cases. For these purposes, it is quite likely that the court met not just in St Andrews but also in the High Street in Edinburgh, near St Giles Cathedral; and occasionally in places like Berwick-on-Tweed and Stirling. Wherever the court met, the application of the universal canon law to local cases meant familiarity with the hundreds and hundreds of cases sent each year to the *Papal curia*—the highest court of appeal—and the responses made which were filtered back to the local church. A canon lawyer like Bisset would see his work as very much a service to the good of the whole church and that is why it was seen as a pastoral task. Canon law was very logical despite the inevitable quirks and peculiarities, but when compared with local secular law in Scotland, England and France, it was actually more humane. One example of this is the fact that in civil law any son born out of wedlock could not succeed to the family property. He could only be provided for by the generosity of the family. This was true even if the parents subsequently married: whereas in canon law, subsequent marriage of the parents legitimised the children.

As expected, the evidence of Bisset at work is mainly in property cases where the title deeds tend to be preserved. These show competence, but what is a more striking tribute to his work is the fact that he achieved an international reputation through what was essentially local interest activities in the legal field.

This international reputation served him well when, in 1296, the war with England—and Edward I's threat to the continued separate existence of Scotland—took Baldred Bisset to Italy and an extremely useful role for Scotland. In 1301 he presented the Scottish case against Edward I at the papal court and won the judgment that the Scots were right and Edward I should desist from his claim to Scotland.

Through no fault of Bisset, political events meant that the Pope got into trouble with the French king and one of the casualties was the Scots case for independence. As a result, the Scots had to wait for years before their case was finally resolved in their favour. It is not without significance that in this muddle the Pope in question was Boniface VIII, one of the few Popes Dante placed in hell in his Divine Comedy.

Baldred Bisset only returned to Scotland for a short time before going back to Italy. An ironic postscript to the story is that when Boniface died he was tried for heresy and other misdemeanours. At the trial Baldred Bisset was chosen to defend him. Ironic, yes, but a very real tribute to Bisset's reputation. Scotland could have had no more distinguished advocate in her service, and that paid dividends in years to come.

Watt, D E R: *A Biographical Dictionary of Scottish Graduates to 1440* (Oxford University Press: 1977).
Boase, T: *Boniface VIII* (Oxford University Press).

12

JOHN DUNS SCOTUS*
Dunce or Subtle Doctor?

AFTER many years of claims that he might have been English, Irish or even Welsh, it is now certain that the scholar known as Duns Scotus, and either dismissed as a 'dunce' or hailed as the 'subtle doctor', was indeed John of Duns in Berwickshire. He was born there in the 1260s and died in 1309. At quite an early age he joined the *Greyfriars*—the Franciscans—and became one of the outstanding intellectuals of his age at Oxford, Paris and Cologne.

In recent years, the separation of his genuine writings from the spurious have made the picture of his teaching clearer. This has added to the respect he had both before and after the Reformation in Scotland, evidenced by the elaborate triumph when Charles I came to Edinburgh for the first time in 1633. A gigantic mountain called Parnassus was built in the High Street and stuffed with books. Among the six statues of men of learning were John Duns Scotus and David Lyndsay, author of *Ane Satyre of the Thrie Estatis*. This conjunction of Catholic and Protestant intellectual activity looks set to be renewed in more recent moves within the twentieth century Roman Catholic Church to declare Duns Scotus a saint, for his thought provides an alternative approach to more traditionally expressed Catholic thought in the line of development stemming from Thomas Aquinas.

To understand the greatness of the thought process of Duns Scotus, it's important to understand that he had to cope with the sort of witch-hunt which scriptural scholars had to face in this century when suspicions of 'modernism' were levelled against them when they spoke of literary forms in the Bible. In 1277 Stephen, Bishop of Paris, condemned 219 philosophical propositions! Not even Thomas Aquinas was exempt. Duns Scotus submitted unreservedly to this and to his superior's demands to observe the guidelines. Despite this restriction, his brilliant mind enabled him despite and within his human warmth and quiet humility to become acknowledged as the 'subtle doctor', the best known philosopher of his age. He had a sheltered life teaching students and emerges as being well liked and popular.

Various factors influenced his quite different system of philosophical and theological thought. He was influenced by the mathematical and experimental studies at Oxford, convinced that no other area of human knowledge can be demonstrated with such perfection. Metaphysics could not prove things so stringently but, he maintained, dealt with more important matters. When it comes to ethics, the science of right and wrong, natural thinking can only show us we should reverence God: and we have to rely on God's revelation to tell us what particular things are right and wrong.

The second major influence was his Franciscan spirituality. He was imbued with Frances' ideals of love and the value of the individual person. In philosophy this led him to emphasise the *will* rather than stress the *intellect* (as Thomas Aquinas had done). This was paralleled in theology where he began with St John's principle that 'God is love' and that all human love derives from God's love in us (as opposed to our love of God). Both the philosophical and theological insights led him in a very warm humane way to invent a word '*haeceitas*' (*this*ness) to stress that the abstract concepts of Greek thought, and Thomas Aquinas' re-formulation of that thought, were less important than the individual human life as it is being lived out. He went so far as to say that Aquinas' thought was effectively suggesting God did not have any free will left in the light of the laws of nature/laws of God construct which Aquinas had elaborated.

In all his thought, it is now clear that Scotus was such an independent thinker that he criticised both the Franciscan and Thomistic schools of thought and did his own thing. More careful analysis shows that he did not engage in a major attack on Thomas Aquinas, but rather on his own contemporaries: men like Henry of Ghent, Gothfried of Fontaines and Aegidius of Rome. His was not a contradictory system of thought, but a parallel and alternative one: his 'lateral thinking' is particularly useful in keeping separate the spiritual life and physical nature.

In theology, Duns Scotus is remembered most for ensuring that in the Western tradition, husband and wife are regarded as the ministers of the sacrament of marriage (rather than the priest), and for his teaching on the Immaculate Conception of Mary, which was defined in the Roman Catholic Church in the nineteenth century. Here again he took a different view from Aquinas and his advocacy of the doctrine was so clear it was known as *opinio Scoti*, the Scotus opinion. What is important is that he saw it as a logical conclusion of the effectiveness of Christ's grace—God's love—taking over and transforming human nature. The Reformers would reject this conclusion of his, but draw inspiration derivitively from his deeply spiritual stress on the love of God above and His gift to our sinful human nature.

Ryan, J K and B Bonasea: *John Duns Scotus* (Washington: 1965).
Coplestone, F J: *Medieval Philosophy* (Burns & Oates).

*   *It is interesting to note that in July 1991 John Dun Scotus was declared 'Venerable' by the Roman Catholic Church.*

13

LAURENCE

Lindores makes its mark

LINDORES Abbey, Angus takes its place in Scottish history from one enigmatic character—Laurence of Lindores. Possibly born around 1373, the first definite record shows him completing his MA degree in Paris in 1393. He was there until about 1403. The main influence on him was Jean Buridan and his study of the Physics of Aristotle and treatise *De Anima* which opened up the whole area of natural philosophy. Although influential before then, Laurence's treatise and logic disappeared in the sixteenth century; but his Physics was preserved in Cracow, Leipzig, Würtzburg and Copenhagen, testifying to the vitality of a ferment of thought— beginning with Scotus and Ockham—which in Paris University showed that *nominalism* (undermining natural philosophical certainties) could be entirely compatible with orthodox Christian theology. Peter D'Ailly, Bishop of Cambrai and John Gerson also showed this when they succeeded to Laurence's tradition at Paris.

Laurence himself had to leave Paris because the Hundred Years War made life difficult for Scots. He arrived in Glasgow sometime after 1403 and was present as the Bishop of Glasgow was dying. It was a difficult time for Scotland, but even more so for the church. There were two rival Popes: in Rome and in Avignon. Scotland supported the Avignon Pope, Benedict XIII. Those tensions were paralleled by others caused by the activities of a group called the Lollards, whose rejection of authority was seen by both state and church as a threat to good order. James Resbie, an English Franciscan, was put to death in Perth about 1408-9. Both situations were to box Laurence of Lindores into difficult positions.

The absence of a Scottish university was becoming more of a problem, with masters and students having to leave Paris and the Scots reluctant to go to Oxford and Cambridge (though some did). Bishop Henry Wardlaw of St Andrews decided to build one and got a bill of authorisation from Benedict XIII which arrived in

1414 with the full range of law, medicine, arts and theology. Laurence may well have been a prime mover for the university. He was certainly appointed there as the first lecturer on the Sentences of Peter Lambard. In 1419 Robert of Montrose endowed a college of Arts and Theology, an experimental college under Laurence.

All this brought future problems because, after Laurence left Paris, the new teachers were Realists who went back to Albert the Great's development of St Thomas Aquinas (Laurence was a nominalist). One of the first Acts of St Andrews was 'no Albertism.' All were to follow Buridan. This meant that there was an undercurrent in favour of Albertism coming from Cologne and (from 1420 onwards) Louvain.

Though liberal in philosophical and theological attitude, Laurence was bitterly anti-Lollard. This showed when he was used as Inquisitor. One case gave him divided loyalty. Benedict XIII, the anti-Pope, was deposed. Called Pedro de Luna, his followers were called *Lunatici*—lunatics. One English Franciscan supporter of Benedict preached to the nobles in Perth to continue supporting Benedict by waiting until he died, then everyone could get together to elect a new Pope. Laurence realised this was ridiculous, but, benevolent towards Benedict because he authorised St Andrews University, he merely banished the Franciscan to a convent in Lanark. The next case was not so easily resolved. Pavel Cravar was a Czech heretic and travelling medical doctor who claimed to have been physician to Ladislaus, King of Poland. The case was compounded by the belief that he was sent to cause trouble by English disciples of the Lollard, Wycliffe, who had gone to Prague for that purpose. Laurence condemned him and he was burned at the stake on 23 July 1433.

Laurence remains an enigma but in the new interest in the line of thought from Scotus on, Laurence's writing may have more lessons for the future than might at one time have been imagined.

Dunlop, A I (ed): *Acta Facultatis Artium Universitatis Sancti Andreae, 1413-1588* (Scottish History Society: 1964).

Durkan, J: *The Scottish Universities in the Middle Ages* (University of Edinburgh: 1971), PhD thesis.

14

ROBERT HENRYSON
The Poet Teacher

ROBERT Henryson (1420-1490) stands as a poet and teacher on the borders of the medieval world of Scottish intellectual life, and the new beginnings which were opening out. Some of his thinking is also remarkably modern. One of the problems in trying to get a picture of Henryson is that we know very little about his life. He was perhaps a cleric in minor orders, but he could have been a priest. He may have been born in Fife—we don't know—but he certainly spent much of his life there.

What we do know is that he came back to the University of Glasgow just after 1451 after studying canon (church) law on the continent. He may well have been lecturing in law at the university, but after a while he moved and became schoolmaster of the school attached to Dunfermline Abbey, staying there for the rest of his life. This may have been a question of returning to his roots, but there is on record a close connection between the abbot of Dunfermline and the University of Glasgow which may have accounted for the move.

There are no records of his work at the school, but there are some records of him being Notary Public in Dunfermline—so it would appear his legal training was not entirely wasted. That apart, however, there are many clues in his writings to show that he did not like lawyers as a breed and that his move to teaching was a move from the distasteful to an activity much more suited to his warm humanist nature and interests. He clearly liked teaching and was interested in its theory. This contrasted with vivid pictures in his poetry of what he considered as 'black oppression' in the Scotland of his day. He blamed this on lawyers. In his writing he portrays ordinary people as sheep kept in their place, cruelly treated by lawyer wolves.

The poetry of Henryson has its pessimistic side but that is secondary to the main characteristics. He wrote extremely attractive religious poetry, some of which could be described as hymns. He shows himself devout without being excessively so and reflects in his work the liturgical seasons of the church's worship. One very beautiful poem is about the Annunciation.

Most of all, Henryson's poetry is very personal and full of warm insights. He's clearly a scholar and a humanist with a sensitivity to real life which makes it clear that he never lost touch with the young people he was teaching or with the life around him.

In some ways, his identification with nature and his sensitivity to animals make him a very special bridge person from the Celtic bards to the modern attempts to build a Christian sensitivity to environmental concerns. In his fables he has the animals behaving like animals—and very acutely observed in the process—but talking like human beings about the social issues of the day. *Animal Farm* had its antecedents that far back into Scotland's history!

Most poets were court figures and here again there is the fact that Dunfermline was still regularly visited by the court at that time. There is, however, no evidence of Henryson at court: only speculation! From his writings, the 'Testament of Cresseid' —a tragedy set in the Trojan War—is more in the style of a poem to be read at court. It's a kind of supplement to Chaucer's poem on the same subject, so would have immediate social acceptance. And Henryson's 'Robene and Makyne' is the earliest Scottish example of pastoral poetry.

Henryson's masterpiece, however, is his 'Morall Fabels of Esope', a metrical version of 13 Aesop fables. These have clearly emerged from his teaching work: in one sense school stories in the Scots standard language of the time; and in another sense the sort of biting stories which might be recounted in the pub or on the street corner on a Saturday night. They are written to be circulated to the new educated middle class and could fairly be described as slightly subversive. He is a true poet ... with messages only possible because of the poet's ability to stand back and acutely observe the society of his day. That vision was shot through with faith.

Fox, D (ed): *Poems of Robert Henryson* (Oxford University Press: 1981).
MacQueen, J: *Robert Henryson* (Oxford University Press: 1967).

15

WILLIAM ELPHINSTONE
'Light from the North'

WILLIAM Elphinstone (*c* 1431-1514) lived for about 83 years, spending most of it at the centre of Scottish life. He died broken-hearted after the tragedy of Flodden, at a time when, despite his age, people still had enough confidence in his abilities to nominate him Archbishop of St Andrews.

We first hear of Elphinstone emerging in 1452 as one of the first graduates from the newly established University of Glasgow. After teaching as a regent there, he took a second degree at Paris before returning to Glasgow to become rector in 1474. Already a priest, he became Bishop of Ross in 1481 and then Bishop of Aberdeen in 1483. There he stood out, both in his own right and as a symbol of a whole range of Scottish churchmen in the fifteenth century who went abroad for second degrees to Paris, Louvain and Cologne, and returned to build up the Scottish universities.

Parallel with Elphinstone's ecclesiastical advancement was his career in the affairs of state. The use of churchmen for offices of state arose from the belief of the Scottish kings that they could trust them. Equally, their training in canon and civil law was ideal for administration. This suitability was one of the main reasons why the kings demanded the right to nominate bishops and abbots for appointment by the Pope. This interface often, however, caused clashes of loyalty. Elphinstone was not immune from such pressure.

In 1498, Elphinstone gained a licence from James IV to found Scotland's third university at Aberdeen. He went on to establish the college of St Mary in the Nativity, better known as King's College, after James IV. The king's crown can still be seen clearly above King's chapel in Old Aberdeen. In this and in other spheres, Elphinstone must go down in history as one of the key educationalists of the fifteenth century. The motto of the university was *Pro Patria,* to stress that it was being founded for the good of the country. Added to that, Elphinstone aimed at the first 'national curriculum' in the grammar schools and universities of Scotland.

He was also characterised as one of the most loyal servants of the crown in his century. He served James II in minor positions, but with James III rose to be finally entrusted with the most important position in the realm, that of Chancellor. He was, however, in trouble after rebellion led to the battlefield of Sauchieburn and the death of James III. He had been too identified with the dead king. Nevertheless, such was his brilliance in both canon and civil law that by the mid 1490s he was back in favour with James IV.

In church matters, Bishop Elphinstone made important additions to the Cathedral of St Machar and set out to reform church life. He also saw the church as having a social responsibility and so had no hesitation in using its master of works to build a stone bridge over the River Dee to make life easier for the community. Church and society for him made an integral whole. Kith and kin meant a great deal to him, and so it seemed quite natural to use a whole 'tribe' of Elphinstones and spread them throughout the diocese to carry out his reforms. We might see it as nepotism; in his age it was the normal way to administer.

As well as looking to the future with a fair deal of visionary thinking, Elphinstone was concerned with cementing the church tradition he inherited. One aspect which was dear to him was that of Scotland's saints. He sent his priests out through his diocese to find the details of those who were regarded as saints, both those stretching back to Columba and those in more recent times. From these he had built up the *Aberdeen* or *Elphinstone Breviary* of 1507. He had two aims: one was to feed popular piety with more saints to match the growth in chapels within the churches; the other was to follow the pattern of all successful reformers, to strengthen links with the past while making changes for the future. The 'light from the north' affected in this way every aspect of church life in the Scotland of his time.

McFarlane, L J: *William Elphinstone and the Kingdom of Scotland, 1431-1514* (Aberdeen University Press: 1985).

Forrester D, and Murray: *Studies in the History of Worship in Scotland* (Edinburgh: 1984).

16

ROBERT CARVER

Rogue Musician?

DEPENDING on people's point of view, Robert Carver (*c* 1490-*c* 1546) was a musician who led Christians astray by pandering to their 'carnal desires', or a musician who enriched Scottish worship with the most uplifting insights from the continental tradition. What is certain is that he was no 'rogue musician', but a composer of breadth and imagination whose work makes it clear that, for better or worse, pre-Reformation Scottish church life was able to reflect the best of developed church music tradition at least on occasions of national importance.

It is still possible to visit the ruin of where Robert Carver lived, but that and a major manuscript of his work is all we have to go on to unravel his significance. He was an Augustinian *canon regular* at Cambuskenneth, across the River Forth from Stirling. These canons lived under church constitutions which laid out for them a regular life of prayer, community and church services, but did not involve them being cloistered like the monks.

Cambuskenneth had close connections with Stirling Castle and the Stuart kings and so—especially since one motet, 'O Bone Jesu', is scored for no fewer than 15 voices and such numbers of musicians would not be found at Cambuskenneth or a normal parish—it seems most probable that Carver's work was composed for the Chapel Royal in Stirling Castle. This was remodelled in 1501 by James IV, and since such Chapel Royals in England and on the continent were complemented by musicians as a matter of course, it again seems highly probable that Carver was in some sense a court composer. Since his main work seems to be dated to the 1520s, he would be associated with the court of the young James V who was prematurely to succeed James IV after the Flodden disaster.

Careful examination of the manuscript, such as has been done by Kenneth Elliot, and discussions of its significance when it was featured in Glasgow's European Year of Culture in 1990, have reinforced the picture of Carver as moving in important circles. His polyphonic music could not have been used in the average parish and would have demanded a bigger setting than the relatively small Cambuskenneth. The manuscript has works important to Scotland, but also five masses and two motets of Carver. They reflect English, Flemish and continental influences and seem to demand that Carver must have studied abroad. He must have been a major investment for the canons.

One mass is particularly interesting, for among the independent strands, the main tune (*Cantus Firmus*) is 'L'Homme Armé' (armed man). This is the only British example of the use of this *cantus firmus* which was often used on the continent even by such a distinguished composer as Palestrina. Robert Carver had been directly in touch with the best, and not at second hand from England.

After the Reformation, the music of Robert Carver disappeared from the churches because the reformers disapproved of music which the full congregation (as opposed to just the clerics behind the rood screens) could not join in. Many Calvinists felt that musical embellishment, like any other, took away from, rather than added to the impact of the Word of God. It's important, however, to realise that Robert Carver would have been frowned on even by some of his contemporaries before the Reformation. One dramatic example of this is Carver's fellow Augustinian canon, Robertus Richardinus, who, writing in 1530, attacked all over-elaborate music as having no place in church: 'Song and chant were introduced for the sake of carnal not spiritual minds: brought into church to amuse people, to tickle the ears of the groundlings. The church music which prevails nowadays does not kindle the true direction but rather melts to distraction. It is unbiblical and unsupported by sound tradition. How did it grow up in this way, especially among the brethren of St Augustine whose rule prescribes that they sing nothing but what you have found prescribed in writing for chant. But some here introduced private masses for their own fancy. Would that they studied the Bible instead.'

Elliot, K: 'Music of Church and Court, 1500-1700' in D Daiches (ed): *A Companion to Scottish Culture* (1981).

17

PATRICK HAMILTON
Forerunner of the Scottish Reformation?

THE burning to death as a heretic of Patrick Hamilton (1503-1528) is one of the relatively few blots in Scottish religious history. He's a young man of whom we know very little, but John Knox in his *History* honours him very much as a forerunner of the Scottish Reformation and said that the 'reek of Patrick Hamilton spread to many the Protestant faith.' All we can say is that it was certainly one influence among many others, and for some who witnessed his death it was crucial. One of these was Alexander Allan, who went on to become professor of Protestant theology at Leipzig, but that didn't directly affect the course of events in Scotland.

Patrick was, on his father's side, related to the immensely powerful Hamilton noble family, and on his mother's to the Stewarts. He was born at Kincavel near Linlithgow and became some sort of cleric at least, for the purposes of receiving the revenues of being Commendator Abbot of Fearn, a Premonstratensian abbey in Ross-shire. He took his Master of Arts degree in Paris, but also spent some time in Louvain in Flanders, which with its study of the biblical languages of Hebrew and Greek, would be more likely the place where he first became impressed with Lutheran ideas.

In 1523 he could be found back at St Andrews where his nascent Lutheran ideas got him into trouble. Perhaps because of his family connections, Archbishop Beaton was reluctant to prosecute. Patrick, however, returned to the continent to continue his studies. Before that, however, he may well also have developed his musical interests. According to Alexander Allan—a canon of St Andrews who went abroad—Patrick composed a Mass for nine voices (the 'Angels') for use in the priory at St Andrews. Presumably this would have been for use on the feast of St Michael, which was a great celebration in St Andrews. John Foxe, the

English writer on the martyrs, writes of how he saw the original document telling this story.

On the continent, Hamilton went to Marburg in Germany where he immersed himself in Lutheran thought. It was a reflection of the times that he went there with Gilbert Winram, who was probably the brother of a St Andrews canon, John Winram, who argued the Catholic position for many years before eventually joining the reformers. In any case it was at Marburg that Hamilton produced in Latin a series of theological propositions called *Patrick's Places*. These in many ways went beyond Luther and so may be the foundation for Knox's claim that Hamilton met Luther and Melanchthon at Wittenberg at this time. This claim is not as yet backed up by any evidence in the records. Be that as it may, *Patrick's Places* claims we have no free will, that there is no Purgatory, that the Pope has no place in the church, that any cleric is as good as a bishop, that vows are wicked, that no one is saved unless predestined, that being in sin means having no faith, that the doctrine of penance for penitents is devilish, and that the baptism of babies is not scriptural. Luther would have been horrified.

When Patrick returned to Scotland, many were also horrified, especially as those who admired him had spread *Patrick's Places* around England. Word would get back to Scotland. Added to this, the atmosphere against Lutheranism had been building up. In 1525 the Scottish parliament passed an act forbidding the importation of Lutheran books. For a while after Hamilton's return it seemed there would not be a problem. There is nothing in the *Acts of Parliament* in 1527 and he seemed to have moved freely in St Leonard's College in St Andrews advocating his opinions with eager zeal (Knox said later on that those who drew from St Leonard's well became Protestant in their faith). It is claimed that he got married soon after his return to Scotland but, when he was finally indicted before Archbishop James Beaton, this fact does not appear and it's hard to see how it would not have been used against him. Regardless of any marriage, he certainly had a daughter, Isobel.

Once again, Archbishop Beaton seems to have given him the

chance to escape at the eleventh hour, but this time Patrick Hamilton was determined to make a stand. He was burned to death in front of St Salvator's College in St Andrews. A stone marks the spot.

And nothing seems to have changed in our modern world—people still die when their convictions are seen to be a threat, but later generations have looked back and found themselves revering Hamilton's memory.

St Salvator's College, St Andrews

Lorimer, P: *Patrick Hamilton, the First Preacher and Martyr of the Scottish Reformation* (Edinburgh: 1857).

Foxe, J: *The Acts and Monuments of the Christian Martyrs* (London: 1843-9), 8 volumes.

18

GEORGE WISHART

Saint or 'Stiff-necked' Rabble-rouser?

GEORGE Wishart (1513-1546) is portrayed by John Knox as a saint put to death by the very epitome of evil, Cardinal Beaton. Yet only a few years before, Wishart was described as a 'stiff-necked' authoritarian preacher who was behind threats to 'cut off the ears' of his opponents at Bristol: and subsequent to that, while some would have loved to have seen him slain, he was yet described as a saint by Tilney at Cambridge.

GEORGE WISHART

George came from an important family at Pittarro in Angus and his mother came from the well-connected Lindsay family. He first appears at Louvain University where he got his degree in 1532, coming out top in the final examination. It was a centre of Greek and Hebrew, as well as the arts, and during his time there he became interested in the Reform movements. In journeys along the Rhine he met Anabaptists in Strasbourg as well as Lutherans.

On his return to Scotland, Wishart became schoolmaster at Montrose in 1534 and was friendly with John Erskine of Dun, who was later to be involved in the Scottish Reformation and become superintendent of Angus. In 1538, he was summoned before the Bishop of Brechin. Wishart says it was because he taught the New Testament in Greek, but more likely it was because of his Protestant theology.

Wishart went next to England where he was licensed to preach by Hugh Latimer, the Bishop of Worcester, who was turning to Lutheran ideas himself. In due course Wishart was accused of the 'worst blasphemy', not just denying the ability of merit to Christians, but even to Christ himself. His supporters were a fiery bunch who threatened to cut off the ears of those who had reported him. He was taken to London and forced to recant in St Paul's before Cranmer. In fact he had to recant three times in a week: at St Paul's, at St Nicholas' Bristol and Christ church, Bristol. How sincere the recantation was is debatable, but his temper showed through at the end of the day when he threw at the officials the faggots (for burning) which he was supposed to carry under his arm round the church as a sign of repentance.

Cranmer sent him to teach at a college in Cambridge, where one of his pupils speaks of how Wishart was influenced by the Anabaptists, particularly in his teaching that they should be hard on themselves but generous to the poor. By this time, he had moved from his previous position to the less sacramental and less ritualistic position of Zwingli and in prison took on the translation of the first Swiss Confession of Faith.

In 1543 he returned to Scotland and found support for his preaching in the remnants of the Lollards in Ayrshire. He showed himself a true Zwinglian by his advice to the lower nobility to go around destroying all images and stained-glass windows. Even Knox noted that this nearly resulted in the destruction of a tabernacle at Mauchline which was 'beautiful to see.' In East Lothian he met and influenced Knox deeply, for Knox would for some time still describe himself as a 'minister of the sacred altar.' From East Lothian, finally, where his preaching failed, Wishart went to Dundee because he had heard of the ravages of plague there, a dramatic example of a love for the poor and unfortunate which marked the whole of his life.

It is at this stage that we find the dramatic confrontation between Cardinal Beaton and George Wishart which was to end in Wishart being burned to death and the Cardinal being murdered a few months later. There were two items on on the indictment for heresy: Wishart's earlier belief that adult baptism alone was valid; and the doctrine of 'soul sleepers' in the period before the resurrection of the body, rather than Purgatory. It was also clear, however, that Wishart could only accept a symbolic presence of Christ in the Eucharist. So there were grounds for heresy claims, but was there a hidden agenda in view of what seems to have been real reluctance in Cardinal Beaton to have him executed?

Wishart has been accused of being involved in a plot to kill Cardinal Beaton, an accusation which has gained credence by the growing evidence of the harsh, violent side to Wishart's charac-

THE BURNING of GEORGE WISHART at ST ANDREWS (HOLINSHEAD 1577)

ter. It is also true that his brother, Hugh Wishart, was procurator fiscal to the Cardinal, and remained so: thus he would have been in a position to pass information to Beaton's killers, some of whom significantly were described as 'earnest professors of Jesus Christ.' Again too, in the final killing of the Cardinal, there are Lindsay connections which again link with Wishart. On the other side, however, is an enigma about a certain John Wigtown, a 'disparate priest', supposedly sent by Beaton to attack Wishart in Dundee; perhaps a heretic trying to buy his freedom, but perhaps the central point of a 'disinformation' story. Be that as it may, Wishart certainly died with courage, dignity and forgiveness. Can one ask for any more?

Sanderson, M: *Cardinal of Scotland: David Beaton, c 1494-1546* (Edinburgh: 1986).

Dickenson, W C: *John Knox's History of the Reformation in Scotland* (Edinburgh: 1949), in 2 volumes.

19

ELIZABETH ADAMSON
Woman behind the scenes

IT has become more keenly appreciated in recent years that, behind the scenes of Catholic Scotland in the 1550s, the Protestant faith was being nurtured in house churches known as 'privy kirks.' John Knox was in Geneva at this time and wrote regularly not just to the men in those privy kirks, but also to the women who were the wives of some of the leading lawyers, merchants and burgesses of the time. In these letters he shows a warmth and respect for women which is quite different from the polemic directed mainly at the Catholic Queen Mary in England, entitled *The First Blast of the Trumpet against the Monstrous Regiment of Women.*

One of the women he wrote to—and therefore one who was at the centre of a privy kirk—was Elizabeth Adamson, the wife of James Barron, an Edinburgh merchant and dean of the Merchant Guild at the time. When John Knox came back to Scotland in the winter of 1555-6, on his great preaching tour to Edinburgh, Ayrshire and the community of Angus and the Mearns, Elizabeth had been ill for some time and Knox met her again.

James Barron himself was a devoted Protestant who had been to Geneva in the 1550s to visit Knox and Calvin. As dean of guild, he was in charge of St Giles' Cathedral and all the altars there, with the arrangements for the priests celebrating mass day by day at these altars. It is the ultimate irony to find him also hosting one of the privy kirks from which 'would grow up the face of Protestantism.'

Elizabeth herself died in the middle of 1556, and Knox in his *History of the Reformation of Religion within the realm of Scotland* has a touching account of what happened. The Catholic priests came to her death-bed offering the sacraments, but she turned them away firmly, despite having been brought up to believe that the sacrament they offered opened the way to heaven. This itself was an act of character and courage, since this happens five years before the Reformation settlement. What Elizabeth did was to insist that her friends gathered round and said Psalm 103. This is the Psalm which reads: 'Bless the Lord, O my soul, and forget not all his benefits: Who forgives all your iniquity, Who heals all your diseases, Who redeems your life from the Pit, Who crowns you, with steadfast love and mercy, Who satisfies you with good things as long as you live so that your youth is renewed like the eagle's.'

The rest of the psalm contrasts the frailty of humanity—our 'days are like grass'—with the steadfast everlasting love of the Lord. Elizabeth went on to say, 'At the teaching of this Psalmie, begane my trubled soule first effectually to taist of the mercy of my God, which now to me is more sweat and precious, then all the kingdomes of the earth war gevin to me to possesse theme a thowsand yearis.'

Elizabeth's story gives a powerfully moving insight into how it came about that so many women in Scotland were among the first Protestants. It illustrates too the power of books among the middle class for Protestantism: the 'religion of the Book' gave them direct access to the riches of Scripture and God's word in a way that did not depend on the quality of the preaching of the priest. Women like Elizabeth Adamson—the 'dear sisters of Edinburgh' in Knox's words—remained the most tenacious supporters of Protestant faith all through Mary's reign. Their strength remained clear—though they were now very old—in the 1580s. In 1584, for example, some of them had to be driven out of town to stop them protesting against the 'Black Acts' of parliament designed to establish royal control over the Kirk.

Many regret that, despite this power and importance, women in Knox's post-Reformation Scotland on the whole lost status rather than gained it. They were not even allowed to be godmothers at baptism and had no vote in kirk sessions. It was to be many generations before women like Elizabeth Adamson were properly recognised.

Laing, D (ed): *The Works of John Knox* (Edinburgh: 1846-64).
Kirk, J: *Patterns of Reformation* (T & T Clark: 1989).

20

MARY OF GUISE
Power and Piety

MARY of Guise (1515-1560)—the mother of Mary, Queen of Scots—illustrates very clearly the heady sixteenth century mix of the search for power and spiritual idealism. She belonged to the great ducal family of Lorraine in France. Her father, Claude de Guise, married a redoubtable woman who gave him a large and talented family and enabled him, through military governships, to advance to centre stage in French politics. The family was conventionally Catholic, but the mother was deeply pious and after her wayward husband's death she ran a convent and outlived most of her family.

Mary herself emerged as a young lady regarded as a great beauty at the court in Paris. Her impact at that time is reflected in her voluminous correspondence in later years with the vast number of court personages who still

MARY of Guise

kept in touch with her when she was in Scotland. She married Louis d'Orleans, Duke of Longueville, in 1534, but after his early death she was narrowly rejected as a wife by Henry VIII (her neck was too short!) and then in 1538, became James V's second-choice wife after his own died after only six months. She gave birth to two sons, James and Arthur, but they tragically died within a few weeks of each other in 1541: she and the king were said to be 'stricken with grief.' By December 1542, she gave birth to a daughter, Mary, in Linlithgow Palace, the week before James himself died.

That daughter was now queen, the only remaining Stewart, so

Mary of Guise had to set aside any thought of returning to France to stay with Mary. She was a fond and affectionate mother who missed her desperately when they were later separated: her daughter in turn almost went mad with grief when her mother died.

These personal things have to be stressed because parallel with motherly love was the Guise family pride and the instinct for power-broking with a daughter, who on being married to the dauphin of France in preference to Edward of England (the other option) became the possible monarch of the four kingdoms of France, Scotland, England and Ireland. It was Mary of Guise who advised Henry II of France that the marriage of Mary to his son was achievable, rather than the English marriage which Henry saw as a clearer empire-building exercise for this 'dynasty.' Mary failed at first to be regent for the young Mary, Queen of Scots, but attained the Great Seal and the Royal palaces which signified regency once Mary technically came of age in 1554. At first she continued the policy of tolerance and prudent discretion she had always shown, believing that though she herself was Catholic, it was wrong to make those who disagreed with her religion suffer for 'being devout.'

By 1558, however, she felt forced by the massive pressures around her—and in particular the English attempts to take over Scotland and build political and Protestant unity—to be confrontational with Protestants and defeat them militarily. A large French expeditionary force landed at Leith (an amazing achievement at that time for a force of 6000 foot soldiers and 1000 horsemen) and she organised Leith into a 'fortified police station' which never succumbed to a three month English siege. Mary led the French to try to take Haddington quickly, but failed and so had to set out to starve them into submission, a difficult task for an army itself very far away from home. Mary exhorted her troops herself, riding into battle on horseback and when the English landed at Inchkeith, she was found declaiming a Renaissance harangue which drew on the ancient Greek and Roman models.

The vision of Mary of Guise was clear. It was to preserve Scotland as a sacred charge for Mary her daughter, by then Queen of France (but only for a brief period before her husband died). It was also to administer part of the great Guise family sphere of dynastic influence. In the spirit of the Holy Roman Empire of old, her Catholic faith was a building block of that dynasty. The odds, however, were too great. A crisis at the French court, triggered by an attempted Protestant *Huguenot* take-over of power, ensured no more support would come to be used against the Protestant cause in Scotland. Mary might still have survived, but her health was failing and she died on 10-11 June 1560 with the English and the lords of the Congregation heading for victory.

Reaction to her death was significant. On the one hand, the lords of the Congregation were so afraid of her ghost that they buried her in a lead coffin in the bowels of Edinburgh Castle until it was taken in a midnight flight to France in 1561. On the other hand, her death was greeted with very great and genuine mourning throughout Scotland ... even among those who opposed her. Such is greatness.

Marshall R: *Mary of Guise* (London: 1977).
Scottish Correspondence of Mary of Lorraine, 1543-1560 (Scottish History Society: 1927).

21

JOHN KNOX
Reformation from Abroad

JOHN Knox (*c* 1513-72) has become identified in the popular mind with every stage of the process surrounding the Scottish Reformation settlement of 1560, but it is at least arguable that his influence was greatest when he was encouraging the growth of privy kirks (small house gatherings of Protestants) and appealing to the Scottish nobles from his exile in Geneva.

JOHN KNOX

From origins in Haddington and being some sort of cleric, Knox was tutor to a rich family when he was introduced to George Wishart, the Protestant preacher who died for his faith at St Andrews in March 1546. This led him to join the murderers of Cardinal Beaton in St Andrew's Castle. When it failed, he was sent to the French galleys for 18 months: a horrific experience which must have taught him to exercise some caution in any future decisions about when to make his presence felt.

February 1549 brought release (thanks to Edward VI), and appointment in 1551 as one of six chaplains to the king. One of the puzzles about him is why he stayed in a ministry at Berwick during these years rather than returning like John Spottiswoode to face the challenge in Scotland. Many of his tracts at this stage are directed to an English audience. After Mary Tudor came to the throne in 1553, Knox fled not to Scotland but to the continent, and finally to Geneva. There he was much influenced by Calvin, while ministering to an exile congregation which, unlike some of the others he was with, was compatible with his developing theology.

In 1555 John Knox returned to Berwick to marry a Berwick girl, Marjory Bowes, to whom he had two sons before her early death in 1560. He was later to marry Margaret Stewart, daughter of Lord Ochiltree, in 1564 and have three daughters with her; but his first marriage seems to have established a very deep dimension, quite at odds with his *First Blast of the Trumpet against the Monstrous Regiment of Women* which, from Geneva, was intended to hit at Mary Tudor in England, and perhaps derivitively, but not so directly, against Mary of Guise in Scotland.

1555 was also the year when Knox came back secretly to Scotland and visited privy kirks in Edinburgh, Angus and Ayrshire. Many letters to 'the dear sisters of Edinburgh' have survived, bearing witness to his warm encouragement from Geneva of the spread of Protestantism from the lairds and nobles down through the various classes of society. At this time too his own transition from the ideas of Wishart and Zwinglian divines, whom he met in England during the reign of Edward VI, to those of Calvin, gradually became complete. During a short spell in Frankfurt-on-Main in 1554, he had drawn varying influences from Zwingli's Zurich, Basle and Calvin's Geneva, but had left them in a dispute about Edward VI's *Prayer Book* and the practice of kneeling at communion. Thus his 'appeal to the nobles' from Geneva, and his preaching when he was invited to return in 1559, was clearly Calvinist, and it was these ideas he incorporated in his *Confession of Faith* which was accepted by the lords of the Congregation in the Reformation parliament of 1560. Thanks at least in part to Maitland of Lethington, his *Book of Reformation* was rejected, and his strictly Genevan ideas were tempered within the drafting committee of 'six Johns' who produced the *First Book of Discipline*. Many of these ideals for a truly social gospel remained unfulfilled in Knox's Edinburgh (as the next years were to be known). Eight schemes of caring for the poor were tried and abandoned in the course of the 1560s.

After 1560, Knox is best known for his confrontation with Mary, Queen of Scots, the Catholic queen invited back to rule Scotland by the Protestant lords, on condition she respected the legal position of the Protestant faith in Scotland, but with the concession that she herself could maintain her Catholic faith and mass in private. From his pulpit in St Giles, Knox preached against Mary on the second Sunday she was back, thundering, 'One mass is more dangerous than ten thousand armed enemies!' He was right: by 1567, 12,606 persons allegedly attended mass at Mary's chapel. The mass, however, was only one part of the story. As Thomas Randolph, the English Protestant ambassador, put it: 'He ruleth the roost and of him all men stand in fear—would to God ye know how much.' Despite being reduced twice to tears, Mary faced up to him in dramatic and fierce debate.

Knox continued to thunder from the pulpit of St Giles but tempered his zeal to the changing political scene. He alienated Lord James by his attacks on Mary, and after the murder of Rizzio, Mary's Catholic secretary in March 1566, he withdrew to Ayrshire. The murder of Darnley and the reaction of the lords to the pre-eminence of Bothwell brought him back into favour and put Mary into exile. Even in the absence of Mary, the assassination of Moray in 1570, and a bitter civil war which had Edinburgh for its battlefield, led him to retreat for safety to St Andrews in 1570. On 9 November 1572 he made his last public appearance at St Giles for the induction of his successor.

GRAVE of JOHN KNOX

Knox died on 24 November and was buried in the churchyard then attached to St Giles. After his death came a major part of his enduring influence with the publication of his *History of the Reformation of Religion within the Realme of Scotland*. It shows a quite unique individual with shrewd insight, a strong capacity for humour and great strength of character.

Dickinson, W C (ed): *John Knox's History of the Reformation in Scotland* (Edinburgh: 1949).

Percy, E: *John Knox* (Edinburgh: 1927).

22

MARION OGILVY

'Behind every successful man ...'

MARION Ogilvy was 'the woman behind Cardinal David Beaton', but a great deal more in her own right. Dismissed as a 'common mistress' of a medievally corrupt archbishop, she has emerged in recent years in the writings of Margaret Sanderson as a person of real strength and achievement. She lived from the 1490s until 1575 and survived her relationship with Beaton to become a power in her family and in the country, and to live true to her Catholic faith as 'Lady of Melgund' in Angus.

ARMOURIAL BEARINGS of
CARDINAL BEATON

The law insisting that priests should not marry had only existed in the church for a few centuries and had often been honoured more in the breach than in the observance. It was widely expected that the Council of Trent would return to the practice of the first twelve centuries and have married priests alongside unmarried ones. David Beaton started to live with Marion Ogilvy when he was only technically a cleric, when marriage 'by habit and repute' was a fairly normal way of entering into it. Priesthood, episcopacy and the cardinal's hat came in a rush in 1537 and 1538, at a time when (since 1534) Beaton had been abroad most of the time as Scottish ambassador to the French court. So they had been together at least since 1524, when David Beaton returned from his first spell in France at the court of King Francis I.

Beaton had achieved brilliant success in France and recognition in Scotland followed when he became Commendator Abbot of Arbroath in that same year. Marion was similarly capable and mistress of her own destiny. Her father was Lord Ogilvy; her mother was Janet Lyle who laid out the pattern Marion was to follow by fighting for her own rights in person at the High Court in Edinburgh from her base at Airlie Castle. By 1525 Marion was an unmarried woman in her thirties, acting as executor for her parents and establishing her own security. She and Beaton chose to be together virtually as husband and wife for over 20 years. His enemies did not despise this arrangement so much, but rather the fact that as head of the ecclesiastical courts, Beaton passed sentence on those who advocated that priests should marry.

That apart, Marion had a stable, happy time with David from 1524 to 1534. They had eight children. At the same time she managed her own affairs and successfully built up a secure base in property in the Angus area. She must have been a familiar figure in Arbroath itself and had learned to sign her own name, leaning so heavily that she split the quill on several occasions!

This shows us the strength of character which enabled Marion Ogilvy to cope with the transformation in David's life when he became Cardinal. He was often abroad or away, and discretion was continually demanded of her: yet she did not forsake him. Knox relates how she was with Beaton on the night of his murder, passing the murderers as she slipped out the postern gate to her St Andrews' lodgings (28 May 1546). She fled by ferry to Angus when the news broke of the murder, but she was back in St Andrews by November (Beaton's body was yet unburied), contesting with Lord Gray, Sheriff of Forfar, her rights to the property he was trying to sequester. She was hunted and harried, but held her own. Margaret Sanderson feels she may have lost her nerve by the summer of 1547, marrying William Douglas for protection. But the marriage did not last: she was *un*married on 15 May and a widow by 18 September (Douglas may have died at the Battle of Pinkie). Marion then clearly re-found her nerve because she continued throughout her long life to fight in the courts. Her base was the castle at Melgund, where her coat of arms and those of David Beaton stood proudly over the windows of the hall in the keep. She died, still respected as the 'Lady of Melgund', in June 1575, and despite all the pressures retained her Catholic faith (as her will makes clear). The enigma of her faith, her morals and character, point to a woman ahead of her time, taking responsibility for her own life in a manner that Germaine Greer would very much admire.

Sanderson, M H B: *Mary Stewart's People* (Edinburgh: 1987).

23

JAMES HENRISOUN

The Visionary Merchant

JAMES Henrisoun, who flourished from the late 1520s to the late 1560s, seems at first sight a hard-headed merchant who skilfully manipulated the turmoil of Reformation times to his own advantage. More and more, however, his vision and influence are being appreciated.

Henrisoun was an Edinburgh merchant with extensive properties in the High Street. His trading contacts with the Netherlands may well have combined with his scathing views about the corruption of the Scottish Kirk (many parish churches 'rent or falling down and the fruites thereof spent in whoredom': most curates ignorant: bishops unable to conduct divine service: and parishioners 'lakketh not onely informacion to morall vertu but also devyn wisdome') as the reasons for him being an active Protestant before 1544. He may well have been a member of a privy kirk, an underground house cell, which operated in Edinburgh in the 1550s.

When James V was building relations with Charles as the Holy Roman Emperor, Henrisoun was arguing the virtues of Edinburgh. His eye was on the post of Conservator of Scottish Privileges (Trade) in the Low Countries, but his first play for power failed. After the death of James V, he was successful during the first months of the Earl of Arran's regency when Protestants were favoured. This changed by the end of 1543 when Arran renounced his stance as a Reformer: Henrisoun was out in the cold. Trade was ruined in any case because of the 'rough wooing' of the Scots by Henry VIII. Before then, however, Henrisoun was off to England to offer his services.

As long as Henry VIII was in power, he was employed at trivial tasks, but once the Earl of Hertford (who had sacked Edinburgh in 1544) became Duke of Somerset and regent for Edward VI, Henrisoun came to the fore. He gained celebrity and notoriety as part of a unionist propaganda team. Clearly his Protestant faith was a large part of the reason for joining with the English. The proposed marriage of Mary and Edward VI was seen as a 'godly marriage', whereas the Scots dealing with France were selling themselves into an 'Egyptian subjugation.' The arguments in Henrisoun's trading are not primarily religious, but they are underpinned by faith. He said that the marriage would bring peace and prosperity—the 'commonwealth'—and from that would flow 'the uncorrupt religion of Christ.'

When Somerset fell, losing his head into the bargain, Henrisoun's return to Scotland was at the invitation of the Catholic Mary of Guise. He had no property to come back to, for it was taken away in 1549 because his dealings with the English were regarded as treason. But Arran gave him a small pension. How this remarkable turn-around took place is a fascinating story. While still

The OLD ROYAL INFIRMARY as it was in the NINETEENTH CENTURY

in England, Henrisoun had heard of a plot by a renegade Scot with access to the cooking facilities for Mary, Queen of Scots (at this time in the French court) to poison her. Henrisoun informed the French, was thrown into prison and only released after the French had been convinced he had saved the young princess' life. Mary of Guise continued to be grateful and gave him a pension herself in 1553, and in 1554 he received back the post of conservator in the Low Countries which he had held before.

Despite his gratitude to Mary of Guise, Henrisoun retained both his religious faith as a Protestant and his vision of a better Scotland: it's illustrated clearly in his proposals to Edinburgh Town Council for a new school, an enclosed roofed market, a playground for the children, a new Tolbooth and the establishment of a hospital. In national affairs, he continued the vision he had already shown in England by talking of the industrial expansion of the textile industry (a vision well ahead of its time). Here he proposed a Forth and Clyde canal.

He survived to see the triumph of the 'incorrupt religion of Christ' at the Reformation. Many of his ideas anticipated the *First Book of Discipline*. Significantly his idea of a 'fair scule' was taken up, and as early as 2 April 1561 he was appointed one of three collectors for the poor in one of the areas of Edinburgh. In 1562 he was one of the first contributors for the hospital of his dreams, which would finally be completed in 1578 (the Royal Infirmary). It would seem too that he left his money to the poor of Edinburgh. Henrisoun is a fine example of a man whose motives were an impenetrable mixture of self-interest and religious response. Therein perhaps lies his importance for this book as one of God's people.

Henrisoun, J: *An Exhortation to the Scottes, to conforme themselves to the honourable, expedient, and godly union betwene the twoo realmes of Englande and Scotlande* (London: 1547).

Merriman, M: 'James Henrisoun and "Great Britain": British Union and the Commonwealth' in Roger Mason (ed): *Scotland and England* (John Donald: 1986).

24

NINIAN WINZET

The Power of the Pen

NINIAN Winzet was born about 1518 and was the priest and schoolmaster of the grammar school at Linlithgow from 1551. There the curriculum was taught solely in Latin and when the Reformation came to Linlithgow like a 'tidal wave' in 1559, Winzet refused to accept the fact that the Roman Catholic mass was celebrated one Sunday and the Protestant rite of John Knox the next. He had to leave his post.

Winzet surfaces next in Edinburgh, publishing several tracts from the press of John Scott, a printer in Edinburgh, in 1561. They contained bitter criticisms of John Knox who was preaching at St Giles. Edinburgh at this time was still very Catholic, as is made clear in a report by the Protestant English ambassador. His statistics show that 1200 attended communion with Knox, but this only accounted for one in six of the adults eligible. The rest were Catholic or scared or confused. This situation encouraged Winzet to try to draw Knox into controversy. Knox—in the manner of the day—should have replied by printed tract also, but he refused. Not even the publication of a rather wicked parody of Knox's *First Blast of the Trumpet against the Monstrous Regiment of Women* could provoke an answer in kind. Perhaps sensing that things were closing in on him, Winzet published in 1562 the *Last Blast of the Trumpet*, containing 63 questions to John Knox demanding an answer. In all of these pamphlets, he showed himself to be not just a scholar but a rabble-rouser.

Winzet's sophistication is evidenced by the fact that his first tract is also a blistering attack on the old Catholic bishops, and he told Queen Mary that bad appointments had caused much of the trouble which bred dissatisfaction. On the other hand, he brought forward skilled arguments against Knox being a lawful minister: 'Name suld tak the honour of ministratioun of Godis Word and Sacramentis on him, except he be laichfillie callit thereto.' He defends mass from charges of idolatry, and shows that to deny Christ's real presence is to brand accepted authorities such as Augustine and St John Chrysostom as heretics. In tackling thorny issues such as good works, the number of the sacraments and the nature of ministry, he shows himself to have clear objectives and to follow them through in an attractive teaching style.

The *Last Blast* was seized at the printer in July 1562 by the radically Protestant Town Council. Mary, Queen of Scots, had been keeping him under her protection and he was linked with one of her chaplains, René Benoist, whose writings were also published by John Scott. Mary could not prevent him, however, from being forced into exile.

He went first to Antwerp, which traditionally had a strong trading connection with Edinburgh and which had a massive printing works. From there he published more pamphlets. Paris was another stopping-off place the next year. When Mary was later in captivity at Sheffield he was her confessor, and after being suspected of involvement in the plotting surrounding Mary, he had a spell of imprisonment. His name was on the list of hunted priests on his next visit to England for a short time in September 1571. In 1572, he returned to Paris before accepting an appointment as abbot of Ratisbon or Regensburg. This was one of the 'Scots' colleges which were in fact Irish but, by virtue of the Scots pulling the wool over the Pope's eyes, they were accepted as Scots. He had finally accepted defeat and by accepting the post had abandoned his native Scotland as a lost cause and contented himself by working for Scots exiles.

Winzet is remembered as the finest pamphleteer of his day and as a shining example of the scholarliness of at least some of the lower clergy in the years leading up to the Reformation. He espoused the cause of reform, but wanted it within what he saw as the structures of Christ's Kirk and not outwith those structures. He was a worthy opponent of Knox and a credit to all he stood for. His exile witnesses to how much he was feared and respected.

Winzet, N: *Certain Tractates* (Scottish Texts Society: 1888-90).
Burns, J H: *Catholicism in Defeat* (History Today: 1962).

25

WILLIAM BROCAS
AND JAMES YOUNG
Hammermen divided

WILLIAM Brocas and James Young represent the rather dramatic divide at the time of the Scottish Reformation in the ranks of the leading craftsmen in Edinburgh. William Brocas represents those in the Hammermen—metalworkers—who remained Catholic, while James Young represents the Protestant group. The struggle mirrored what was happening in society at large.

The involvement of the church with the guilds showed the more positive side of Catholic cult and worship in the first half of the sixteenth century, for the church had clearly responded to the changes in town life which stemmed from the craft guilds being given incorporated status in the burghs. The guilds took pride of

place in the great processions at Candlemas and Corpus Christi around the blessed sacrament. In everyday life each craft had an altar and their own saint: then they would prescribe and pay for masses to be said for the living and the dead. The Hammermen, a powerful guild with 85 masters and as many apprentices, had gone one stage further: they had their own chapel, the Magdalene chapel in the Cowgate, built in 1547 as the last Catholic chapel to be opened in Edinburgh. With the Reformation, the guild was split.

TABLET on the
CHAPEL of ST MARY MAGDALENE,
showing the ARMS of the HAMMERMEN

William Brocas remained a devout Catholic, but William Barber, the chaplain, became exhorter (assistant minister) at Lasswade by 1565. In 1560, however, just as a minority radical town council swept into power in Edinburgh, so also a small radical group under James Young took over the Hammermen. William Brocas was accused of gathering with a group of 40 Hammermen at the Boroughloch (the Meadows today) and was taken before the Protestant town council. At the illegal meeting William Brocas had been elected deacon of the guild.

Three months later, in August, William Brocas was called before Mary's Privy Council to defend himself as best he might. He refused to budge from his principles. No one—he said—would seduce him from the loyalty he owed to the queen, and no one would seduce him from his Catholic faith either.

As a result of his stand the sequence of events is clear. In 1560 the Protestant minority gained control. After William Brocas' stand, the majority Catholic group took over and so did he. William was, however, dismissed by the Council and the guild was methodically purged in favour of James Young and his sympathisers. Finally, after Mary, Queen of Scots was deposed in 1567, the Protestant minority took over again and gradually turned that minority into a majority. William Brocas faded from the scene.

James Young triumphed, but on the way he was involved in a whole series of assaults on Catholics. In 1566 Mary tried to use the great feast of Candlemas (2 February) to attract some of her nobles back to the mass and celebration. Two days later, James Young and three colleagues made an unsuccessful attempt to murder the Dominican John Black, one of Mary's priests. Then on 9 March 1566, the very same night that Rizzio—Mary's Catholic stalwart secretary—was murdered in front of Mary's own eyes, a Protestant gang succeeded in murdering John Black and disappearing into the confusion of the night. Opportunism, power-play and violence then settled the religious allegiance of the Hammermen, rather than religious conviction. From that point on, the guilds would gradually pass from the centre-stage of religious observance and celebration.

Register of the Privy Council, volume 1.
Lynch, M: *Edinburgh and the Reformation* (Edinburgh: 1981).

26

JOHN BLACK

Catholic preaching changes—too late!

FROM the time of the Fifth Lateran Council at the beginning of the sixteenth century—which set out a programme of reform which could in large measure have made the Protestant reform unnecessary—the Black Friars, or Dominicans, were in the forefront with the Franciscans, in trying to bring reform to Scotland. Dominicans were to be split, however, as the reform movement failed to make the progress they wished. As early as 1543, a frustrated Dominican reformer John Adamson had to face riots when he turned to Protestant-style reforms. John Black represents in our story those who wished reform to take place within the established Catholic Church.

We first meet John Black as a Dominican based in the Dominican House situated, as was their wont, on the edge of Edinburgh as it was then. It is the site today of High School Yards, for the town ended at the junction of St Mary's Street and the Cowgate, where there is now a Salvation Army hostel. Early in 1559 the friary was sacked by a Protestant mob and later in the year John Knox was made the minister of Edinburgh by being made minister of St Giles. At the same time, John Black was celebrating mass in the Abbey church at Holyrood (the ruin now beside Holyrood Abbey). He seems to have been active and successful round about the city for he was imprisoned in 1562 after being violently assaulted. Mary, Queen of Scots intervened on his behalf and took him into the relative safety of Edinburgh Castle.

By 1565 things were changing. As many went to the mass at Holyrood that Easter, so it was said by the English ambassador, as went to hear John Knox at St Giles'. In 1566 Mary began on a positive campaign of attracting Protestants back to the Catholic faith. John Black was one of two men appointed to celebrate mass and to preach in her chapel at Holyrood.

This specific mention of preaching may well have been the

first Scottish implementation of the decrees of the Council of Trent which launched in the Catholic Church what is often termed the Counter-Reformation. The decrees of 1564 pointed to a renewal of preaching. Even John Knox noticed the difference, for he notes that John Black preached in a different way in 1566 from the way he had preached in 1559.

John Black was a marked man and this increased when rumours were spread that he had a sexual liaison with the wife of a leading Protestant councillor, John Watson, the treasurer of Edinburgh. The times were violent, with Protestant and Catholic murder gangs roaming the city. There even seem to have been segregated Catholic and Protestant public houses. The stakes were high, for in 1560 the minority Protestant party was given power by political *fiat* rather than gaining or earning power. Time had eroded their position and by 1566 only one of the original radical party which brought in the Reformation was still on the Town Council. John Black was seen as at least a symbol of the reasons for failure and so there was an attempt on his life two days after the major celebration of Candlemas when Mary tried to attract her nobles back to the mass. Involved in the assault were James Young, a powerful craftsman from the Hammermen Guild, a tavern owner Andrew Armstrong, Thomas Brown and William Johnston (craftsman or small merchant). That was 4 February, 1566. On 9 March—the very night when Rizzio was murdered before the very eyes of the pregnant Mary (and she may well have been an intended victim)—a Protestant gang succeeded in murdering John Black. It was an effective means to eliminate him and his influence without making him a martyr and a rallying point of popular support. The man behind the murder kept well in the background and the political upheaval covered up the religious killing. Good preaching, it seems, makes people edgy or even afraid!

Lynch, M: *Edinburgh and the Reformation* (Edinburgh: 1981).
McRoberts, D (ed): *Essays on the Scottish Reformation* (Glasgow: 1962).

27

JAMES HAMILTON
Vacillator or Survivor?

JAMES Hamilton, the 2nd Earl of Arran from his early twenties, was only a heartbeat from the throne of Scotland all his life. He has been portrayed variously as a weak vacillating man caught up in the pressures which led to the Scottish Reformation, or as a

JAMES HAMILTON

remarkable survivor from those same pressures. He died peacefully in his bed in 1575—most in his position were not so fortunate.

Arran took over the vast Hamilton lands in 1529 at the death of his father, and later on in 1548 he received a grant of the duchy of Chatelherault from Henry II of France. Had James V died without a child, he would have been king. Later on, if either Mary, Queen of Scots or James VI had died without children, he would

also have become king. This was not to be, but at the death of James V in 1543 he became Regent of Scotland and tutor to the young queen: these offices he held through thick and thin until 1554.

He seems to have been raised as a conventional Catholic, but in the early months of the regency he surrounded himself with Protestants, the ones who 20 years later would lead the Reformation. He had a vision that Scotland would become Protestant by Mary marrying the Prince of Wales, son of Henry VIII. This caused him, on one notorious occasion in the early years of his regency, to be pelted by the wives of Edinburgh on his way to St Giles. Pressures built up and he had to return to the Catholic fold, not least because the validity of his claim to the throne depended

66

on the possible annulment (Catholic) of his father's first marriage, but also because Mary's betrothal to the French dauphin pointed equally realistically to that being the future.

Once back with the Catholic Church, he used his position as regent to advance the church career of John his brother (half-brother to be precise, because of illegitimacy). He appointed him Bishop of Dunkeld and then, two days after the death of Archbishop Beaton, Archbishop of St Andrews. Rome was so suspicious that John's consecration was delayed for three years. Nevertheless Arran and Archbishop Hamilton worked as a team, the one in the state and the other in the church, right up to the Reformation. It was John's advice of course, in those early days of the regency, not to offend the church, which led Arran to move away from the 'glitter of Protestantism.' Arran's son, however, was a committed Calvinist and was imprisoned in France for his faith.

During these years as regent, Arran has been described as weak, vacillating, indecisive, reduced to tears at the slightest provocation, a poor general. The final insult was that he was kicked out of his job by a woman. This was when Mary, Queen of Scots came of age and appointed her mother—Mary of Guise—as regent in 1554. More recently, this has been regarded as unfair, for he was in many ways the longest survivor of his period. He held on for twelve turbulent years surrounded by towering characters such as the Earl of Angus, Lennox, Mary of Guise and Henry VIII. He saw Mary of Guise into her grave and was able to see the overthrow of Catholicism in Scotland in the face of continuing majority support. To assess Arran as a politician and leader of Scotland, we have to realise that he conducted Scottish affairs at a time when his country's independence was under greater threat than at any time since the fourteenth century. At no point did he surrender Scottish independence when a lesser person would have: and he even brought in the French to preserve that independence from England.

In 1560 Arran made a clear decision that the hour had come for Protestantism. He joined the lords of the Congregation and most feel that without him they would have failed. And yet he supported Mary, Queen of Scots until the murder of Darnley. Even then, Mary fled to his house in 1568 and he led the final futile defence of her crown.

Perhaps the most critical assessment of his life is his role as head of the Hamilton family. Throughout Europe great families sought to further their interests as dynastic families. By this criteria, he was outstandingly successful. The Hamiltons outlived the Tudors and the Stewarts. Though he had a son who became insane, other sons and daughters did well and significantly there are no recorded attacks on him by his offspring in an age when these were the fashion. And his faith? It comes at the crossroads of all the other aspects of his life: there are clear convictions, but less black and white distinctions, than we are now accustomed to.

Donaldson, G: *Scotland: James V to James VII* (Edinburgh: 1965).

Finnie, E: *The House of Hamilton: patronage, politics and the Church in the Reformation period* (Innes Review xxxvi: 1985).

28
GEORGE GORDON
'Pope of the North'

GEORGE Gordon, 4th Earl of Huntly, was born just before Flodden (*c*1510) and died tragically at the battle of Corrichie in 1562. He was the last of the old-fashioned Catholic magnates of Scotland, known as the 'Pope of the north' in the Reformation controversies and political upheavals which eventually destroyed him.

Huntly, the grandson of a natural daughter of James IV, and a member of a powerful family given the status of an earldom by James II, performed the function of loyal lieutenant in the north and held the office of sheriff of Aberdeen. These roles, when added to his vast lands, gave him immense power. In 1542, when Mary became queen at a week old, he was on the council of regency and went on to attain the high office of Chancellor in 1546 after the murder of Cardinal Beaton. When, during the 'rough wooing' by England of the infant queen (to force her marriage to Edward), the English defeated the Scots under the Earl of Arran at the battle of Pinkie, he was captured but managed to escape to the relative safety of the north.

Throughout the 1550s, Huntly's Catholic allegiance was clear. So also was his power and influence in the north, both politically and in church affairs. A kinsman was Bishop of Aberdeen and a cousin became Bishop of Galloway before becoming a Protestant in 1559. It's a symbol of the confusion of the times that Huntly's first son became a Protestant, his third son was a Catholic and executed at the time of his father's death, and his grandson was a Catholic!

Despite his Catholic status and general support for Mary of Guise, Huntly fell out with her and landed in jail in 1557. This probably led him to support the rebellion of the Protestant lords of the Congregation in 1560—somewhat reluctantly—and he saw the return of Mary, Queen of Scots as the ideal opportunity for the

Catholic faith to make a return in Scotland. When she was being approached by the Protestant lords, Huntly made separate representations that if she came to Aberdeen, he would raise three shires to rebuild a Catholic Scotland. Mary, however, did not trust him because of what had happened with her mother, Mary of Guise. Added to that, there is growing evidence that Mary, in coming to Scotland, had at least one eye on the throne of England to which she had a better claim than the illegitimate Elizabeth. For both Scottish and English consumption then, it seems that after her return to Scotland in 1561, she may have felt it necessary to establish her credentials as a respecter of the Protestant character of any country she ruled. At the very least, in the light of a proposed meeting she was to have in Nottingham with Elizabeth, she needed to show her authority.

In any case, she set off on a traditional royal progress to the north, accompanied by Thomas Randolph, the English ambassador. She deliberately provoked Huntly by taking the earldom of Mar from him and giving it to Lord James (her half-brother). She went on then to effectively declare war by making Lord James Earl of Moray as well.

William Maitland went ahead of the progress to Huntly's base at Strathbogie. Huntly was absent, but his wife invited Mary to attend mass in his private chapel. This she couldn't afford to do since this would have broken the terms of agreement by which the lords had agreed her return to Scotland. It was in order for her to have her own mass at Holyrood, but no more. It was as if the last Catholic card had been played in the confrontation. Lord James' military prowess ensured defeat for Huntly at the battle of Corrichie. Huntly died of apoplexy, falling off his horse in the middle of the battle. His lands were posthumously forfeited. With the passing of the 'Pope of the north', one of the last remaining hopes for Catholics disappeared.

White, A: *Queen Mary's northern province* (Innes Review xxxviii: 1987).
Donaldson, G: *Mary, Queen of Scots* (London: 1974).

29

JOHN ERSKINE OF DUN
The Reformer who spanned Four Generations

JOHN Erskine of Dun (*c*1508-1591) spanned four generations in his 83 years. He saw Scotland transformed from a Catholic country struggling to reform itself into a Protestant country, where the *majority* who were still firmly Catholic at the time of the Reformation had become very much a small *minority*. A chat with him in his old age would have provided fascinating insights into the events of the century. He was a Protestant long before Knox and survived him by 20 years.

John Erskine was born at the family farm of Dun, located in the area of Angus and the Mearns. He may have attended St Leonard's College in the University of St Andrews, but certainly went on to become provost of the burgh of Montrose. He became a Protestant in the 1530s. Since he took a French wife, he may have changed faith when he met and married her in France. As an early Protestant, it is not surprising to find his opinions lay somewhere between Luther and Zwingli. Being a landowner and a powerful man in his own right, this was an important advance for Protestantism: by 1550 there was a network of about 30 lairds in Angus who were Protestant.

In his links with Edinburgh, Erskine went to a privy kirk there and met John Knox during his visit to Scotland in the winter of 1555-6, inviting him to preach in Angus. Knox preached there in private houses as was only to be expected: his target audience was the lairds. George Wishart had preached in public in the 1540s: he was caught and burned to death. Knox would not make the same mistake. He preached in private right up to 1559.

When it came to 1559, John Erskine was elected as spokesman for the lords of the Congregation. He wrote to Mary of Guise to say that she should observe the division between the 'two regiments' and not interfere in Christ's kingdom. It was already significant then that a laird should be recognised as a leading ecclesiastical figure.

After the Reformation, Erskine was appointed superintendent of Angus and Mearns to appoint ministers in turn. His incredible energy and organising skill meant that in a couple of years, 95 per cent of the parishes were filled with ministers or readers. The General Assembly began to criticise the quality of his appointments but certainly couldn't complain about the number. Another end result of Erskine's direct involvement in so many appointments, however, was that the character of the church in Angus and Mearns had a quite different and more moderate feel than the rest of Scotland.

At times, Erskine called himself bishop, much to the fury of Andrew Melville. He was too closely attached to Mary, Queen of Scots' household and was present at some of the famous interviews between John Knox and Mary. Essentially he was there to smooth the waters, even though his own Protestant faith was firm and unshaken. In this he was fairly successful.

In 1571, and then crucially in 1584, Erskine was a firm supporter of Episcopacy. When James VI tried to impose his will on the church in this direction, Melville and 20 Melvillian ministers were forced into exile. Erskine however was happy to fit in with his wishes for he acknowledged the role of the 'Godly prince.' In this he balanced out Knox's position, which could have led to total confrontation, and illustrates how crucial the role of the lairds was in bringing about the Protestant Reformation. In 1578, we find him assisting in the compilation of the *Second Book of Discipline*.

In many ways, the role of John Erskine should in hindsight be seen as important as that of John Knox. The Scottish Reformation was brought about not by the revolt of the common people but by people like Erskine. Was he too much of a moderate to die for his Protestant convictions? To answer that properly perhaps we should remember that not a single noble in the sixteenth century died for their faith, neither Catholic nor Protestant. Erskine certainly lived for his faith and used his power to establish it.

Bardgett, F D: *Scotland Reformed: The Reformation in Angus and the Mearns* (John Donald: 1989).

Hewat: *Makers of the Scottish Church at the Reformation* (Edinburgh: 1920).

30

MARY, QUEEN OF SCOTS

The Woman of Destiny becomes its Victim

MARY Stewart (1542-1587), daughter of James V and Mary of Guise, was born in Linlithgow Palace on 8 December 1542. She became 'Queen of Scots' six days later when her father died. Had destiny decreed, she could legitimately have been Queen of France, Scotland, England and Ireland. Instead, after spells as Queen of France and Queen of Scots, she was beheaded at Fotheringay in England by Queen Elizabeth I, who was highly sensitive to Mary having a more legitimate claim to the English throne than she had. The woman of destiny had become its victim.

MARY, QUEEN of SCOTS

In many ways the deadly cocktail which destroyed her was the mixture of political and religious divides. As a child she was ripped away from the tender care of her mother and sent to France, in order to foil the plot of the Protestant Arran and the invading English armies to marry her forcibly to Prince Edward of England and ensure a Protestant Britain. Instead, she was to marry the French dauphin and after ten exciting and loving years of education at the French court, she became Queen of France.

Mary as a child was extremely attractive, a lively young woman, charming and outgoing, but who suffered severe bouts of ill-health and a mental instability which led her at times to break down in tears. She missed her mother but found in Henry II of France a sensitive father who belied his rough exterior by spending time with each of his extended family. Catherine de Medici, as a substitute mother, was a waspish, often difficult character who had no real love for the Queen of Scots. The future Francis

II was her playmate before becoming her husband, and his sister Elizabeth, who married Philip II of Spain, was her best friend. When she came to France they all laughed at her rustic French and her Scots accent, but by the age of twelve she spoke French beautifully and was well on her way to becoming one of the most cultured and best educated women of her age. Destiny was in the air and all the educational vision available enabled her to play a full role in an age when powerful women were emerging right across the European scene.

Tragedy, however, walked hand in hand with that destiny. Sadness at the sudden death of Henry II in 1559 led to the excitement of her husband's coronation as Francis II of France. Then, in December 1560, came the equally sudden death of her sullen lumpish 16 year old husband whom she had gently but regally encouraged and partnered through the 18 months of his reign. The next dilemma came when the very lords who made Scotland Protestant invited her back as a Catholic queen, on the understanding that she would respect the Protestant character of Scotland. When she returned, her treatment of the Earl of Huntly, the most powerful Catholic lord in the north, and his death in the course of a populist progression through Scotland (almost a 'meet-the-people' tour) to establish her glittering personal rule as queen, points to the very real possibility that her eyes were set—in the spirit of all she imbibed at the dynasty-orientated French court—on her next marriage and the extension of her rule in Scotland to the throne of England.

JOHN KNOX in St GILES

Research in Mary's library in Scotland has linked with research on her upbringing at the French court to show a woman who was not only learned, but *convinced* of her faith. She began her rule by striking a good political balance

74

and a balance between her religious practice (despite Knox's insistent confrontations) and a clear respect for Protestantism. Marriage to the Protestant Lord Darnley (who strengthened her claim to the English throne) and his conversion to Catholicism, combined with the popular pressure of the crowds attending her masses rather than Knox's services, led to her trying to convert the other lords. More tragedy—first the murder of her adviser Rizzio and then the murder of Darnley her husband—led her to the fatal mistake of marriage, willingly or unwillingly, to the roguish James Hepburn, Earl of Bothwell for political ends.

The birth of her son Charles James—whose name pointed to her continuing vision of a European destiny—was the high point of her reign. After surviving nearly fatal illness in the Borders, she went in triumph to the glittering celebrations of the Catholic baptism at Stirling. The birth, however, gave the enemy lords an alternative; their hatred of Bothwell was the rallying point. In Lochleven Castle, she was forced to abdicate in favour of her son, now restyled King James VI. Even then she was only let down by poor military tactics at Langside and she compounded her fate by going into exile in England, followed by involvement (either

The ARMOURIAL BEARINGS of MARY, QUEEN of SCOTS

willingly or as an inevitable symbol) in successive plots which led to her execution by Elizabeth I. Even at the end, Mary, Queen of Scots played with dignity the martyr's role which she had perfected during her life. This was mirrored by an inner faith which always seemed to add a deeper dimension to both her successes and failures in politics, intellectual achievements and in being a queen, a woman of destiny.

Lynch, M (ed): *Mary Stewart: Queen in Three Kingdoms* (Oxford: 1988).
Cowan, I B: *Mary, Queen of Scots* (Saltire Society: 1987).

31

ALEXANDER GORDON
A Curious Bishop

ONE of the most curious figures of Reformation times, Alexander Gordon (*c* 1516-1575), had almost too many jobs for us to list here. Was he jack of all trades and master of none? Or was he a complex character defying Knox's claim that 'in religioun there is no middis?' While it was a question of God or the devil for Knox, many like Alexander Gordon fell somewhere in the middle.

Alexander was the brother of George Gordon, 4th Earl of Huntly, the man they called the 'Pope of the north'. The earl was the greatest Catholic magnate in the land before he was destroyed by Mary, Queen of Scots in what was either an attempt to prove her credentials to respect the Protestant character of Scotland or England, or merely a tragic joust in the usual manner of Stuart Kings and the feuding lords. Certainly family loyalties were to be one of many pressures on Alexander's decision-making.

Alexander was probably born in Huntly. As a younger son he gravitated towards the priesthood. He may have attended St Andrews (perhaps at St Leonard's College with its Protestant ideas) and then went on to Paris or Louvain. We know for sure that he had a series of unsuccessful attempts to become Bishop of Caithness, the Isles, and Archbishop of Glasgow. His only consolation was to become titular Archbishop of Athens. In 1559 he was elected to the diocese of Galloway, only to become one of the three Scottish bishops who became Protestant at the time of the Reformation (Galloway, Orkney and Caithness were the others).

What was his motivation? He may have been dissatisfied, as so many were, with the slow pace of the attempted Catholic reforms. Alexander he had a common-law wife, Barbara Logie. Like many in Scotland he expected that the reforming Council of Trent would, by the mid 1540s, allow the marriage of the clergy, as in the old tradition of the church. But time dragged on without change. Many began to suspect that no change was imminent (which was the case). Despite this, Alexander Gordon, Bishop of Galloway, turned up at the Protestant centre of Perth in early 1560, admitting not just to the existence of Barbara (with whom he had lived for 14 years), but also to their five children. It must have been extremely attractive to priests like Gordon that the reformers legitimised marriage among the clergy and, perhaps more importantly (because no-one seemed to get too alarmed about them living together), legitimised the children of that union. They otherwise would not have been able to inherit in the law of the church.

The born-again Protestant Bishop of Galloway had an indifferent career in the church, perhaps because he seems to have been a moderate Protestant, unwilling to go to the wall or the stake for his beliefs. He was attacked by the Protestant reformers for not proceeding fast enough with the imposition of reform in his diocese of Galloway: he seemed more inclined to let things be.

Perhaps some of his many jobs caught up with him in the reign of Queen Mary. Traditionally the post of Dean of Stirling's chapel royal went with the bishopric of Galloway. With Mary this became, after 1561, one of the great Catholic centres. From 17-19 December 1566 it was the venue for the baptism of Mary's son Charles James, proclaiming him Prince of Scotland, Lord of Rothesay, the next great Catholic prince. The baptism was followed by a pageant in which a fort stood (amid fireworks) as a symbol of the triumph of the Stewart monarchy against all attacks from their enemies.

Another little-known sideshow of Alexander Gordon is the fact that he was both a lord of session and a minister of Mary's privy council in 1566. The final irony came in the civil war when, in common with the rest of the Gordons of Huntly, he was, as a Protestant bishop, found fighting on the side of Catholic Mary. He was disciplined for this. The times were certainly confused! Allegiances were mixed between the political and the religious, and many, like Alexander Gordon, were somewhere in the middle.

Ross, A: *More about the Archbishop of Athens* (Innes Review: xiv: 1963).
Donaldson, G: *Alexander Gordon, Bishop of Galloway and his work in the Reformed Church* (Trans. of 12c Dumfriesshire and Galloway Nat. Hist. and Antiq. Soc. xxiv: 1947).

32

REGENT MORTON

Rapacious Lord or Pious Reformer?

REGENT Morton (*c* 1516-1581) was second son of the second son of an Earl of Angus, but by marriage has as his full title James Douglas, fourth Earl of Morton. His importance rests in the fact that, as head of the Douglas family in the south of Scotland, he led the pro-English faction in the years which spanned the Scottish Reformation and played a crucial role in achieving and making effective the Scottish Reformation settlement. His detractors would see him feathering his own nest and advancing his family interests at every point along the way; his admirers would find in his piety when facing death an enduring spiritual motivation.

REGENT MORTON

Morton emerged in the pro-English faction in the confusing years of the early 1540s, but had a brief spell of pro-French allegiance which led to him being captured and imprisoned by the English. He was one of the few who signed the 'First Bond' of the lords of the Congregation which came to nothing, and then was in the party who finally carried through the revolt against Mary of Guise and the French, which with English help, established the Reformation of 1560. He became Chancellor to Mary, Queen of Scots in 1563, was dismissed for his part in the murder of Rizzio, had at least foreknowledge of the murder of Darnley and became the leader of the king's party after the death of Regent Moray, before becoming regent himself in 1572 (he even took bribes from Elizabeth I in 1571).

During his regency, Morton worked to import English ideas

both politically and religiously. He was responsible for two carbon copy acts of English bills brought in by Elizabeth. In 1573 he brought in the Test Act which forced holders of church benefices to be Protestant and sign the Protestant 'Confession of Faith.' Then in 1575 he enacted a Poor Law designed both for poor relief and for the punishment of idle beggars: ideas in the tradition of Knox but modelled on the English act. During this time he is accused of rapaciousness, a high-handed treatment of nobles and clergy, and an attempt to restore episcopacy proper. One example of his struggles with the radical clergy was over a scheme to accept realistically the shortage of ministers and appoint one minister in charge of three or four parishes. The ministers demanded that one minister to one parish should be established forthwith.

At the end of the day, power struggles brought about his downfall. The earls of Atholl, Argyll and Mar engineered a palace revolution with the twelve year old King James in Stirling Castle declaring he no longer needed a regent. Morton resigned without fuss, but in six months made something of a comeback by regaining charge of the Privy Council. His enemies took their revenge against him finally in 1580, but for fear of his English allies took six months to get him to trial. He

The 'MAIDEN'

was beheaded in Edinburgh's Grassmarket on 2 June 1581 by means of the 'Maiden', a guillotine-like device which, rather ironically, he himself had imported into Scotland.

There's a fascinating interplay between Morton's last movements and John Knox. On his death bed in 1572, Knox charged Morton at the beginning of his regency to use the riches, power, wisdom and friends he had: first for God's glory to maintain the church and the ministers; and second for the benefit of the king, the realm and his true subjects in the land. If he did, God would bless him. If not, God would bring him to a shameful death. In

Morton's Confession before his death, there are clear echoes of that charge. On the one hand Morton had a fatalistic view of the trial, knowing all too well his enemies were seeking his life irrespective of whether he was 'as innocent as Stephen or as guilty as Judas.' On the other hand there is a very deeply pious acceptance of God's will and a claim that with the ministers he always did what he thought best at the time. 'As concerning religioun and doctrine, as it is now preached and professed in Scotland, I ever meanned alwayes weill in my heart to it.' In dying he said, 'I am sure the king sall losse a good servant this day'; and exhorted the people, 'I testifie, before God, that as I professed the Evangell which this day is taught and professed in Scotland, so also now willinglie I lay down my life in the professioun thereof.' How much of this is Calderwood's re-writing of history is not clear, but the contradictions of politics, career and religious conviction create enigmas today as then.

Calderwood, D: *History of the Kirk of Scotland* (edited by T Thomson) (Wodrow Society: 1843), volume iii.
Hewitt, R: *Scotland under Morton* (John Donald: 1982).

33

JOHN CARSWELL
Reform goes Gaelic

JOHN Carswell (1520/25-72) is important to our story of God's people when we try to assess the claim that the Reformation neglected Gaelic-speaking areas of Scotland. In truth perhaps there was more attention to Gaelic-speaking Scotland than might be suspected: yet at the same time there was a great persistence of the old Catholic faith.

Carswell was a native of the parish of Kilmartin, Argyll. He graduated from the University of St Andrews in 1544. By 1551 he had taken orders and was treasurer to the Cathedral of Lismore. He became priest to the parish of Kilmartin in 1553 and of Southwick and Kingarth in Bute in 1558. More significantly to our story, he was also chaplain to the Earl of Argyll: in that capacity he was an active Protestant while still exercising his priestly ministry. As with many of the period, it was not a matter of double standards, but rather that the dividing line between what we now label Catholicism and Protestantism were far from clearly defined. Whether he was a Lutheran or a Zwinglian or a Calvinist is of course again a matter of speculation and probably of impossible definition in an age of searching for the right way to reform the church. Catholic, Lutheran, Zwinglian and Calvinist are all identikit labels of where to place a whole range of searchers.

Some evidence of his part in the scheme of things is in his translation of the *Book of Common Order* into Gaelic. This was the book used by the English exiles in Geneva at the time of the Catholic Queen Mary Tudor in England. Although published in 1567, it certainly had its origins a lot earlier than that. By this time Carswell had been appointed one of the five superintendents, his district being that of the old diocese of Argyll and the Isles. Mary Queen of Scots made him Bishop of the Isles in January 1565 but it was later on, in March 1567, that he was formally presented as the Protestant Bishop of the Isles and Abbot of Iona.

And so it is against this background of being the first and foremost representative of the Reformers to Gaeldom that we must assess his translation of the *Book of Common Order.*

It was printed at the press of Robert Lekprevik, the Edinburgh printer to the General Assembly and took about two years of *meticulous* work to set up the Gaelic letters. This was the first Gaelic book ever printed in Scotland or Ireland and Carswell was acutely aware this. The translation is entitled, significantly in Gaelic, *The Form of Prayers* (*Foirm na n- Urrnuidheadh*). The language is generally the standard literary Irish of the time, not the vernacular Scottish Gaelic: but in the added catechism (*Calvin's Small Catechism*) the language is simpler, with Scottish syntax and vocabulary in evidence.

The Irish connection in the main part of the project is interesting especially since Carswell added a Gaelic poem in traditional style. It seems he visited Ireland in 1545 in the train of Donald Dubh, but he may have studied there at the bardic schools. The predominantly Irish literary Gaelic and the poem, however, may have come from what he learned of literary style from 'the MacEwans, the hereditary bards to the Earls of Argyll and the Campbells of Glenorchy.'

The prologue to the book reveals much about Carswell and his relationship to the Earl of Argyll: 'For the mighty, just-judging, gentle-speaking Lord Archibald Campbell, Earl of Argyll and Lord of Lorne, Justiciary of Scotland, also styled lieutenant in the lands of the Hebrides and Master of the Household of the kings of Scotland, Mr John Carswell, minister of God's gospel, prayer and earnestly beseeches God diligently and fervently to strengthen and increase the spirit of wisdom and of understanding and of truth in him, and that he may obtain eternal joy from God the Father through Jesus Christ our Lord.'

Carswell was aware of the criticism from the 'Papists' for his work, but was also clear about his motivation: 'The principal reason which moved me to perform this task was, in the first place, the love of God, and for fear that he would accuse me of wasting the talent, that is the gift he had given me, (secondly) the love of God's Church, and in order to help my Christian brethren who have need of teaching and of comfort, and who lack books.' As a result, his influence spread throughout Gaelic Scotland and to Ireland. And as a consequence of this, many requests followed from Ireland for Gaelic ministers to be sent to them.

Thomson, R L (ed): *John Carswell's Gaelic translation of the Book of Common Order* (Scottish Gaelic Texts Society: 1970).
Thomson, D S (ed): *The Companion to Gaelic Scotland* (Blackwells: 1983).

34

MAITLAND OF LETHINGTON

Evil Genius by Nature as well as by Name?

MAITLAND of Lethington (1528-1573) came from an East
Lothian family which can be traced back to Anglo-Norman times.
His name means 'evil genius': this is quite ironic for he was held to
be just that by his contemporaries. But he was unquestionably one
of the most gifted men of his age. Elizabeth I
regarded him as 'the flower of the wits of Scotland', but his enemies saw him more as the
Machiavelli of his day; or, as George Buchanan
his arch enemy, said: 'the chameleon.'

In 1540 Maitland attended the University of
St Andrews and it was perhaps significant that
he was a member of that hotbed of Protestant
ideas, St Leonard's college. After further study
at university in Paris, where he appears to have
completed his legal training, and possibly at

MAITLAND of LETHINGTON

other European seats of learning, Maitland returned to Scotland.
His Protestantism and his legal training were to be strong features of his career, with him rising to the position of a lord of
session during the reign of Mary, Queen of Scots.

In 1554 Maitland entered the service of the then Regent of
Scotland, Mary of Guise, as assistant secretary to bishop David
Panter. In 1558, he succeeded Panter as secretary of state, the most
significant appointment of his entire career. By 1558 the position of secretary was a position of great power throughout Europe
(witness the careers of William Cecil and Thomas Cromwell in
England and the Perez brothers and De l'Aubespine family in
Spain and France). What made Maitland's appointment even more
exceptional was that he was the only native Scot in a position of
executive power in Mary of Guise's French dominated government. It was an appointment Mary of Guise was to regret, for
Maitland was to betray her.

Maitland acted as a double agent for the lords of the Congregation (the vehicle which was eventually to carry through the Reformation), passing valuable inside information to them before openly defecting to their side in October 1559. He was instrumental in the successful procurement of English aid which was to prove decisive in the eventual victory of July 1560.

Maitland had met John Knox during the 1550s and there is evidence that Knox actually converted Maitland during a meeting of the privy kirk at the house of Erskine of Dun, another major Protestant. Almost as soon as the victory of the reformers was achieved in 1560, however, Knox and Maitland clashed over the form the new kirk should take. As the speaker in the Reformation parliament, Maitland cast a moderating eye over the Scots Confession of Faith. He was a vociferous supporter of parliament's rejection of the radically Protestant *Book of Discipline* which Knox had helped produce, and it is doubtful if Knox ever forgave him.

Maitland's brand of Protestantism was of a quite different stamp to Knox's. There were not many laymen who could quote chapter and verse back at Knox, and Maitland was also conversant with such European reformers as Luther, Bucer, Melancthon, Calvin and even more obscure ones such as Musculus. Knox came to denounce him as an atheist. Maitland was certainly a cool politician rather than a hot gospeller, but he was nonetheless a convinced Protestant whose own preference it seems would have been for an Anglican-type church settlement with state control as exercised by the English monarchs.

Maitland can be regarded as something of a classic Renaissance figure, very much at home in the dazzling court of Mary Stewart. He even had a long and controversial romance with Mary Fleming, one of Mary's four Marys, whom he eventually married in 1567. It was Maitland's second marriage—his first wife had died—and despite the fact that many thought the two were incompatible (Kirkcaldy of Grange believed Mary Fleming was 'as fit to be his wife as I am to be pope'), the two shared a happy married life together before Maitland's death in 1573.

If in his personal life Maitland managed to remain free from scandal, he made up for it in other ways. After being pardoned for his role in Rizzio's murder, Maitland helped depose Mary Stewart at Carberry in 1567 and was instrumental in the creation of the regency of Lord James. He said his main motivation was to rid Mary of Bothwell's influence, but for a long time after the threat of Bothwell had been removed, he was still seen openly on the queen's side, particularly during the civil war of 1567-73. This was only after Langside and during Mary's exile in England. He emerged as the leader of the queen's party opposing the king's party of Mary's infant son Charles James (known as James).

The civil war witnessed an intense propaganda campaign by both sides. It was during this time that Knox, Buchanan, Bannatyne and other king's men propagandists denounced Maitland. The civil war was not however a sectarian conflict. Many devout Protestants supported Mary and many Catholics were found in the ranks of the king's party. As ever, both sides sought to pose as the true defenders of 'the religion.' At this time Knox accused Maitland of being an atheist and of believing 'heaven and hell to be but a bogle of the nursery.' But Maitland was a match for Knox; he even threatened the reformer with the discipline of his own kirk session for his slanderous libel. Knox only avoided this embarrassment by his death eight days later in November 1572.

The king's party had the backing of the English army and finance, after the wave of common fear after the St Bartholomew's day massacre of French Protestants in Paris made the prospect of a 'French Catholic' queen intolerable. Maitland and Kirkcaldy of Grange held out in Edinburgh Castle, the last bastion of support for the queen, until starved of food, money and military support, they were forced to surrender. Maitland died in a prison cell within six days of his imprisonment. Was it suicide in keeping with Maitland's love of the classics, imitating the great Romans when they faced defeat? We'll never know, but it certainly saved him from the public humiliation of the hang-man's rope. And perhaps we'll never know either whether he was a Machiavellian, evil genius or a brilliant man in the right place at the wrong time.

Calendar of State Papers, Scottish and Foreign.
Russell, E: *Maitland of Lethington.*

35

LORD JAMES
'Blessed are those who die in the Lord'

LORD James (1531-1570) was James Stewart, Earl of Moray, and Regent of Scotland for the young King James VI from 1567 to 1570. Perhaps the key to an accurate understanding of Lord James is to acknowledge the effect on his character of being the illegitimate son of James V by long term mistress Margaret Erskine. The King seems to have favoured Lord James more than any of his prodigious illegitimate offspring and part of this seems to have been a genuine affection for James' mother with whom it seems he seriously entertained the prospect of marriage. Regrettably for Lord James this never came to pass and as a bastard he was unable to inherit the crown. This set the scene for a tempestuous relationship with his half sister Mary who, as the only surviving legitimate child of James V, became Queen of Scots.

LORD JAMES

Some have argued that the establishment of Protestantism in Scotland owed more to him than anyone else. The epithet of the 'good regent', however, owes more to the propagandising efforts of George Buchanan than to Lord James' actual achievements (Buchanan has been portrayed as the defence lawyer of Lord James reputation). Not everyone, however, was as kind. Sir James Melville unfavourably described the regent as an unskilled tennis player, lacking any finesse, forever chasing the ball all over the court. But in fact, Lord James was far from short on political guile.

His own influence and great wealth began in 1537 when he was appointed by his father as the commendator of St Andrews Priory. His mother later married Sir Robert Douglas of Lochleven and thereby opened up a strong connection with one of the greatest families in Scotland. Lord James' great friendship with the Douglas Earl of Morton was to be important, particularly during the years of his regency.

Lord James seems to have been attracted to Protestantism from an early age. He visited France in 1548 and 1550, when he apparently met Knox and was converted to the faith. Thus began a friendship and alliance that prepared the way for the Reformation settlement of 1560. Lord James was the most dynamic of all the leaders of the Congregation and his contribution to the victory of the reformers in 1560 was immeasurable.

Following the death of Mary's husband Francis II, and her impending return to Scotland, Knox and Lord James had a profound difference of opinion as to how to respond. In March 1561, Lord James travelled to France to invite Mary to return to Scotland and offered her the shrewd advice, 'For the love of God madam do not touch religion not for any man's advice on earth.' Lord James promised Mary that if she would accept the religious situation as it stood in Scotland, then he would ensure she was able to practice her own Catholic faith. Knox was furious and his anger was to deepen as Mary's reign progressed. He blamed Lord James for not supporting his demands for the parliamentary sanctioning of the full endowment of the new kirk, which was still desperately short of money. He believed that Lord James had been bought off by Mary: he had led her forces against the rebellious Earl of Huntly and her creation of him in 1562 as the Earl of Mar and then in 1563 as the Earl of Moray certainly gave some credence to that view.

The situation was to change drastically in 1565 when Mary married Darnley. Quite possibly Lord James would have opposed any Scottish marriage for Mary as it would have reduced his power, but the son of the Earl of Lennox was the limit. He attempted a *coup d'etat* which failed miserably, resulting in him seeking asylum in England. Within a year, however, he was back in Scotland, arriving somewhat suspiciously the day after the Rizzio murder, and was received once more back into Mary's favour.

Lord James never allowed Mary back into *his* favour, however, and within a year proved that he had learned some hard political lessons from his failed *coup* of 1565. He turned a judicious blind eye to the murder of Darnley in February 1567, choosing to 'look through his fingers', and then played an absolute master stroke. In the spring of 1567, following the Darnley murder, he gained Mary's permission for a discreet leave of absence to travel abroad, fooling Mary as to his real intentions by naming her as executor of his will. As Lord James well knew, it was Mary who was in more danger than him. He had left other devious men behind him, including his ally Maitland, who were more than capable of doing the dirty work of deposing Mary who had, by this time, fallen completely under the influence of Bothwell. Consequently in June 1567 at Carberry field, Lord James was conspicuous by his absence but, as he had planned, was in the perfect position to return home with a seemingly spotless reputation in response to the calls for him to accept the regency. He had at last attained the power and position he had always wanted, but his tenure of it was to be brief.

In May 1568, although heavily out-numbered, he displayed his military brilliance by routing Mary's troops at Langside, and thus strengthened his controversial position as regent. With their common hatred of Mary, both he and Knox patched up their differences. Yet even with the support of the Kirk, Lord James was not a popular regent. He succeeded in turning two thirds of the nobility against him and his assassination at Linlithgow in January 1570 came as no great surprise. It was a perfectly planned operation with even a 'getaway' horse at the ready for the assassin, James Hamilton of Bothwellhaugh.

At his funeral, John Knox moved a congregation of 300 to tears with his elaborate praise, 'blessed are those who die in the Lord.' He probably saw James as doubly blessed for having seen the error of his ways and returned to the fold of the godly. It was then in his 'martyrdom', as Knox put it, that Lord James achieved the glory he had struggled to achieve in his life.

William Croft Dickinson: *John Knox's History of the Reformation*.
Lee, M: *The Earl of Moray*.

36

JOHN DURIE

Monk turned Rabble-rousing Reformer

JOHN Durie (*c* 1537-1600) is one of many Duries who figure in the Reformation century in Scotland. Andrew Durie was abbot of Melrose and then Bishop of Galloway who is said to have died of shock after a Protestant riot in 1558. His brother George was abbot of Dunfermline and keeper of the Privy Seal: he died in 1561. George's son was a John Durie who was active as a Catholic priest in the south-west of Scotland and lived on until 1587. Whether our John Durie was any relation to these Duries, we don't know. All that we do know is that he was a Benedictine monk at Dunfermline and was probably a Catholic monk there as late as 1567.

Our John Durie then was a late convert to Protestantism and this came about when the Reformed Kirk was recruiting for more ministers. Some of his colleagues at Dunfermline stayed on as monks into the 1570s, some left to become readers in the Reformed Kirk, but John became a fully-fledged minister, and a radical and talented one at that. He worked in Penicuik, Colinton, South Leith and then finally in Edinburgh with Knox's successor James Lawson, who himself became a convert only after he returned from France to Scotland in 1567.

Durie got into trouble for refusing to submit to the Regent Morton: the independence of the Kirk was to him central. When Esmé Stewart, Duke of Lennox, took over, he suspected him of being a Papist agent and accused him publicly of going to the brothels of Edinburgh. He had to flee Edinburgh, but the abortive Ruthven Raid in June 1582 caused so much confusion that he was able to return in triumph. At the Gallowgreen (the Grassmarket), it was reported that he was met by a crowd of 200, 'but ere he came to the Netherbow their number increased to 400, but they were no sooner entered but they increased to 600 or 700, and within short space the whole street was replenished even to St Geiles Kirk; the number was esteemed to 2,000. At the Netherbow they took up the 124 Psalm, "Now Israel may say", and sung in such a pleasant tune in four parts, known to the most people, that coming up the street all bareheaded until they entered the kirk, with such a great sound and majestie, that it moved both themselves and all the huge multitude of the beholders ... with admiration and astonishment.' What is significant about this is that the route taken for Durie's re-entry is a deliberate parody of the procession route of Mary, Queen of Scots in 1561.

This was not the end of the trouble for, largely due to the preaching of Melvillian ministers like Durie, the Kirk was tarred with the image of revolution in the eyes of James VI. Durie was again called before the Privy Council in December 1583 for approving the Ruthven raid. He was warded to Montrose. As minister of Montrose, he received a gift of stipend from the abbey of Deer and the bishopric of Brechin and another stipend gift in 1590.

Nonetheless, Durie returned eventually to Edinburgh. Somewhat chastened, he led a quieter life. He'd passed on the torch of radicalism, however, to his son Robert (1555-1616) who was 'the faithful friend and companion' of James Melville. He was in trouble during his father's life but eventually was driven out of Scotland for life in 1605, ending up as minister of Leyden.

John Durie had come late to the Reformation scene, but had made his mark. He had had the courage to call such powerful characters as Lennox and Arran 'abusers of the king', and had proved his strength of conviction by being prepared to lose everything rather than deny his principles.

Cowan, I B: *The Scottish Reformation* (Weidenfeld & Nicholson: 1982).
Lynch, M: *Edinburgh and the Reformation* (John Donald: 1981).

37

GILBERT KENNEDY
Dithering on the Catholic-Protestant divide

GILBERT Kennedy (1541-1576), 4th Earl of Cassillis, is a good example of many at the time of the Scottish Reformation who appeared at times to be (rightly or wrongly) like lost souls searching, or at least like confused people finding it difficult to decide their religious and political loyalties and finding it almost impossible to avoid family pressure in the decision-making.

Gilbert Kennedy's family was divided on religion but were basically Catholic. His childhood must have been overshadowed by the towering character of Quentin Kennedy, commendator abbot of Crossraguel. He condemned abuses in the church in *Ane Compendious Tractive* (1558), but disputed powerfully and ably with the Protestant reformers, including John Knox, whom he encountered in a somewhat dramatic confrontation at Maybole in 1562.

At the age of 18, Gilbert had to make up his mind on the Protestant question. In the end he went to the Reformation parliament in 1560, went to the John Knox service on Sunday and the Catholic mass on Monday, and continued to dither for years, especially since the return of Mary, Queen of Scots led many to think that the Catholic faith might be re-established.

Marriage to the sister of Lord Glamis, a good Protestant, settled the matter for him: at least in the area of religion he dithered no more. In addition, the effects of the Wars of Religion in France created a climate of fear that a Catholic monarch might crush Protestantism by force. This was balanced, however, by family considerations. At that time, there was great pressure to follow family attitudes. Nobles only are granted power and so if there was any faltering by the noble from the family line, the powers-that-be would pull the plug on him. The Kennedy line on religion was mixed and so that gave much more room for manoeuvre. There was no 'Berlin Wall' type division between Catholics and Protestants: intermarriage was common.

This mixture of religious attitudes became even more complicated on the Scottish scene when it was a question of political allegiance. The nobles of Scotland could never be categorised as sticking to decisions about politics on religious lines. Gilbert Kennedy illustrated this clearly, for mostly he fought consistently for Mary, Catholic or not.

The one exception was with the Confederate lords after the murder of Darnley in 1567. Kennedy was happy that Mary should be deposed at Carberry, but only as a temporary measure to get rid of the hated upstart, Bothwell. Immediately, however, on Mary's escape from Lochleven Castle, he joined with the 18 earls who, in six days, rallied a quite superior army behind Mary at Langside. They were led—tragically for Mary—by the Hamiltons whose military prowess was legendarily poor. They 'snatched defeat from the jaws of victory.' Mary then compounded the defeat by her flight to England.

Despite backing the wrong side—and he continued on the side of the 'queen's men' for much of the long civil war which followed—Gilbert survived until 1576 in relative obscurity. His dithering was typical of many then and perhaps indeed many in every age.

Donaldson, G: *All the Queen's Men* (London: 1983).
Roberts, D M (ed): *Essays on the Scottish Reformation* (Glasgow: 1962)

38

ANDREW MELVILLE
The True Architect of Scottish Presbyterianism

MARY, Queen of Scots today would feel that the shape of Scottish Presbyterianism owes more to Andrew Melville (1545-1622) than to John Knox. Born at Baldovie in Angus, he went to the University of St Andrews in the early days of the Reformation

CONTEMPORARY VIEW of GENEVA

in Scotland, but he only stayed there for a short time. He then went on to Paris to study under the up-to-date Royal Lecturers. Poitiers was the next stop where he studied law and even took part in the famous siege of Poitiers. But things remained dangerous so he went on to Geneva where he enrolled for study at the Academy

(the University). He also took up a post teaching in a preparatory college for the University and stayed there until 1574.

Melville's return to Scotland in 1574 was a return by invitation —by the Bishop of Glasgow, no less!—of a scholar who was well-equipped to carry out his set purpose of transforming Scottish education and to play a crucial role in what was to be a real religious revolution. In Geneva he had studied Hebrew under Cornelius Bertram and had received a great deal of encouragement from his uncle, one of the Dundee Scrymgeour family, who was professor of civil law at the Academy. In line with the promises he made to his uncle, he embarked on a programme of simplifying education by reducing the scope of rhetoric and in general reducing the stress on style rather than content. He brought the Frenchman, Peter Ramus, into the curriculum: this was predictable for when Ramus was expelled from Geneva for attacking Aristotle, Melville went to Lausanne to learn from him. At the end of the day—despite major failures in record-keeping—Andrew Melville made Glasgow a 'market place for learning.' Greek and Hebrew were put on the same footing as theology and the arts. He was a charismatic teacher, but he made the students work extremely hard and very few lasted the pace.

Melville was also to influence the University of Aberdeen and (indirectly) the new University of Edinburgh, but St Andrews was particularly important. He went there in 1580 with the idea of drawing all the theology students into St Mary's College. He wanted to bring in two English Puritans, Cartwright and Travers, but their appointment was blocked. Nevertheless, despite again neglecting administration, he attracted students from across the breadth of the continent. He was known as 'the light and leader of our schools.'

Parallel with the intellectual work, Melville became more and more involved in religious politics. For two years he was the central character in a committee set up by the General Assembly: it produced a draft of the *Second Book of Discipline* in 1578. This gave Scotland church government based on that of Calvin's successor Beza at Geneva. By 1581, 13 presbyteries—the vital core of the Scottish presbyterian system had been set up.

In 1584 he had to flee the country because James VI's new adviser, the Earl of Arran, did not like him—and imprisonment loomed in Blackness Castle. He used the time to go, with two other ministers, to the English puritans at Oxford and Cambridge. Once Arran was out of favour, Melville came back to Scotland in 1585. From that time on, he fought for the independence of the Kirk from James VI, despite the fact that his own university posts had been given to him courtesy of the Earl of Morton and state appointment. From 1590-1597, Melville was rector of the University of St Andrews, but after more tussles with the king—whom he dubbed 'God's sillie vassall'—he was deprived of the rectorship in 1597. It was mostly because of the conflict with the king, but it was also because people found him very difficult to get along with. He stayed on as dean of the Faculty of Theology and in 1606 he was actually invited to London to arbitrate between James VI and the Scots ministers. Because of a bitter epigram about English ritual practices (and a fiery debate with Archbishop Bancroft), he landed up in the Tower of London and was subsequently never allowed back to Scotland.

In 1611 he was freed thanks to the intercession of the Duke of Bouillon who appointed him professor of Biblical Theology in Sedan within what was an independent French principality. He died there, an embittered man. During those last years he wrote a few poems, but although he has been recognised as a distinguished poet, he never fulfilled his true potential due to his involvement in religious politics. His university work was outstanding but it would have benefited from better organisation and better human relationships. He had an alternative career in the 1590s as a kind of unofficial Latin poet laureate. He was deeply interested in Scottish history and began a verse epic—'Garnelus'—on the origins and history of the Scots: but only 158 lines of it ever reached print. However, in terms of church organisation, both his ideas and his fight for those ideas, remained as an important rallying point for Scottish presbyterianism.

McCrie T: *Andrew Melville* (Edinburgh: 1819).
Autobiography and Diary of Mr James Melville (Wodrow Society: 1842).

39

GEORGE BUCHANAN
Poet, Historian or Revolutionary?

ONE of the challenges with George Buchanan (*c*1506-1582) is to assess what has proved to be most significant in his many talents —religious, political, poetical, historical or educational. Buchanan was born near Killearn in Stirlingshire, son of a Gaelic-speaking laird and well-connected mother Agnes Heriot (from the important Edinburgh family of that name). He returned from study at Paris and St Andrews determined on educational reform which would reduce logic and disputation in favour of grammar and rhetoric. In this he opposed his old teacher John Mair: his tool was to be the introduction of the *English Renaissance Grammar* by Thomas Linacre (a friend of Thomas More) and to do this he translated it into Latin. After tutoring the young Earl of Cassillis, he tutored (from 1536-38) James, the second eldest of James V's many natural sons.

GEORGE BUCHANAN

Buchanan infuriated Cardinal Beaton with a biting Latin satirical poem attacking the Scottish Franciscans and was imprisoned. But he was allowed to escape from the castle of St Andrews to London and thence to the continent where his teaching reputation and skills developed with such distinguished pupils as Montaigne. He also wrote and performed plays. In 1547 the King of Portugal invited him to Coimbra to teach, but he was then arrested by the Inquisition. During his time in prison he began his Latin paraphrase of the Psalms, one of his most popular works. It contained a beautiful poem in honour of Mary, Queen of Scots when it was published finally in 1566.

In 1552 he was in England again, but then returned to France, his affection for France and his support for the Guise family increasing. He wrote a celebration of the capture of Calais by France from England; tutored the sons of the rich and powerful in Italy and France; then, in addition to being a cleric of Glasgow archdiocese, he became in 1558 a canon of the French diocese of Coutance.

Buchanan came back to Scotland in 1561 shortly after the return of Mary, Queen of Scots. He moved easily in the complicated world of Scotland in the early 1560s and became a favourite of the queen, reading each evening to her from Cicero or Virgil. He praised her in elegant Latin verse. He sung praises of her marriage to Darnley, no doubt encouraged to do so by the Lennox connections of his birthplace.

However, this Latin court poet of a Catholic queen was also a convinced Protestant. He had already begun to acquire English friends and friends among the 'English' party of the Scottish nobles, notably his former pupil, the Earl of Moray. It was Moray who invited him to reform the University of St Andrews and Buchanan produced an extremely interesting plan of it for Moray. Again too, he played a significant role in the General Assembly from 1563-68: supposedly as a lay member, although we have seen his clerical status in both France and Scotland.

The dramatic events of 1565-7, the conversion of the Lennoxes to the Mass, the murder of Darnley and the deposing of Mary, forced him to decide where his real loyalties lay. Darnley's murder enraged him and moved him further away from his expected loyalty as tutor at court, his pension from Crossraguel and his patronage. He was Moderator in 1567 when an excited Assembly met, only ten days after Mary's defeat at Carberry, to lay plans for completing the religious revolution begun in 1560. His appointment in 1566 as principal at St Leonard's College at St Andrews, which became the key seminary producing ministers for the Kirk, became critical in the uncertain years after 1567. He was there off and on until 1570 when he 'simply went away.'

Buchanan entered more deeply into the political intrigues of the time when he went, as secretary to Moray's commissioners, to see Elizabeth I, regarding the fate of Mary, Queen of Scots. The knife had turned completely. He presented the case against Mary with brilliant viciousness and claimed the 'Casket Letters' which implicated her in Darnley's murder were genuine. He satirised the Guise family and wrote pamphlets ridiculing Maitland of Lethington, Mary's advocate in Scotland.

Meanwhile he was also writing works of a different nature: an elegy on Calvin's death, for example, and a book of poems published along with a work by Theodore Beza, Calvin's successor at Geneva. Buchanan retained the royal connection with his tutorship of James VI at Stirling and was keeper of the Great Seal from 1570-78. But continuing involvement with religious and secular politics meant that the poetry, on which his continental reputation was based, tended to suffer. In 1579, however, he produced a powerful political pamphlet *De Jure Regni*: although in the form of a dialogue it was more of a scathing monologue justifying rebellion. His last years were given over to his massive *History of Scotland*, completed in 1582. It is valuable as a sharply-studied view of the turbulent years he lived through: he falters between admiring the work of Hector Boece and criticising him. But although it is beautifully written it is not history as we expect it.

Buchanan left a mixed legacy. He had been tutor to the most important Protestant noble in the Reformation generation. His other pupil, James VI, far from turning out a 'godly prince', turned against his old teacher. The *Dialogue* and *History* were censored by parliament in 1584. The *History* especially became a kind of handbook for revolutionaries for more than a century. The Covenanters, it was said, rode to war against Charles I with the *History* in one saddlebag, the Geneva Bible in the other.

Buchanan seems to have concluded his days as a sharp, angry old man rather than the carefree poet of his early years. The young man who became somewhat of a Scottish legend for his brilliance on the continent seemed to promise more than he actually fulfilled in Scotland.

McFarlane, I D: *George Buchanan* (Duckworth: 1983).
Williamson, A H: *Scottish National Consciousness in the Age of James VI* (Edinburgh: 1979).

40

JOHN WELSH

Married to Knox's Daughter

JOHN Welsh (1569-1622) was born in south-west Galloway and educated as one of the first graduates of Edinburgh's Town College (the newly established University of Edinburgh). He graduated MA in 1588 and took up his first charge as minister of Selkirk in

JOHN WELSH

1589. Marriage to one of John Knox's daughters ensured his part in the family tradition of ministers which was so much the backbone of the Church of Scotland ministry in post-Reformation years. He belonged to the second and third generations of such ministers and therefore in the tradition and influence of Melville's advocacy of a presbyterian system of government, with ministers of equal rank working within a close-knit structure of church courts. Like Andrew Melville, he suffered exile because of his resistance to James VI's interference in church matters.

Welsh progressed from Selkirk to Kirkcudbright and then Ayr in 1604. He appears to have been a competent and conscientious parish minister, but in the post-Melvillian purge he was arrested, tried at Linlithgow, imprisoned in Blackness and driven into exile. Like many who suffered this fate he went to France: to Nérac and Saint Jean d'Angely. At this stage he took a 14 week crash course: letters still survive from this time addressed to 'Robert Boyd of Trochrig' (Trochrague), a leading academic and divine. They are a strange mixture of French and English, illustrating the fact that Welsh was not a top-flight academic, but rather a foot soldier. This made his life in France more difficult. Had he been more academic he could have easily joined the brain drain of the seventeenth century which took so many Scottish intellectuals to France and the Netherlands. This competent parish minister became in effect a second class exile. His wife who, like all of Knox's family, was educated in England, must have been a major support to him in his enforced exile from familiar surroundings.

Life in France was far from easy. Prayer books of whatever kind—Anglican or Presbyterian—were suspicious to a man like Welsh: so he preached without preparation for up to three hours at a time. His local synod took pity on the congregation and told him to stop and keep to the set forms where his lack of French would not be so devastating. Despite these niggles, however, the way Welsh was able to transfer to the French scene illustrates the major movement of Scots back and forth to the continent both before and after the Reformation. In some ways there was a greater cross-fertilisation of continental and Scottish life then than now.

Another aspect of the background to Welsh was the strain in France between the Huguenots and the Catholics. Welsh became a victim of the crackdown on Protestant congregations which came as Richelieu built up his civil and clerical power, moving from government positions back and forth to his diocese of Lucon before becoming Cardinal in 1622. Welsh had left by then, part of that movement of Scots returning furious because of the oppression of Protestants by Catholics in France and by Anglicans in Ireland—determined to do better in Scotland.

This led to the revolution against Charles I (1637-8). Welsh would have been in the vanguard of that had he survived. Despite repeated attempts to return to Scotland, James VI would not allow it. Welsh died in London in 1622. He had even thought of going to Nova Scotia in Canada, another avenue for ministers like himself seeking a niche to exercise their ministry. After his death, his wife was at last able to return to Scotland. She died in Ayr, 1625. It is a sad story and another example of one of God's people, a man of conviction, prepared to suffer for his principles.

Letters of Mr John Welsch in Wodrow Miscellany (Edinburgh: 1844).
Foster, W R: *The Church before the Covenants* (Edinburgh: 1975).

41

JOHN OGILVIE

A Catholic Martyr

JOHN Ogilvie (*c*1579-1615) is the only case of a Roman Catholic being put to death in post-Reformation Scotland by the judicial sentence of a properly constituted court. We have to ask what made him different? We have no real answers to that question in the little we know about his origins: before 1598 the details are very confusing—it has even been disputed whether the facts we have belong to the man honoured today by Roman Catholics as Saint John Ogilvie. In some ways this illustrates that what is essential to this story is the manner of John Ogilvie's suffering at the hand of the torturers and his courage in dying, rather than the rest of life—it certainly frustrates any attempts to round out his personality.

Most probably John Ogilvie was born *c*1579, son of a Protestant laird in Banffshire. He may be the John Ogilvie who, at the age of 13, went abroad to the Protestant Helmstedt University. This John Ogilvie became a Catholic and in 1596 went to the Scots college of Douai (then at Louvain). When Douai shut down with money problems, he went to the Scots Benedictine monastery at Regensburg in 1598. What is certain is that the John Ogilvie of our story went in 1598 to the Jesuit college at Olmutz in Bohemia where he became a Jesuit novice in 1599. What characterised Jesuit training was its thoroughness, and so we can be sure that the man who died in Glasgow was the product of their intensive contribution of spiritual training with studies in philosophy and theology. John Ogilvie taught in Central Europe during his training before going to France in 1610. Ordained in Paris, he then taught at Rouen.

The oddest characteristic of his return to work secretly in the Jesuit mission in Scotland is that he only worked here for two periods of less than six months. He arrived late 1613 in the footsteps of Jesuits who, since 1580, had been working behind the scenes of Scottish life with clandestine Catholics. For them and those who sought information, they brought in books and engaged in combative dialogue about Catholic teaching. In this first period (about four months) John Ogilvie was active in the north-east of Scotland and Edinburgh. He saw his mission clearly: 'to unteach heresy.' We have only odd glimpses of what he did there, working for example with advocate William Sinclair and James McDonald who was a prisoner in Edinburgh castle for cattle-stealing.

The next puzzle is John Ogilvie's journey to London in the early spring of 1614 for an interview with James VI. We don't know what business he had with the king, nor why he went on from there to France, especially since he had an English safe-conduct from James. Had he grasped some great vision that by convincing the scholarly James he could short-circuit the struggle to restore Scotland to the Catholic faith? Be that as it may, something may well have gone badly wrong and James may well have determined at this time that Ogilvie was dangerous: and this could provide the background for Ogilvie being singled out for death later on.

Whatever the background and whatever went wrong then, or later, Ogilvie went to Paris shortly before Easter. He got a flea in the ear from his superior and was sent back peremptorily to Scotland. He arrived at the end of May or early June and worked in Edinburgh and the west of Scotland before being betrayed by a spy and commuted to the Bishop of Glasgow's jail. Archbishop John Spottiswoode was James' religious agent in Scotland and he was the principal protagonist in the months of interrogation and disruption. Torture in Edinburgh was frighteningly reminiscent of modern psychological methods: Ogilvie was kept awake for eight days until on the point of death and almost out of his mind. James ensured Ogilvie was tried by a special commission of five judges and given five questions, in answer to which he declared his conviction that the 'divine right' of kings did not bestow spiritual jurisdiction. That was reserved to the Pope. Ogilvie was condemned, but unlike his associates whose sentence was committed to exile, he was hanged for treason on 10 March 1615 (by the new style calendar: it was 28 February in Scotland).

John Ogilvie's reminiscences, smuggled out of prison, revealed a saintly courageous man to seventeenth century Europe. A beatification process in 1628-29 collapsed because there was no bishop in Glasgow to further the cause. Once the bishopric was re-established, the cause began again at the turn of this century; and in 1976, after the remarkably striking cure from cancer of the Glasgow docker John Fagan (when only a few hours from death), the seal was set on the general acceptance among Catholics of his sanctity. The irony is that he died witnessing to the same independence of Christ's Kirk which Covenanters died for in a later age.

Relatio Incarcerationis et Martyrii P Joannis Ogilbei (Scottish Catholic Archives: 1615).
St John Ogilvie SJ 1579-1615 (Third Eye Centre: 1979).

42

SAMUEL RUTHERFORD
Brilliant Bigot or Caring Pastor?

SAMUEL Rutherford was born about 1600, son of a small laird or landowner in Nisbet near Jedburgh in the Scottish Borders. Some admire him as the most learned Presbyterian theologian of the seventeenth century; others revere him as the epitome of all that is good and unique in the Scottish kirk minister's pastoral care; others still question his political stance that in the 1630s and 40s shook the Stewart monarchy to its foundations in the wars of the Covenant.

He went to Edinburgh University in 1617, graduated Master of Arts in 1621 and was appointed as a regent or tutor before becoming professor in 1623. Despite having permission from the principal for his marriage, it led to his dismissal in 1626 and by 1627 he became minister of the remote parish of Anwoth in Kirkcudbrightshire. This quiet setting was the cradle of the intellectual development that led him to become the most learned Presbyterian theologian of the seventeenth century. This isn't just a matter of his appointment to St Andrews University in 1639, nor of his starring role in the Westminster Assembly in 1643, nor appointments to Edinburgh again in 1647 and as principal of St Mary's College in St Andrews in 1648, nor even the fact that he turned down offers of two chairs in the Netherlands—rather it was his writings that revealed the man: *Lex Rex* (*The Law of the King*, directed against Charles I) and *The Due Right of Presbytery* were both written in 1644. They shook the great thinkers of the state by their directness. More importantly, their arguments were arranged in tight syllogisms, were packed with references to contemporary theologians from French Jesuits to Dutch Calvinists, as well as the ancient fathers of the church: a challenging treasure house for the whole Covenanting Movement over the 1640s and 50s!

What makes Samuel Rutherford stand out today is the background to his intellectual achievements and political energies. At Anwoth he was foremost a pastor who showed the unique potential of the Scottish minister for the good of his parish. He was the first in the history of the reformed church to think that democracy in the congregation should extend to all: tenants, apprentices *and* women. The complexity of this man is perhaps summed up by the way he overcame personal tragedy. His wife died in 1630 after a painful illness lasting 13 months: 'My wife is in torment, night and day. Pray for us ... God hath filled me with gall and wormwood, but I believe (which holds my head above the water) it is good for a man that he bear the yoke in his youth.' More testing came with the early death of two of his three children by his second marriage. Meanwhile he worked tirelessly for the congregation, rising every morning at 3 am to find time for prayer, since most of the day was taken up with visiting the sick and catechising from house to house. Yet another crisis—his suspension for seditious preaching in 1636 and exile to the 'Siberia' of Aberdeenshire—brought another flowering. During that year he wrote almost 300 letters to the whole range of society from nobles to cottars, high-born ladies to farmers, lawyers to ministers. These were read out to the congregation and became a catalyst for change in the 'conventicle' gatherings in the hills which were to fuel the Scottish Revolution of 1638. They are full of tender, mystical, almost erotic imagery, balancing movingly pious words about the Kirk as the bride of Christ with grim warnings to nobles like the Earl of Casselis, 'If you the nobles, play Christ the slip now, when His back is at the wall, then may we say that the Lord hath casten water upon Scotland's smoking coal.'

He battled for the Covenant through the 1640s and 50s, maintaining, even after it was a lost cause, that the extreme party, the Protesters, were the 'witnesses of Jesus Christ.' He was certainly a 'witness': in his humiliation at the Restoration when he was deprived of his parish (1661); when he had his writings burned by the hangman; and when he thwarted his enemies by dying before they caught up with him. His greatness ensured he could never be dismissed as a 'brilliant bigot': 'I believe the Lord will build Zion [in Scotland] and repair the waste places of Jacob'—of such is Christian hope!

Bonar, A A: *Letters of Samuel Rutherford* (Edinburgh: 1891).
Henderson, G D: *Religious Life in Seventeenth Century Scotland* (Cambridge: 1937).

43

ROBERT LEIGHTON
Saintly Bishop or Ecclesiastical Opportunist?

ROBERT Leighton (1611-1684) may have been born in London, for his father Alexander Leighton was living there at that time. Alexander was a doctor who was more interested in promoting Presbyterianism than practising his trade: he published *Sion's Plea against the Prelacie* in 1628 which led to imprisonment by Archbishop Laud, who also had him scourged, pilloried, branded and his ears cut off. Alexander would have been horrified to know that his second son was also destined to become a despised prelate.

Shortly after his father was imprisoned, Robert went to Edinburgh University, graduating there in 1631 then heading for the continent, travelling and studying widely in France and the Low countries. He seems to have had dealings there with Catholic Jansenists (Pascal was a leading one) for his later writings show their stress on a holy life for individuals rather than church structures.

When King Charles faltered in the late 1630s, Robert returned to Scotland, his father was released (1640) and Robert became the parish minister at Newbattle through the Earl of Lothian. Though this involved subscribing to the Covenants, Leighton moved out of sympathy with the anti-royalist and anti-English sentiments of the time. By the end of the 1640s he spent less time at Newbattle and began to take a more political role. In 1652 he was sent to Cromwell to plead for the release of Scots prisoners taken at the Battle of Worcester. Cromwell took a liking to his spiritual qualities and put pressure on Edinburgh Town Council (then garrisoned) to appoint Leighton Principal of Edinburgh University. Opportunism or merit? Whatever, Leighton was a great influence at the university. Sir Robert Sibbald in his autobiography says Leighton made him realise that the church-state struggle was not important: one should build an inner life away from outward skirmishes. Leighton certainly spent days in his room at prayer. As for his preaching, while it had been lost on his parishioners, Gilbert Burnet and others thought a great deal of his fluid teaching style. But his wider vision was not so appreciated: a colleague criticised him for using the spiritual writings of Catholic Thomas á Kempis.

In 1660 the restoration of Charles II led Leighton to his greatest mistake when the government persuaded him to become a bishop in the period of transition. He was taken in by Archbishop Usher's scheme that bishops should be merely superintendents; and by puritan Richard Baxter's view that being a bishop was compatible with equality of ministry, provided one was not too political or authoritarian. When Leighton was ordained in 1661, he chose Dunkeld for his See since it was the least renumerative. After being enthroned in Holyrood, he tried in Dunblane to promote episcopacy as low-key. He was a model bishop who did not impose his views in his regular synods, a remarkable contrast to the ways of the more autocratic Archbishop Sharp. At the end of the 1660s Leighton designed and worked for a 'scheme of Accommodation' to bring the presbyterian and episcopalian parties together, but both Charles II and Sharp disagreed and instead intensified the persecution of the Covenanters. Leighton went to the king to resign in 1665 but paradoxically (and reluctantly) had accepted appointment as Archbishop of Glasgow by 1670, with consequent responsibility for the south-west where Covenanters were most persecuted. He refused enthronement until 1671 after a series of fruitless conferences aimed at reconciliation. By 1674 he was so out of tune with the government policy of persecution that he resigned and retired to England.

His last ten years were spent in his sister and brother-in-law's house, Broadhurst Manor, Sussex. There he preached in the church of Horsted Keynes where he was eventually buried. He also built up a remarkable library, confirming his intellect as the finest of his day. This library of doctrinal works, patristics, Hebrew and Jewish studies was left to Dunblane. He also left money for bursaries at the University of Glasgow. The spiritual gifts so admired by Coleridge, evidenced in those of his writings published at the end of the seventeenth century, are still admired today.

Burnet, G: *History of My Own Time* (Oxford: 1897/1900), 2 volumes.
Knox, E A: *Robert Leighton, Archbishop of Glasgow* (London: 1930).

44

JAMES SHARP
Murdered on Magus Moor

'ALTHOUGH the deed was foully done, the loon was well awa.'
This judgment on the Archbishop of St Andrews, James Sharp
(1613-1679), after he was murdered by a band of Covenanters in
Fife, has been reinforced by studies of his correspondence: it shows
him as a man, ducking and weaving for the
main chance in the complicated political and
ecclesiastical intrigues of the time. Perhaps,
however, he suffers from us knowing too
much about him and he was no worse than
anyone else in such confusing times.

ARCHBISHOP SHARP

James was born in Banff, the son of the
sheriff-clerk, and with this head-start went
to King's College, Aberdeen with an eye to
being a minister in the established Episcopalian Church of his day. Then he was a
regent at St Andrews University and minister at Crail in 1649, a
ministry which was so popular that parishioners resisted his transfer to Edinburgh at a later date.

Unlike the high-principled Samuel Rutherford, who was his
boss at St Andrews, Sharp seemed to swim with the tide. It was the
era of the Covenanters and Cromwell; and though he had a spell
of imprisonment in 1651 in London, he was chosen by the moderate resolutioner party in the Kirk to go to London in 1657 to
try to ensure presbyterian government in Scotland. This was during the negotiations when General Monck was inviting Charles II
back from the continent. He met Charles II twice at Breda and
his letters are full of apprehension for presbyteral government.
What followed next was regarded as betrayal by those who sent
him, for he co-operated with the Earl of Middleton and then the
Earl of Lauderdale in the re-establishment of episcopacy in Scotland. He himself accepted the archbishopric of St Andrews in

1661. He demurred at first to demands that he be re-ordained in Anglican orders, but eventually he gave in, provoking the comment that he was 'a typical Scot: he would strain at anything and in the end swallow everything.'

He was now on the move regularly between St Andrews and Edinburgh where the Privy Council were the agents of Charles II in Scotland. Charles himself did not involve bishops in government, but Sharp was still a key figure for the Privy Council in the question of whether ministers would accept the new order of things. The Earl of Lauderdale did not completely trust him, but was prepared to use him. Many of the 'resolutioner' ministers Sharp had represented accepted both bishops and patronage, but the 'protesters' refused. Out of 900 ministers, 270 refused. The worst opposition was in the south-west of Scotland and in some parts of Fife. Archbishop Burnet stood no nonsense in the southwest and made things worse. Archbishop Sharp was more diplomatic and conciliatory but nonetheless came to be associated with the government's persecution of Covenanters and Conventicles. The government sent the troops to problem areas and this provoked the Pentland Rising. Sharp still went along with the government and was hated for it by the extreme Covenanters.

In 1668 one of them, James Mitchell, took a shot at Sharp: it missed but hit another bishop in the wrist. The cry went up—'a man has been killed!' The significant answer rang out—'oh no, it's only a bishop.' The end came on 3 May 1679. Sharp was travelling with his daughter back to St Andrews. Some of the Fife lairds were out looking for the sheriff of Fife, but when they found the archbishop they decided, 'the Lord has delivered our enemy.' They ordered out the terrified old man and told him to 'pray for his soul.' He was shot and hacked to death. Had he asked for it—or was he a tragic victim of the times, a minister and archbishop trying to do the best for Scotland's Kirk? The lairds went on to the west and raised the second Covenanting rising which in turn was crushed at Bothwell Brig. Right or wrong, it was too late for Sharp.

Buckroyd, J: *The Life of James Sharp* (John Donald: 1987).

45

MARGARET LAUCHLINSON
AND MARGARET WILSON

Drowned for their Faith

MARGARET Lauchlinson and Margaret Wilson must surely take their rightful place in the list of God's people, even though we know very little about them. Probably drowned for their faith by judicial sentence, they represent a whole generation of strong-faithed women who were very often the driving force of the 'godly bleeding remnant' of those described as extreme Covenanters in the south-west of Scotland.

The background to the story of the two Margarets was the 'killing times' in the mid 1680s, after the main body of Covenanters had made an accommodation (a 'deal', if you like) with Charles II and James VII. Groups of Covenanters held out and were particularly strong in the south-west of Scotland. They had to worship in the outside conventicles and even there they risked civil penalties. The churches were closed to them.

Under the leadership of James Renwick, the 'apologetical declaration'—a powerful statement of the Covenanting position— particularly angered the government. The government decreed that suspects should be asked to disown the 'declaration', and if they refused they should be shot or hanged. What made the legislation particularly horrific was the addition that women, if notorious, should also be put to death. But they should not be shot or hanged as a matter of public decency: instead they should be drowned.

Here the two Margarets enter the scene. Margaret Lauchlinson was 60 years old and a widow. Margaret Wilson was only 18. We don't have any idea how or when they were captured, but know that they were sentenced on the 13 April 1685. The sentence was that they should be ritually drowned by being tied to stakes at low tide in Wigton Bay and there watched until the incoming tide drowned them. In those days of *public* executions (meant to deter others, but pandering to the worst in human nature as the crowds gathered to watch) this was a particularly horrendous scenario.

It has been verified about this particular sentence that people were shocked: they appealed to the Privy Council in Edinburgh, which ruled Scotland in the name of the king. At the end of April, a stay of execution was issued but—tragically—it was addressed to the magistrates of Edinburgh when it should of course have been addressed to the authorities at Wigton.

Here the mystery starts, for we cannot ascertain whether the execution actually took place as decreed. A local source fairly near the time indicates that it did indeed proceed and recounts several details which would point to its authenticity. It appears that as the tide came up, the Town Officer took his halberd and held each of their heads in turn under the water to drown them more quickly and mercifully.

Nonetheless the story of the two Margarets is a story of an age of savagery in Scotland, and a story of faith, courage and religious conviction that continued to inspire in Victorian Scotland and even today challenges our complacency with the consequences of religious division when entangled with political debate.

Privy Council Register.
Reid, H M B: *The Professor's Wallet* (1910).

46

ISOBEL YOUNG
Strangled and burned

ISOBEL Young is a well-documented example of the countless number of witches burned in Scotland during the savage witch-hunts which swept many Lowland areas of Scotland (the Low-lands, the East Coast, Fife and Lothians in particular) in bursts between 1591 and 1662. An Act against witchcraft had been passed by the Scottish parliament in 1563 and one of the first to burn was an unfortunate woman at St Andrews, who was chained to a pillar and forced to listen to a sermon by John Knox. Witch-es were more commonly female, but Major Weir of Edinburgh is a well-documented exception. The last execution of a witch was at Dornoch in 1727: the Act of 1563 was repealed in 1736, although

Major Weir's Land, Edinburgh

it is true to say that popular belief in witches lasted much longer.

East Barns near Dunbar was where Isobel Young lived, the spouse of George Smith, portioner (tenant farmer). By the time she was accused publicly on charges of witchcraft, she was a widow and about 60. The indictment said that her reputation for witchcraft was long-standing: the charges went back over 40 years, 24 charges in all, only twelve of which, however, were sustained at the trial.

The indictment for the trial has not survived, but the proceedings have, with the prosecution's summary of the indictment and the defence's denials. The case was brought in 1629, one of the years in which there was a national panic about witches. (The other years were 1591, 1597, 1649 and 1661-62.) In such years accusations of witchcraft became almost an epidemic. James VI became interested in 1590 when a group of witches were accused of having conjured up storms during his recent voyage to Denmark to fetch his bride Anne. He and his courtiers had encountered the latest witchcraft theology in Denmark, and launched a campaign on their return to purify the land of witches. Fear and suspicion spread, as many of those accused were pressed to provide names of 'accomplices.' With Isobel too, there was the crucial damning fact that she was named as an accomplice by two other witches in 1628. This led straight to her arrest and local gossip began to build up the case.

Normally a confession was extracted from a suspected witch by means of sleep deprivation and aggressive interrogation, or less frequently by witch-pricking to try to find the devil's mark, or other torture in rare cases. Unlike many so-called witches, Isobel had the means to defend herself. Without that, it would simply have been a matter of the local laird going to the Privy Council in Edinburgh and getting authority to organise a jury, try the accused and have her executed. With Isobel, however, it was a case for the Court of Justiciary in Edinburgh. Her lawyers made shrewd points and seem to have convinced many of the assize (the jury) that she was the victim of false accusations from people who had fallen out with her, and her husband before her. One such was from 20 years before, when William Meslot and his wife Margaret Ogill paid more than Isobel and her husband were offering for a piece of land. Isobel was said to have issued angry threats, taken her hat off and turned three times anti-clockwise to call down a spell on the offending couple. Margaret Ogill swore that cattle had died as a consequence. Some other witnesses nonetheless—and this must have taken courage—stood up in court and said that, though their cattle had died, they could not in all conscience say it was Isobel.

Though many charges were rebutted, enough stuck and she was condemned to be taken to the Castlehill in Edinburgh, strangled to death and then burned: all her goods would be confiscated.

Isobel's tragedy was part of a more widespread witch-hunt which occurred in both Catholic and Protestant areas of Europe in the sixteenth and seventeenth centuries. Belief in witches was normal for orthodox theologians of the time. The Bible seemed to them to show that the Devil was active in the world and had human agents. Ordinary people believed something slightly different: that some people had supernatural powers (with unclear origins) which could be used to heal or to harm. What many theologians did was take parts of this folklore, combine it with the many New Testament stories of demonic activity, and develop the theory of the 'demonic pact', whereby a witch received powers from the Devil in return for her soul. The solution to this threat was clear: 'thou shalt not suffer a witch to live.' In the search for a 'godly state', God's enemies were also the enemies of the state, and the land had to be purged of them. Present controversies about some Christian groups seeing satanic ritual abuse rather more often than the facts seem to warrant, may have significant parallels with the witch-hunts of old.

Gillan, S A (ed): *Selected Justiciary Cases 1624-1650* (Stair Society: 1953), volume i.
Larner, C: *Enemies of God* (Chatto and Windus: 1981).

47

ANNE
God's Duchess?

ANNE, 3rd Duchess of Hamilton (1632-1716) has what can only be described as an adventure story of a life. Her father was the first Duke of Hamilton, Charles I's leading Scottish adviser and courtier, and so she was born in a house near Whitehall Palace in London. One elder sister died in infancy and her mother died in 1638 leaving another young sister and three little brothers. The three sons died soon after. Her father was embroiled in the civil war on the royal side, although he came from a Covenanting family and his mother had him well warned that 'if he came to Scotland with a royal army, she'd shoot him personally.'

The father leased a house in Chelsea for a few years, but eventually decided his elder daughter Anne should stay with their formidable grandmother in Hamilton Palace (the family had lands from the island of Arran in the west to Kinneil Castle at Bo'ness). It was the opposite end of the Protestant spectrum from that which Anne had been used to and these five years were formative. Meanwhile her father was executed in 1649: feeling that he couldn't leave his titles to a 17 year old girl, he left them to his younger brother. He in turn was wounded at Worcester fighting Cromwell, but before he died 12 days later he left the title to Anne. Thus at 19 she became duchess of Hamilton, with a string of other titles —though the confiscation of her lands by Cromwell meant major problems. She lived first in Arran and then—with a faithful retainer—in a hut behind Hamilton Palace.

Marriage came next: an unlikely choice, for the groom was William Douglas, Earl of Selkirk, the younger son of a Roman Catholic family, and Anne's father had specified that any member of his family who married a Roman Catholic would *not* get the title! It was a love match and Douglas had to deny his faith. He was a meticulous man, as evidenced by the carefully tied up receipts discovered by Dr Rosalind Marshall. By careful management he paid enormous fines, and with Charles II paying back some of the money his father owed, they were able to return to Hamilton Palace. At Anne's insistence, Charles created her husband Duke of Hamilton. They had 13 children. Though as a couple they made a dramatic contrast with her soberly dressed and he in magnificent satins, they worked well together.

Anne was semi-regal with an enormous reputation. She said she would not influence politicians but inevitably did. She was a devout presbyterian and ministers came to her for advice. She gave communion cups to needy kirks. She cared for her estates and everyone on them, setting up schools throughout for the poor. By 1707 she was the leader of the patriotic anti-union party, but even afterwards her influence continued. People remembered how she had always tried to stay outside the arguments about church government but had protected the conventicles as long as there were no breaches of the peace. She and her husband had then supported William and Mary and their rule in Scotland.

Many didn't like Anne's husband for he was curt, surly and drank too much, but there is nothing in the 30,000 letters and vast number of accounts to suggest there was any trouble between them. He had an illegitimate child, but then so did her father before. One note to her speaks of 'how lucky I was to have found such a virtuous person as you.' She was devastated when he died in 1684 and wept for months. Nonetheless, she carried on working for the welfare of her tenants. 'God's Duchess' might be no exaggeration!

Marshall, Rosalind K: *The Days of Duchess Anne* (Collins: 1973).

THOMAS NICHOLSON
Bishop 'in his Grand Climacteric'

THOMAS Nicholson (1642?-1718) was appointed as the first post-Reformation Catholic vicar-apostolic (bishop) in 1694 in what he called 'his grand climacteric', namely at the age of about 53. He tried to decline on the grounds of age and rheumatism, but was to take on a new lease of life when he finally returned to Scotland in secret to take up his dangerous clandestine role, organising the scattered remnants of the Catholic Church in the Highlands and Islands of Scotland.

The story begins with his birth into the well-to-do Episcopalian family of Lord Kemmay at Birkenbog, Banffshire. Thomas had at least two brothers who attained positions of importance in Scottish life and he himself was very clever. This he proved at Marischal College in Aberdeen where he studied Greek, Mathematics and Philosophy. His name is noted in the *Fasti* of the university. After graduation, he went as a young man of 21 to the University of Glasgow as regent, where he taught Mathematics. This involved taking the oath of allegiance to the king and to the Protestant faith. By 1682 all regents were required to take the Test Act oath. Nicholson refused to take the oath because he was thinking of becoming a Catholic. He had met some of the academics who were turning to the Catholic or High Anglican faith at that time. Archbishop Laud's high church views had of course encouraged the trend and Charles I's marriage to a Catholic had started many thinking in that direction. The story goes that Nicholson went to a minister friend to discuss these issues. The minister pointed to the children playing around him to explain why he couldn't become a Catholic: '*These* are my reasons.' Nicholson shrugged his shoulders: 'I have no such reasons.' His mind was made up.

Thomas Nicholson studied at Douai on the continent and was ordained as a priest. From there he went to Padua under cardinal

Barbarigo and taught there his specialist subjects of Mathematics, Philosophy and Greek. During this time he suffered terrible ill health, part of which may have been due to his harkening for his native Scotland, the 'land of cakes.' At a later stage in his life, while chaplain at a Benedictine convent at Dunkirk, he even sent to his mother in Scotland for his tartan nightshirt!

After Padua, Nicholson came to Scotland in secret as a missionary priest, but with the crackdown in 1688 he was arrested and imprisoned first in the Tolbooth and then in the castle in Edinburgh. His older brother was a lord of session at the time. He got him released on bail on condition he left the country and did not come back.

This was when he stayed in Dunkirk as a chaplain for six years knowing well that King William would in no way have given him a passport to return. Then came the bombshell: his name was put forward as a bishop in 1694. Nicholson wrote to William Leslie, the Scottish agent, that he was too ill and close to death, but the appointment still went ahead.

The remarkable thing is that when Nicholson managed back to Scotland in 1697, his health recovered. He was to live for another 20 years and in his first years back travelled all over the Highlands and Islands in secret. This involved journeys on foot up and down mountains, very often on his hands and knees.

He was based at Presholme on the estate of the Catholic Duke of Gordon, with a butt and ben as a hideout. The times were difficult, with many Catholics losing their lands, but many still taking the risk of harbouring the visiting Jesuit priests, priests from orders and the occasional secular like Nicholson. Nicholson used almost 26 pseudonyms and in his letters back to Rome he incessantly complained about the lack of teachers and priests. Three hundred of Nicholson's letters survive to this day, written in old Scots in seventeenth century writing, some folded to the size of a postage stamp in order to be concealed in a glove or shoe. Anyone caught carrying the letters would have been arrested.

Nicholson emerges as a kindly, wise, prudent, down to earth man. He wasn't emotional, but clearly an academic. He is described as slow of speech and since his eyesight failed in his late fifties, his writing got worse and worse. He took great delight in baptising children, confirming young people and marrying young couples: he especially loved the company of young families. His last years were spent at Presholme and he left the travelling to an assistant, Bishop Gordon. Nicholson died quietly and peacefully at the age of 76, a quiet man who achieved great things quietly in a turbulent age.

Blairs Collection (Scottish Catholic Archives).
Anson, P: *Underground Catholicism in Scotland* (Montrose: 1970).

49

ROBERT BARCLAY
The Quaker Theologian

ROBERT Barclay (1648-90) is one of those Scots who are more honoured abroad than in their native home. Some regard him as the one truly original theologian Scotland ever produced. Voltaire, in his four letters on Quakerism, said that Barclay's defence of Quakerism was 'as good a work as it could be'—from Voltaire that was a compliment indeed.

Robert was born to a landed family near Inverurie just outside Aberdeen. His father, Colonel Barclay, was an early convert to Quakerism, which began in England in the early 1650s. The Colonel was a powerful man in the Aberdeen area, but was imprisoned in Edinburgh castle at the Restoration in 1660 because he had been in Cromwell's parliament. One of those he had met there, John Swinton, had become a Quaker. Through him, so did Colonel Barclay; and then, at the age of 18 when visiting his father in Edinburgh Castle, Robert too was converted.

One early Quaker meeting place was in Colonel Barclay's home and several notable people in Aberdeen joined the group. It was at this time that Robert wrote the works which have conveyed his insights to the present day. The background to that was a great deal of opposition from the Church of Scotland. The presbyterian elders were able to use the Conventicle Act (brought in against the non-conforming Covenanters) against the Quakers. They were suspected of being English allies, or even fifth columnists. It was even said that they were clandestine Catholics.

Even today there are only about 600 Quakers in Scotland. George Fox, their founder, had made several journeys into the south of Scotland. He visited Edinburgh and Glasgow but was bundled out because of his stance against Calvinism. Quakers wanted to stress the availability of Christ to every human being (in the form of a 'seed' or inner light) and so found Calvin's idea of the predestination of some to damnation repugnant, as it eliminated the call and moral responsibility on everyone to make a positive response to God. In this they saw themselves as a movement (rather than a church) calling everyone back to the central challenge of Christianity.

Another interesting aspect of Robert Barclay is that he was related on his mother's side to the Stewarts. This meant that he got to know James VIII when he was Regent in Scotland before reigning in his own right. When Barclay went to London, James and he were on good terms. The common interest was toleration for all: James for Catholics, Robert for Quakers. That apart of course, Robert was just as scathing about Catholics as anyone else. The only parallel between the two religious approaches has been between the Quaker use of 'silence' in their worship and the Catholic and Orthodox atmosphere of silence and reverence for the presence of Christ in the Eucharist. Many early Quakers may have been influenced by monks who had been thrown out of their monasteries and missed the silence of contemplative spirituality.

While in London, Robert got himself appointed governor of the colony of East Jersey in the United States of America (now half of the state of New Jersey). He never actually went there, but did the necessary administrative work, raised funds and helped to write the constitution. Barclay's influence was not in the colonial outreach, however (though that is partly the reason why there is more interest in him in America than in Scotland); it is his writings which have remained his main influence. In them he shows himself intelligent and well read, with a good theological mind and a deep lay spirituality which was quite distinct from the clerical or monastic. He was a very human, family man. People spoke of his equanimity of temperament and his dignity, even when he landed for several spells of imprisonment in Aberdeen's Tolbooth. Above all, however, he was responsible for the first and only systematic exposition of Quaker theology's: *Apology for the True Christian Divinity*. It is still read today, although its formal style of argument makes it dense and difficult to read.

Freiday, D (ed): *Barclay's Apology in Modern English* (Arthur Elberton, USA).
Trueblood, D Elton: *Robert Barclay* (Harper, USA: 1968)

50

EDWARD HICKHORNGILL
'Now you see him, now you don't!'

EDWARD Hickhorngill appears fleetingly on the face of Scottish history, symbolising an approach to Christian faith which found no lasting place at the time, but was to become significant in later centuries. On 20 October 1652, he was ordained an Anabaptist minister with prayer, fasting and the laying-on of hands in Hexham, North England. He was then sent from the Garrison church there as a 'minister and messenger', to be pastor at the Cromwellian garrison in Leith. There are letters preserved in Hexham—evidence of his work there—concerning typical Baptist concerns of the time as to whether ministers should be paid or left to support themselves from their normal jobs in secular life. The instinctive feeling was that establishing a class of 'professional ministers' led to the same dangers they were objecting to at that time in the established Church of England.

By 1653 Hickhorngill was gone from Leith. We get an impression of a man moving—as many did in Commonwealth times—from one denomination to another. He is described as a 'sometime precious but now deluded brother.' This could indicate that he had joined the Society of Friends, or one of the Baptist groups such as the Ranters. Be that as it may, we know that with his companion minister Stackhouse, he had some success with baptism of the soldiers at the garrison and with the adult baptism of some of the native Scots. Working from his base at the Citadel in Leith, these baptisms took place in the Water of Leith at Bonnington Mill. There was also activity at the other Cromwell garrisons at Dalkeith and Perth. Hexham kept in touch with the work in Scotland. *A Confession of Faith* for Baptists was published by the Leith Garrison church in 1653. The impression is given of serious Bible study balanced by a new free style of worship, breaking away from the ritual structures of the Establishment: lots of young people crowding into the church, responding to the words of the preacher. The Baptist ministers engaged the ministers of the Church of Scotland in debate, very much in the tradition of a church which had John Bunyan imprisoned for ten to twelve years for refusing to give up non-conformist preaching. In Scotland there were the same suspicions of these radical attitudes, but also resentment of Baptist ministers because they were not trained as ministers. They were dismissed as mere soldiers getting into the pulpit and preaching. Perhaps because of this there are no records of Baptists in Scotland at the time, except one reference to the conventicles in Edinburgh of Congregationalists and 'water doupers' (water dippers).

This quotation in Nicholl's diary (1653) is worth noting again: 'Anabaptists daily increased in this nation where never none was of before, at least dare not avow themselves but now may make open profession thereof so that thrice in the week on Mondays, Wednesdays and Fridays, there were some dipped at Bonnington Mill between Leith and Edinburgh, both men and women of good rank. Sometimes there would be sundrie hundreds of persons attending and fifteen persons baptised in one day by the Anabaptists!'

There were others like Hickhorngill in Scotland. A certain James Brown was an army chaplain in Fairfax's regiment and is on record as having debated with the minister at Cupar. The subjects were predictable: original sin; infant baptism; limited atonement of Christ. These Anabaptists in Scotland were not Calvinists, but rather 'General Baptists', and therefore Armenian: this would not increase their popularity. In the records at Cupar, there is a long account of three Anabaptists brought before the kirk session so there must have been a measure of success.

Cromwell's soldiers were recalled in 1658 and thereafter there is no record of Baptists in Scotland until Sir William Sinclair of Keiss in Caithness founded a Baptist church on his estate in 1750. He became bankrupt and moved to Edinburgh, but the church survived. Those who quarrelled with the established Kirk had joined the Baptist rather than Secession Church and the tradition remained, proof that the Baptist Church could flourish in a Scottish context.

Laing, D (ed): *Nicholls Diary 1650-57* (Bannatyne Club, Edinburgh: 1836).
Bebbington, D W: *The Baptists in Scotland, A History* (Baptist Union in Scotland: 1988).

51

WILLIAM CARSTARES
'Cardinal Carstares'

HIS opponents called him 'Cardinal Carstares', an ironic tribute to the power of the Presbyterian churchman William Carstares, who at the height of his power from 1695 to 1702 was more influential than any prime minister of Scotland could have been.

The road to that role had been a testing one, so he was clearly a man of deep principle and energy. Born in Glasgow in 1649, he was educated in Edinburgh, but very soon showed the same strength of character which led his Covenanting father to rebel against Charles II. Utrecht in Holland was a more congenial place of study and there he will have learned of William of Orange for the first time. The seeds of the future were sown.

The next years are shrouded in mystery. William Carstares travelled back and forward between Holland, England and Scotland. We hear of him in London from 1672-75, and then imprisoned in Edinburgh until 1679. He was accused of being implicated in the Ryehouse plot against Charles II and the Catholic Duke of York. He was captured in Kent, imprisoned in London, and sent back by ship to Scotland to be tortured in the lower Parliament building, for torture was not allowed in England. His one and a half years must have been a severe test of his resolve, but undaunted, he escaped back to Holland and an official post as confidential chaplain to William of Orange. From that point on he accompanied him at every stage and so was with him when he came to take over the throne of England, landing at Torbay and going on to Ireland and the Battle of the Boyne.

The measure of a man like Carstares is often how they survive the death of their patrons. When William died in 1702, he came back to Scotland and even more glittering achievements, at least in the realm of religion. Chaplain to Queen Anne, minister of Greyfriars, and then St Giles High kirk, he was four times Moderator of the General Assembly between 1705 and his death in 1715. During this time he was also principal of the University of Edinburgh and was responsible for the conversion of the Town's College into separate university faculties after the Dutch system. The union of the Crowns owed much to his statesmanship.

How did he use his power? In an era when others persecuted Episcopalians bitterly, he insisted on the tolerance he himself had not received in earlier times. He certainly represents an era when there was no question of the Kirk not being involved in politics, but he used his political influence to nurse the newly established Church of Scotland through the difficult period of strong episcopal influence from England (William would have preferred both churches to be the same), to the stage when the threat to establishment had passed. Carstares represents the reality that steadfast fidelity to perceived Christian tradition can be more effective than raging fanaticism. The Kirk remains established, but relatively free, due to his legacy. His sort of tolerance takes a long time to learn and some never learn it.

Jacobites: *Cardinal Carstares* (1693-1702).
Dunlop, A I: *William Carstares* (Saint Andrew Press: 1967).

WILLIAM CARSTARES

52

ALEXANDER SHIELDS
From the Bass Rock to Jamaica

ALEXANDER Shields (1660-1700) was born at Earlston in the Scottish Borders but begins to make his mark in our history of God's people when, in 1685, he was arrested as a Covenanter objecting to the English imposition of episcopacy on Scotland. It was tragically a question of Protestant persecuting Protestant, with religious and political issues inextricably linked.

He was sent to join his fellow Covenanters in the makeshift Bass Rock prison which had no suitable buildings. The barren isolated rock that is now a bird sanctuary was owned by the Earl of Lauderdale, the leading activist in the persecution of the Covenanters. In a sense it was the first private prison!

After he was set free, he fled to the Netherlands, 'that republican centre of sedition' which was to seventeenth century Europe what Gaddafi's Libya is to present day radicalism. From this point, Shields becomes a very effective political polemicist. He wrote the *Life and Death of James Renwick,* one of the great inspirational characters of the Covenanting movement (Renwick was born in Moniaive, ordained in Holland in 1683, and executed in 1688 after being caught preaching in the fields and accused of stirring up sedition).

Shield's most outstanding work, however, is *A Hind let Loose*, one of the most radical tracts ever written by a Scot. In the *Hind*, Shields appears as a very learned and accomplished scholar. Unsurprisingly he quotes Buchanan, Knox and Calderwood from Scottish Reformation thought. More unexpectedly, he quotes the distinguished Jesuit scholar, cardinal Bellarmine. This is because the Jesuits were the first to attempt a theological defence of the killing of tyrant rulers, partly as a justification of the murder of Henry IV of France. Shields is, however, proud of being in the tradition of Knox and Buchanan in what he wrote. What stimulated his own thinking was his anger at the rise of absolutist kings (with the doctrine of the 'divine right' of kings) and his conviction that there was an international Catholic conspiracy against Parliament and Protestantism, the one often being the tool of the other. Shields advocated that it was the right not of the nobles as Knox said, but of the people themselves, to depose kings: 'Man is born by nature as free as beasts,' and is not subject to anyone. In England he would have been placed at the radical end of the Leveller tradition. Perhaps so, but others trace a line of thought stemming from John Locke, the philosopher who gave birth to so many liberal thought movements and who shares with Shields the Dutch connection with the liberal theologians Limborch and Le Clerc. Whatever is true, his writings are evidence of one of the most interesting minds of the seventeenth century.

Tragically, an early death of fever in Jamaica in 1700 prevented him publishing a mature political philosophy. Interestingly, he had become, after the Glorious Revolution, chaplain to the Cameronian Regiment. This returned him to his roots but paved the way for his participation on the tragic Scottish misadventure to Darien which buried so much Scottish money and hopes. While there he tried to convert the native Indians in true colonial style, but he showed an unusual sympathy and identification with them. In the appalling sufferings of the second Scottish expedition to Darien, when the English ensured that they would not even get humanitarian help, Shields remained a total optimist right to the last; but condemned his fellow colonists as 'too many knaves and too many fools and too many lairds and too many lairds' bairnes, who think it below them to work and find themselves disapoynted of their big and phantastick hopes of getting goupings of gold for the uptakin.' He concluded: 'I think it is a wonder of mercy that so many of us are escaped considering our wickedness and sillie management.' Alexander's faith and intellect always seemed to combine to produce something quite different from his contemporaries and insights far ahead of his time.

MacPherson, H: *The Cameronian Philosopher: Alexander Shields* (Edinburgh: 1932).
Smellie, A: *Men of the Covenant* (London: 1911).

53

EBENEZER ERSKINE
Man of the People

OPINIONS have been divided down through the years as to whether Ebenezer Erskine (1680-1754) was a thrawn rigid Calvinist who perpetuated the Kirk's tendency to split into warring factions, or whether he was a prophetic man of the people whose spiritual convictions helped to preserve the Kirk from any danger of becoming merely an ecclesiastical prop for the powers of state.

His father taught him by example that principle counted for more than advancement in the Kirk. In 1662 he was thrown out from his charge as minister at Cornhill on Tweed in the purges following the Restoration and ended up as a prisoner on the infamous Bass Rock in the round-up of Covenanters. This period of confusion means that we don't know if Ebenezer was born on the Bass Rock (unlikely) or somewhere in the vicinity of Dryburgh Abbey. The changed political service after William of Orange brought Ebenezer's father the position as minister of Chirnside, again in the Borders. Ebenezer went to the parish school and then studied divinity at the University of Edinburgh. A spell during his studies as domestic chaplain to the earls of Rosyth gained him enough influence to be appointed minister of Portmoak in Kinross-shire shortly after ordination.

There he engaged in the practical, dynamic ministry he passionately believed Scotland needed. His preaching on Sunday was backed up by a lecture on Scripture on Thursday and a constant tour of his parishes on both formal visitation—solemnly introduced by 'May God bless this house'—and informal contacts where he would relax and share a meal. He was to marry twice and to have lots of children. Both reinforced his commitment: his first wife—Alison Turpie—was a Fife-born woman of deep spiritual character and influence; his second wife was the daughter of an Edinburgh minister. It could be argued that Ebenezer would gladly have remained in the relative obscurity of Kinross-shire but it was not to be. He finally yielded to a call to Stirling in 1731, and soon after his evangelical party commitment in the Kirk got him into trouble with the moderate party. He was unjustly accused of heresy at the General Assembly after supporting a friend of his who brought out a reprint of a book encapsulating old-style Calvinism (*Marrow of Modern Divinity*). This controversy was a warning of the major crisis which lead Ebenezer to the founding of the Original Secession Church (which itself was to split into two in his own lifetime and into four parts later on).

At the root of the dispute was the 1712 Patronage Act which gave the landowner the right to appoint ministers. The last straw for Ebenezer was a controversy over the appointment of a minister to Kinross which the people clearly did not want. This sort of imposed ministerial appointment was disliked by everyone in the Kirk, but the moderates accepted it, partly, it is said, because it meant the appointment of more ministers who had the requisite social graces. The General Assembly responded to the Kinross controversy by strengthening patronage in the sense of not even requiring the 'Call' document to the minister to be signed by the congregation as well as the landowner. At the Synod of Perth and Stirling, Ebenezer Erskine preached against the Assembly with powerful and scathing eloquence: 'I can find no warrant from the Word of God to confer the spiritual privileges of his house upon the rich beyond the poor.' He said that the act favoured 'the man with the gold ring and the gay clothes unto the man with the vile raiment and poor attire' … 'What a miserable bondage would it be for a family to have stewards or servants imposed upon them by strangers who might give stones for bread or a scorpion for medicine.'

The Kirk was shocked. The General Assembly censored him. In December 1733 at Gairney Bridge near Kinross he set up a defiant group in the company of three other ministers. He was finally deposed as a minister in 1740. His protest led to him preaching in the fields before a meeting place in Stirling was acquired. In 1747 the controversy between Burghers and Antiburghers found him believing his group had become too extreme and so he stayed with the Burghers who believed the civil oath did not compromise the Kirk's independence.

But his health and spirit seemed broken for what proved to be the last seven years of his life. Ebenezer Erskine stood for a kirk tradition which condemned the 1707 union, dancing and repeal of the Witches' Burning Act, but gave dramatic impetus to the conviction that Scotland needed to hear God's message. It seemed rigid, but quite remarkably Erskine, as a measure of the man, is noted for telling his congregation not to fear Calvin's teaching that some are predestined to hell: 'You have no more need to worry about Predestination than about people in Mexico—God is good, leave it to Him.'

Fraser, D: Article on 'Ebenezer Erskine' in the *Dictionary of National Biography* (1831).

54

ROBERT KEITH

Factious Priest or Builder of Bridges?

BISHOP Robert Keith (1681-1757) is a good example of a cleric who developed from his own background to play a role which was quite unexpected. Born at Uras in Kincardineshire, his father was a laird of the cadet branch of the hereditary earls Marshall: thus Robert was very much in the tradition of the bishops in the Scottish Episcopal Church who came from the landed gentry. He was, however, a lively spirited man who not only looked back to the Stewarts, but also stood out against overdue influence by the Old Pretender (and was attacked as part of a 'factious group of priests' by his agent, Lockhart of Carnwath). Keith took no part in the '45 Rebellion and his restraint and discretion about political matters was perhaps a critical element in the survival of the Episcopal Church in the savage repression that followed (only five members of a congregation were officially allowed to worship together at any one time, though people stood outside the churches to join in the services).

Bishop Robert Keith was proud of his origins. Educated in Aberdeen at Marischal College, he then became a tutor to Lord Keith James, the future field marshall who distinguished himself in the service of Frederick the Great in Prussia. He became deacon in 1710, was chaplain to Lord Erroll and travelled abroad with him before being ordained priest in 1713. He took up his first charge in Edinburgh's Canongate at the Episcopal meeting place in Barringer's Close. He became bishop in 1727 and took up the Episcopal area of Fife (once part of the former St Andrew's diocese) in 1733.

These are the bare facts of his career, but the inbuilt pride was easily recognised in his presentation to field marshall Keith of a copy of his *History of the Scottish Reformation*. This book paradoxically illustrates that there was far more to Bishop Keith than a cleric who had advanced not so much by merit, but by family connection. The book, and his wide range of excellent letters, show panache, style and quality of mind. His *History of Mary, Queen of Scots* (1755) is an important reference point for attempts to unravel her complex character and history.

But more importantly, Keith exercised a central position in two controversies which could have destroyed the Episcopal Church: the first was the question of the royal prerogative claimed by the Old Pretender after 1720 with regard to the appointment of a new Bishop of Edinburgh and other bishops, too. Many in the church felt that it was not only right (and parallels in Presbyterianism reinforced this) for the priests to choose their bishop and get royal approval afterwards, but that such a reversal of the king's prerogative would be more acceptable to future generations in the church.

Second, balancing the first and following the same sort of divide, was the controversy over 'usages in Scottish Liturgy.' Some wished to have features of Edward VI's *First Prayer Book*: these were the English Anglicans, and some similarly minded Scots, who refused to swear the oath of allegiance to a Hanoverian king. The difficulty was that the liturgy had things left out in the Scottish Reformed version which Keith realised were not essential and should not be pushed. Particular points of sensitivity were praying for the dead, the use of water mixed with wine at communion and prayers of offering (all suggesting the view of the Eucharist being a sacrifice, an idea inextricably associated in Scottish thinking with Roman Catholicism).

From 1731-32 Keith was the architect of a concordat to try to achieve a solution, at least on paper, to the controversies: in 1743 he presided as primus in discussions to establish canons of law for the church. It was all building a future, but doing so with discretion towards the political scene.

Bishop Keith was a family man who moved to Bonnington in 1752 where a daughter succeeded to the family home. He seemed far from being a 'factious priest.' Perhaps quite the reverse!

Article on 'Robert Keith' *in the Dictionary of National Biography*, volume X, pp 1214-1216.

55

JAMES KIRKWOOD

A Moderate among Extremists

THERE are at least three James Kirkwoods noted in the history books in late seventeenth century Scotland. One was schoolmaster at Linlithgow and Kelso, being dismissed from both and writing about it afterwards. The second was minister of Minto, deprived for refusing the Test Oath in 1685 and going on to be deprived as a non-juror in England in 1702. He was also an advocate of parish libraries.

The third James Kirkwood is our concern. We catch up with him when he was parish minister at Sanquhar in Dumfriesshire in the early 1680s. He is typical of the class of minister put into churches after the 1660 restoration of the monarchy when, in 1662, the ministers who wouldn't accept bishops and patronage were expelled from their parishes. In the south-west of Scotland this was the majority. People despised the 'king's curates' who were imposed on them: they were caricatured as being poorly educated and of poor character. All in all, 270 left their churches in 1662, a move which was reversed in 1688-89 when many more than the 270 were thrown out either because they couldn't accept presbyterianism or because they couldn't accept William and Mary on the throne. In the south-west, mobs physically rabbled out the ministers from the churches and manses. The ministers were beaten up and it is interesting to note that women were particularly strong in leading the mobs. Had he not died in 1684, Kirkwood would have been one of those thrown out.

James Kirkwood of Sanquhar is notable because he was clearly far from being a 'king's curate.' From the little we know of him, he emerges as a strong, capable man who stood for moderation and reason in a climate of extremes: covenanting extremists on the one hand and episcopalian persecutions on the other.

It is said, for example, that though he was Episcopalian by conviction rather than convenience, he had sympathy for those who wouldn't come to church. He arranged with them that if they turned up in the churchyard, he would put in a good report on them so that they could avoid the penalties laid down for non-attendance at the established church.

The story goes too that he was playing quoits near the River Nith when two Covenanters arrived on the scene, pursued by the dragoons. Not knowing who he was, the Covenanters came across the river and asked where they could hide. 'Take your coats off and join in the game,' said Kirkwood. So they did—and escaped arrest. No one would have suspected friends of the king's minister.

One last story concerns the Earl of Airlie. He had been sent with the *Highland Host* to stay and pillage, to punish the south-west for its rebellion against the king. He sent for Kirkwood to entertain him, no doubt with a hidden agenda. Kirkwood got more and more restless as the night went on for he wanted to get back home to prepare his sermon. Time and time again the Earl decreed, 'Just another glass.' Eventually Kirkwood went home drunk. But he managed to make it to the church for the morning sermon only to find the Earl sitting in the congregation. He launched into an impromptu sermon on the text, 'The Lord shall destroy the wicked and that right early [Airlie!].' If that wasn't bad enough, every time the hour glass timing his sermon was about to run out, he turned it round: 'Just another glass,' he smiled.

James Kirkwood stands as a contradiction to the caricature of the imposed ministers of the Restoration, but also perhaps as an illustration that a good man can always rise above the pressures of the age

Brown, J: *History of Sanquhar* (1891).

THOMAS GILLESPIE
'God chooses the Weak'

DESCRIBED as a man of delicate constitution, melancholy, shy, reserved and retiring, Thomas Gillespie (1708-1774) was a man of conviction who rejected the narrowness of the original Secession movement in the Kirk. Ironically he ended up by establishing the Relief Church. This was established 'to bring relief to oppressed congregations in Scotland' against the imposition of unwelcome ministers by patrons.

In some ways the story of Thomas Gillespie is also the story of his mother and his wife. He was born in the Duddingston area of Edinburgh of a farming and brewing family. His father, however, died while Thomas was still very young, the only son of his father's second wife who responded to the crisis by carrying on the business. She suggested to Thomas at the end of his teens that he should journey down to the Borders to listen to the preaching of Thomas Boston. He was converted and went to the University of Edinburgh to train for the ministry at the age of 20.

Through the influence of his mother, who had joined the Secession Church, he left the university during his final year in the Divinity Hall. Next stop was the Secession Theological Hall in Perth which he left after ten days in fundamental objection to its strictness and its demands that there should be no relationship with other Christians. The Protestant Dissenting Academy at Northampton—which was founded by the distinguished writer Philip Dedridge—gave a home to this remarkable Scots idealist. Subsequently he returned to Scotland and was inducted into the Church of Scotland as minister of Carnock in Fife.

Crisis came on the issue of patronage within the Presbytery of Dunfermline. The patron of the parish of Inverkeithing was determined to impose his own choice, despite the opposition of 95 per cent of the elders and families. The General Assembly decided that the Presbytery had to ratify the patron's choice. Gillespie and others refused, but since Gillespie alone spoke publicly and his own background was still regarded as somewhat suspect, he alone was deposed from his charge. Here enters the second powerful woman in his story. He came back home after the Assembly in the dead of the night and announced to his wife, 'I am the deposed minister of Carnock.' Unperturbed, she responded at once, 'Well if we must beg, I will carry the meal-poke.'

Thomas did not try to go into his church to preach, but during that whole summer preached in the open air in Carnock. It is legendary that there was not one wet Sunday that whole summer. All his electors and elders followed him to a barn and then a proper church in Dunfermline. At the next communion session in Carnock itself, the offering was only a quarter of what it had been.

History turned full circle when, in 1761, in the establishment of the 'Presbytery of Relief', he was joined by Thomas Collier of Colinsburgh in Fife and Thomas Boston of Jedburgh, the son of the preacher whose sermon had first brought Thomas Gillespie into the church. It wasn't, despite appearances, that Gillespie wanted to be outside the mainstream church. This was evidenced after his death in his congregation, for it split into those who felt they should rejoin the Established Church and those who felt they should stay outside to continue to witness against patronage. The task of witness to conviction went on and the principle of the Kirk's independence was to be slowly established. The Relief Church grew to 116 congregations when, in 1847, it joined with the United Secession Church to become the United Presbyterian Church, before in turn the long tortuous path of re-unification brought it back into a Church of Scotland which had accepted that ministers should not be imposed on congregations.

An end to patronage was not his only prophetic witness. He also stood for open communion and invited 'all who hold to Christ as Head of the Church' to his communion services. He died on 19 January 1744: as any passing visitor can now ascertain on a tablet in Dunfermline Abbey. With the commemorative tablet, the reluctant rebel had come home.

57

DUGALD BUCHANAN
The Gaelic Bard

THE beginnings were unlikely. Dugald Buchanan (1716-68) was born in Ardoch, a hamlet in Strathyre in Perthshire. His father was a miller who was also involved in farming. Dugald spent most of his working life in Perthshire, a threshold county embracing the Gaelic Highlands and the Lowlands. The main family language was Gaelic, but Dugald was to move freely between the two cultures, speaking both languages with equal fluency: and in the process he never lost that closeness to nature which marked the early life of his family.

Dugald was educated at a parish school run by the Society in Scotland for the Propagating of Christian Knowledge. From there on he was self-taught, taking advantage of being tutor to a local wealthy family to begin a lifetime's acquaintance with the classics and with English literature in their library. He was to familiarise himself with Puritan literature and the hymns of Isaac Watts which were to add to the mixture of influences which made him a towering character in Gaelic literature.

A varied career followed. He was apprenticed to a joiner working around Kippen and Dumbarton. Farming was his next occupation, and then in the 1750s he was appointed by the Society for the Propagation of Christian Knowledge and the 'Forfeited Estates' (a government body set up to administer the estates taken away from Jacobite lairds and landowners). His kindred had been on the Jacobite side but he had not been. He was regarded as a Whig but was sent to Struan Estate to remove all traces of Jacobite influence. He set up a number of schools, doing such a good job that he was honourably mentioned in dispatches to the government.

In the 1740s Buchanan had deep spiritual experiences with a 'conviction of sin' which had to be atoned for. He travelled around to Communion Services and in 1742 could be found at the Cambuslang Revival, listening to the English evangelical preacher, George Whitefield. In 1744 he attained 'peace for his soul.' In his diary of his spiritual experience he writes: 'On my way back home, I sat down to rest and in a minute's time all my doubts were dispersed, the gates of brass and the iron bars of unbelief were broken in a thousand pieces and my captive soul was set at liberty.' He went on to say, 'and before I rose, my tongue was loosed to sing the high praises of my God and at the same time Jesus Christ the sun of righteousness arose upon me with healing under his wings.'

It is significant that it was after this that he began to compose (1750), sometimes in English like some verses in his journal, but notably in Gaelic. He was so self-critical that most poems were destroyed and in fact only eight survive to the present day. It is on these that his reputation rests. He celebrates the natural world as God's creation and sees this world as being accountable to God at the day of judgment. His thought is not original, but his style, command of language, care with words and clear desire to awaken people to God's judgment made these hymns powerful at a time when people were searching for a new expression of faith. He borrowed from Isaac Watts and Edward Young but transformed them in the translation. These hymns are still sung with perhaps the most moving one being reminiscent of both Charles Wesley and Isaac Watts in its sensitivity to the sufferings of Christ on the cross.

Buchanan stayed within the Church of Scotland, but when visiting Edinburgh in 1767 he went to the Relief congregation and gained immense popularity with his sermons in Gaelic. This independent streak and distaste for patronage may well have been the reason he was blocked from becoming a minister as he wished. He remained a school-

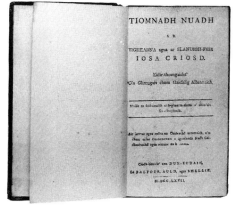

TITLE PAGE of GAELIC BIBLE 1767

139

master but went round Perthshire as a itinerant preacher, often in the open air. In this way he had more influence than if he had been a minister confined to one parish.

He was a serious-minded intense person, but capable of humour in his poetry, if only about how death levels the great and pretentious. His imagery of the beauty of his beloved Highlands is integrated in his writing in a way that is quite different from the rather dour nineteenth century Gaelic hymnody. If he had lived longer, his influence would have been enormous. But he died just after working on the translation and printing of the Gaelic New Testament. He hurried back home when he heard that fever was raging among his people: he himself succumbed. His generous caring shortened his legacy, but of course also added to it.

MacLean, D: *The Spiritual Songs of Dugald Buchanan* (John Grant: 1913).
MacBean, L: *Buchanan the Sacred Bard*.
Thomson, D: *Introduction to Gaelic Poetry* (Edinburgh University Press: 1990).

58

WILLIAM ROBERTSON
History teaches

ONE of the central convictions of William Robertson (1721-93) was that a movement such as the Enlightenment, though at first sight threatening, should be harnessed rather than opposed in communicating the Christian message.

William was a son of the manse of Borthwick in Midlothian and proceeded from there to the University of Edinburgh, by which time his father was a minister in Edinburgh itself. At the age of 23, he accepted a presentation by the patron to the rural parish of Gladsmuir. He must have been a spirited young man, for at the time of the '45 rebellion he volunteered for the defence of Edinburgh. The rebellion over, he rapidly progressed to a brief spell in a smaller Edinburgh parish before taking up a joint ministry in the prestigious Old Greyfriars kirk with a quite different character Erskine, whose story is told in a separate chapter. The joint ministry is a remarkable testimony to both ministers, for they led quite opposing parties in the Kirk while ministering together to the one congregation and respecting their individual ministries.

Not only was William Robertson an eloquent preacher, but he very rapidly became the leader of the moderates in the Kirk and as such influenced the church to play a leading role in the Enlightenment. In this regard he was friend and ally to both John Hume and Alexander Carlyle: and friends with intellectuals like Adam Smith, Lord Kames and Adam Fergusson. He was a club-going man, to be found regularly in conversation at the 'Poker Club' and other social or intellectual gatherings.

The basic influence of William Robertson lies in two main areas, ecclesiastical politics and literary work. To take ecclesiastical politics first of all, he led a group of 'young Turks' in the 1750s, ministers committed to a determined campaign to take over the General Assembly for their views. They wanted to free the church to manage its own affairs but believed that reinforcing the law of the land was the best way to achieve it. They believed that the patronage of well-educated and 'enlightened' landowners was the best way to encourage the appointment of literary and moderate ministers. In this case William Robertson achieved real personal ascendancy in the 1760s, and this partly from the power of his personality and partly from his literary achievements as a historian.

These literary achievements mark Robertson out as a leading figure of the Scottish Enlightenment. Public recognition was his in a rapid succession of honours. He became a royal chaplain in 1761 to add to his prestige as minister of Old Greyfriars. In 1762 he was appointed principal of the University of Edinburgh and in 1764 the king's historiographer. Part of this success derived from the acclaim given to his *History of Scotland 1542-1603* which he published in 1759. But his most valuable work came later: his *History of Emperor Charles V* (1769), a work which was highly praised by such distinguished scholars as Voltaire in France and Gibbon in England. The breadth of his interests became clear with his *History of America* (1777) and an enquiry on *The Knowledge which the Ancients had of India* (1791), just two years before his death.

William Robertson is perhaps, with the breadth of connection between pastoral ministry and academic brilliance, the impossible dream for ministry today—that is, the coming together of Christ's message with the cutting edge of current academic thought. Indeed, he remains a challenge for those who would divide the presentation of the gospel from the rigor of intellectual respectability. What is truth? The question came to a crunch in 1779 when he supported a Catholic Relief Bill in an unsuccessful attempt to push it through parliament. Mobs attacked his house on the issue and he had to take refuge in Edinburgh Castle. He resigned from the General Assembly the following year and lived out the rest of his life quietly as a gentle, kindly, scholarly man.

Stewart: *Life of William Robertson* (1801).
Gleig: *Life of William Robertson* (1812).

59

JOHN ERSKINE

'Shall I go to War with my American Brethren?'

THE pamphlet *Shall I go to war with my American Brethren?* (published in 1769) is a typical example of John Erskine's work, courageously questioning the Government policy that was leading to war with the American colonies. The support given to that policy by leading establishment figures like Dr Johnson was set aside in convictions which arose from a blend of evangelical commitment (as one of the two great leaders of the evangelical party of the time) and the Enlightenment insights into the social implications of being a human being. John Erskine shows clearly that one needn't be rigidly fundamentalist and unbending to be a committed preacher of the 'good news' of Christ.

Born about 1721, John Erskine came from an aristocratic background. His father was a professor of Scots Law. At the University of Edinburgh, his aristocratic propriety did not prevent his figuring in public debate with William Robertson (a future principal of the university) about the Cambuslang Revival of 1742. Robertson thought it a return to seventeenth century fanaticism. Erskine thought it a sign of the impending millennium, the perfect age at the end of time. The debate convinced him that revivalism was what Christianity was all about. Even before his ordination he wrote a pamphlet boldly declaring that the professor of Divin-ity at St Andrews was not good enough for the job. In restrained but

GREYFRIARS KIRK

he argued that the professor had not answered the Deists properly and so had failed to preserve the fundamentals of Christian faith.

He became minister of Kirkintilloch in 1744, Culross in 1753, New Greyfriars in Edinburgh and finally Old Greyfriars from 1767, until his death in 1803. At Old Greyfriars he occupied the pulpit in tandem with the leader of the moderate party in the Kirk, his old sparring partner, William Robertson, now the principal of the University of Edinburgh. In an era of powerful religious and political passion, it is the key to understanding Erskine to learn that his deep convictions about heart religion allowed him to respect as an equal someone like Robertson whose religious principles were so different and so liberal. That respect allowed them to stay on good terms. Erskine was himself a part of the eighteenth century Enlightenment of which Robertson was such a leading figure.

Evangelicals, both in eighteenth century Scotland and today, have been caricatured as stick-in-the-mud traditionalists. It was true that Erskine was proud to be a Calvinist but, as his biographer noted, he was not attached to 'vulgar Calvinism.' It was not just a matter of his aristocratic background, or even having 25 publications in his own right and 20 more which he edited, that attracted people like Sir Walter Scott's parents and other well-to-do professionals to his congregation. It was much more. He was happily married with a family, he could be 'warm when occasion required it', but as we have seen he could strike out with power for a good cause. He preached the Enlightenment and Reformation values of benevolence to the poor, with free coals being distributed in winter to the sub-standard houses down below in the Grassmarket. In religion he was a reformer who advocated the reduction of sermons before the communion season to one, but an increase in the number of communion services from once to four times in the year. To preach the unchanging gospel demands change.

Moncreiff Wellwood, Sir Henry: *Account of the Life and Writings of John Erskine, DD, Late One of the Ministers of Edinburgh* (Constable: 1818).
Bebbington, D W: *Evangelicalism in Modern Britain* (Unwin Hyman: 1989).

60
ALEXANDER CARLYLE
'The Grandest Demigod I ever saw'

SIR Walter Scott's description of Alexander Carlyle (1722-1805) as 'the grandest demigod I ever saw' was a tribute to his handsome, portly figure, his silver locks and large head, a man who physically stood out from his peers at his prime in Edinburgh society. 'Jupiter Carlyle' was the more common title he was known by. It was not, however, a mere matter of looks: it was also a tribute to his personality and his place at the centre of both the social and intellectual life of his day.

Alexander's father was William Carlyle, a minister of Prestonpans, a man well connected to many East Lothian families. In 1735 Alexander went to the University of Edinburgh and so was an eyewitness to the Porteous riots which were described so vividly by Walter Scott in *Heart of Midlothian*. It was typical of how Carlyle always managed to be at the centre of what was going on. In 1743 he graduated Master of Arts and this was followed by two years at Glasgow, then three years at Leyden University to gain breadth of knowledge from continental schools of thought. In between, however, in 1745 he volunteered to defend Edinburgh against Prince Charlie!

In 1848 he settled in as minister of Inveresk where he was to stay as parish minister until his death. He was a good parish minister, a fascinating preacher and a man concerned for the poor, active in the welfare of the poorhouse and committed to education and parish visiting. He even established a Sunday school in his later years, a sure sign that he was constantly rethinking his ministry. In 1760 he married and enjoyed a long and happy life with Mary and his children. All of this is often lost sight of in the legendary 'Jupiter Carlyle': his entertaining *Autobiography*, which was published over 50 years after his death, only outlines one side of his life: his towering presence in the social and intellectual circles of Edinburgh.

Much of Scottish life was shaped at that time by the sparkling life of the Edinburgh clubs and intellectual gatherings. David Hume, John Home, Adam Smith and Adam Fergusson were only some of the great intellectuals of the day who met in the taverns and clubs, having long discussions into the night. Alexander Carlyle was at the centre of this intellectual life. Like other 'moderates' in the Kirk of the time, he believed that Christ could only be at the centre of God's people in Scotland if the church was at the centre of the cultural life.

John Home was a particular friend of Carlyle and so it was natural for them to work together on the play 'Douglas.' Carlyle was at the rehearsals but also at a performance. This actually landed him in trouble and in 1756/57 Alexander Carlyle was called before presbytery to account for his actions. But the rebuke was reduced to an admonishment by the synod and this was confirmed by the Assembly.

Alexander Carlyle wrote a number of pamphlets which illustrate the wide range of his interests and involvement. In 1759 he was at the centre of the Scottish Militia controversy. It was the time of the Seven Years War and so the militia was there to defend the shores, but also to nourish in people a sense of Scottish patriotism and civic virtue. It was unsuccessful because the government was wary still of the Jacobite sympathies of many Scots.

Not only was Carlyle involved in Scottish circles but he was also active on the London scene. He seems to have been too proud and conscious of his dignity as a minister of the Kirk to have been a lieutenant to others in the moderate party. He was Moderator of the Chapel Royal in 1789. All in all, he seemed to have enjoyed life but also taught in the process that Christianity was about living—and drawing all of life into that new life

Carlyle, A: *Autobiography.*

61

JOHN HOME
God or the Devil?

MANY in the Church of Scotland in the eighteenth century felt that John Home (1722-1808) faced a choice between God and the Devil. In choosing the world of drama when the Kirk made it impossible to be both minister and dramatist, it seemed as though Home chose the Devil. Many today, however, feel that this man witnessed, at some personal cost, to the fact that God was able, through drama, to deepen human communication and uplift the human spirit just as much as in the more direct forms of His communication.

John Home was born in Leith, the son of the Town Clerk, in a house marked by a plaque just off Bernard Street. He was clearly well connected and so the path into the ministry was a smooth one. Leith Academy was followed by the University of Edinburgh, although in his early twenties we find him—as with other ministers—fighting with the Hanoverians at the Battle of Falkirk. He was captured by the losing Jacobites, but a daring escape from Doune Castle enhanced his reputation when he returned to quieter tasks.

As minister of rural Athelstaneford, he very quickly became prominent in the moderate party of the church: as such he saw the church as deeply involved both in the arts and in the improvement of society, both in agricultural and industrial matters. He wrote a play, a tragedy called 'Agis', and took it to London. There it was rejected by the theatrical impressario Garrick. Garrick did not like his next effort either ('Douglas'—founded on the ballad of Gil Morrice). But when Home managed to put it on in Edinburgh, it appears that some of the locals certainly liked it. One is reported to have proudly proclaimed 'whaur's yer Willie Shakespeare noo?' It is generally considered to creak very badly as a play, although it has been presented on occasion in recent years.

However, Edinburgh presbytery was not amused, for many

regarded the theatre as 'the devil's playground.' A couple of his friends in the ministry were disciplined for merely attending a performance. Some tried to excuse themselves. One man—the minister at Liberton—said that he seen the performance from behind a pillar! Jupiter Carlyle of Inveresk, however, stood by Home and did not apologise.

Pressure built up on Home and, feeling that his future in the church was now in some doubt, he decided to resign from the ministry. He got in with Archibald, third Duke of Argyll (who built Inverary Castle), who in turn got him a job as secretary to the Earl of Bute (Prime Minister briefly in George III's reign). He tutored the future George III and was given a pension for his trouble. Added to this he was given a sinecure job as 'conservator of Scottish privileges in the Netherlands', a job which arose from the small town in the Netherlands (now twinned with Culross) to which Scottish merchants used to have to go to pursue trading in the Netherlands.

In terms of being a playwright, Home had moderate success due to his new patronage. Garrick produced 'Agis' and the next play 'The Siege of Aquilea.' He had three other plays, occasional poems and, in prose, *A History of the Rebellion of 1745* which must have benefited from his personal memories. He certainly didn't rival 'Willie Shakespeare'!

John Home married somewhat late in life in 1770, and then retired to Edinburgh in 1779 where he lived quietly until his death in 1808. In this period he returns to some significance in the history of God's people in Scotland, for he spent his time in the clubs of Edinburgh where the 'moderate' ministers met to further their ideal that church and state should cross-fertilise one another in building the people of God. In an age when even Ramsay the poet got into trouble for writing poetry, Home helped to keep alive a different Christian vision.

Mackenzie, H (preface ed): *Works of John Home* (1822).
Article on 'John Home' in *Chambers Biographical Dictionary* (1984).

62

JOHN WITHERSPOON
The American Connection

IN the early church, persecution in Jerusalem brought the first dramatic steps in the spread of Christianity. John Witherspoon (1723-94) represents the spread of Scottish Kirk influence in the American Colonies, due to disillusion with the trends current in eighteenth century Scottish church life.

JOHN WITHERSPOON

Witherspoon is variously described as being born at Yester, near Hadding-ton or at Gifford. He studied at the University of Edinburgh at the same time as the future 'moderate' minister Alexander Carlyle, who was later to say that Witherspoon became an evangelical 'because he didn't have much success with the ladies.' That apart, he certainly did become an evangelical minister at Beith and then Paisley, but continued to develop his intellectual interests. He deplored the moderate clergy's acceptance of patrons' rights to impose ministers on parishes and their acceptance of liberal and secular values as part of Christian faith.

His publications illustrate his interests: *A serious Enquiry into the nature and effects of the stage* (1757); two on *Justification* (1756); and *Regeneration* (1764). Most significant, however, was his earliest major publication in 1753, attacking the 'moderates' in the Kirk. *Ecclesiastic characteristics* has all the passion of an early work. It is a bitter parody of the 'Our Father' which some thought blasphemous. It savages the moderate ministers for believing in classic pagan philosophies and in modern agnostic philosophers.

Interest in the history of the American Colonies gave him a

way out of his growing disgust at the pre-eminence of the moderate clergy in the General Assemblies of his day. In 1786 he emigrated to America to become president and pastor of Princeton College, New Jersey: as such he is honoured to this day as the second founder of the University of Princeton as it now is. Paradoxically much of his influence on Princeton was in line with what would more usually be associated with the 'moderates' than with an evangelical like he was. Freed from the polarisation of Scotland, he is reckoned to have been one of the channels by which 'common sense' Scottish philosophies became influential in America. Major work by Andrew Hook has developed our appreciation of that connection.

When it came to the rebellion of the American colonies, he was very much on the side of the rebels. Part of this might have been his resentment of the 'establishment' so loved by the moderates, but his evangelical identification with his people would also be important. As representative of New Jersey he played his part in the Continental Congress and was one of the signatories of the Declaration of Independence.

While in America, John Witherspoon retained contacts with his fellow evangelicals in Scotland. They were already worried about the government's attitude to the colony, arguing that 'if they can get tough with liberals in America, they could get tough with radicals here in Scotland.' In any case the evangelicals were always ready to be 'agin the government.' One of John's personal friends, John Erskine, published a very famous pamphlet *Shall I go to war with my American Brethren?*

The American connection was two-way then and has perhaps remained so ever since, at least in the affairs of the Scottish Kirk.

Works quoted.
Article in *Chambers Biographical Dictionary* (1984).

63

ARCHIBALD McLEAN
From Glassite to Scotch Baptist

ARCHIBALD McLean (1733-1812) is one of many 'searchers for the ideal' which mark the story of God's people in Scotland. It took him from the Glassite Church to the Baptist Church.

The McLean family came from Mull, but Archibald was brought up in East Kilbride. He was apprenticed to a printer in Glasgow and about that time joined the Church of Scotland, after hearing George Whitefield at the Cambuslang Revival. The parish kirk must have seemed dull by comparison for he joined the Glassite church in Glasgow in his search for a deeper spiritual experience.

The Glassite Church was founded by John Glass in Dundee when he was deposed for independency. His was a strict form of church government and behaviour which kept quite separate from other Christians. It was said of them—quite remarkably for the eighteenth century—that they 'wouldn't pray with you but would dance with you.' Glass' son-in-law, Robert Sandeman, wrote a powerful book which deeply disturbed Congregationalists in England and New England alike. He died in Connecticut. The Sandeman family remained associated with the Glassite Church, with Dundee the main centre and London featuring as well as the Edinburgh church which was in Barony Street and only finally closed in 1989 (though some still meet locally).

Archibald McLean, however, journeyed on. He and Robert Carmichael, a former Secession minister, were chatting one day about Baptism. They went to their Bible and decided—it would seem quite independently of other influences—that infant Baptism was not properly Biblical and that only professing adult believers should be baptised. They were disciplined by their church and so left and found the Baptism they sought from a Dr Gill in London. Subsequently, they gathered a group at Edinburgh and started Baptisms at Canonmills. This was the foundation of what is now Bristo Baptist church (1765). These baptisms made quite an impact for they were reported in the *Scots* magazine in 1765. They came to be called 'Scotch Baptists' because they were a quite unique bringing together of different strands of church life. Ministers were not paid lest they became a separate ruling caste and generally—to avoid one man domination—at least two elders were appointed in each congregation. The services were in one sense old-fashioned, with rituals of foot-washing and the kiss of charity, but very intensely spiritual.

McLean travelled widely in the central belt of Scotland and generally the spread of Scotch Baptist churches paralleled the spread of Glassite churches. In a very short time, we find congregations in London, Nottingham, Beverly, Hull, Whitehaven and Liverpool. In Scotland itself, however, the numbers probably never exceeded a thousand active members at the one time. They suffered from their idealism, falling out with one another because of their careful attention to details of observance. Because of divisions in 1810 and 1834, there were three churches in Dundee and three in Glasgow which didn't speak to one another in the latter year. Nevertheless Bristo church carried on a very vital existence. The group only stopped calling themselves Scotch Baptist in 1927: they retained the tandem ministry of elder alongside ministers until then, before falling in with wider Baptist traditions.

Looking further afield, the only Scotch Baptists remaining outside Scotland are in North Wales where they worship in Welsh. There it was the writings of McLean which had such lasting impact. His wider vision had fruits too in his welcoming of the Baptist Missionary Society to Scotland, raising a lot of money for them. Who can measure the enduring influence of that alone?

McLean, A: *Collected Works* (Elgin: 1847-54).
Bebbington, D W (ed): *The Baptists in Scotland. A History Baptist Union in Scotland* (1988).

64

ELSPETH BUCHAN
Woman of Revelation

IN writing this book it has been difficult to find out enough information about individual women to be able to devote whole chapters to them. Elspeth Buchan (1738-1791), however, is an exception. She takes her place not so much because of a contribution to the enduring history of Christianity, but because she showed, in an eccentric way, how women were capable of very real leadership even in during male-dominated centuries of the Kirk.

Elspeth was the daughter of an innkeeper in the north of Scotland, between Banff and Portsoy. She was brought up as an Episcopalian. Although she would have had little formal education —most women did not—she became a keen student of the Bible. As a young girl she was sent to Glasgow to work in domestic service to the owner of pottery works. She married a pottery worker and left the Episcopalian Church to join her husband's church, the Secession Church of Ebenezer Erskine: a very real conversion experience which made her immerse herself in the Bible. Thus her own interpretations began to develop.

We know that in married life she had at least one son and two daughters. When she left her husband on the next stage of her spiritual journey, her son stayed with him, while the two daughters continued at her side through all the stormy years that lay ahead.

Elspeth Buchan believed she was a prophetess of the second coming of Christ, to usher in the millennium. She stands in a long line of Christians who, before and after her, have taken a quite simplistic reading of the complicated literary apocalypse, the book of Revelation. Since all the accounts we have are from her enemies, she was probably less eccentric and more attractive than portrayed: for when she moved from Glasgow to Irvine, leaving her husband and launching a new church, she attracted both a lawyer to sign up, and a minister of the Relief Church who left his charge and joined her. Mainly however it was the humblest and poorest who joined her.

At first she held meetings in the former minister's house, Revd White, but feelings ran so high in the town that a mob threw them out. She was joined by 40-50 followers as she moved south through the villages of Ayrshire, ending at Closeburn, some two miles from Thornhill, 13 from Dumfries. There they lived as a community in a barn: a primitive form of communism, based presumably on the picture in the Acts of Apostles. Though there were husbands and wives in the group, they all lived in celibacy, presumably following the strictures of Paul in 1 Corinthians, for those expecting the imminent return of Christ. Those with a craft continued to work, but did so free for others, attracting people in that way.

Things became more extreme. Elspeth told them Christ would come the next day—and he didn't. Some returned to Irvine, claiming that threatened defectors were locked up and soaked in cold water. She asserted money would fall from heaven, making followers hold a cloth outside for hours with her. When they gave up she carried on, later bringing in five pounds, claiming their 'lack of faith' had delayed the happening. Another time she took them outside for their 'last day', when they would levitate into heaven to meet Christ. When they didn't she accused them of having 'no faith and of being too fat.' She ordained a fast of 40 days and nights and when some fell ill she would only give them spirits and water.

The climax followed swiftly. Elspeth had earlier been accused of being the Virgin Mary, which she denied although declaring she was the 'daughter of Christ.' In 1791 when she knew she was dying, she declared she *was indeed* the Virgin Mary; also the woman in Revelation 12, clothed in the moon and stars and driven into the wilderness where she wandered before coming to Scotland. She said she would only *appear* to die and so when she did, her remaining followers kept her lying there until forced to put her standing up in a coffin in the barn. Neighbours were so disgusted that they got a Justice of the Peace to enforce her burial.

But with her died a dream and the sort of extremism which becomes attractive in times of rapid change such as the industrialisation of her times. Has she a message or a warning for today?

Train, J: *History of the Buchanites* (1833).
Article in *Chambers Biographical Dictionary* (1984).

65

DAVID DALE
Christian Capitalist

DAVID Dale (1739-1806) would have been taken aback to be described as in any sense a Christian capitalist: he was born at Stewarton in Ayrshire of a very simple farming family. He began life as a herdsman and though he ended by being a well-read and successful man, he was even then almost entirely self-educated.

David's first step up the ladder of life came when he was apprenticed to a Paisley cottage weaver. Not content with this he began travelling the country buying up homespun yarn, before expanding his interests into every aspect of the marketing of textiles. He became established as a yarn and linen merchant in Glasgow.

The door of opportunity opened up, however, when he was introduced to Richard Arkwright, inventor of weaving machines. They agreed to build a mill to take advantage of the water power of the Falls of Clyde as they tumbled down to what was to become New Lanark. But Arkwright got all wrapped up in court cases about his patents so David was left on his own. He built the largest mills in Scotland (1775).

Dale continued to stay in Glasgow but at New Lanark he showed an immense care for the underprivileged and for orphans. To the cynical twentieth century observer it might look like exploitation, but within the lights of the time it was genuine Christian caring. There was a shortage of available workers in central Scotland at the time so Dale got all the parishes of the Church of Scotland to refer to him any orphans and people in poverty that the kirk sessions were trying to help. The only stipulation was that they must learn a trade. He provided sanitary and well-heated accommodation, school outside working hours and paid wages which were quite reasonable by the standards of the day. It was largely a Lowlands workforce, but on one occasion he took on 200 Highlanders at once: they had been heading for the United States when their boat was driven back by bad weather.

One incident has always made his critics think again: when the mill burned down, Dale, unlike any other owner of the time, insisted on paying his workers all the time the mill was being rebuilt. He clearly had a developed awareness of his social obligations as an employer. This awareness was a by-product of his Christian faith.

David Dale had been born into the Church of Scotland. By the time he had become established in Glasgow, however, he had thrown his weight behind the 'Presbyteries of Relief'. These 'Presbyteries' had emerged from the objections raised about ministers being imposed on congregations because of the landowners right of patronage. In this he was typical of many self-made men of humbler origins, and indeed of rising tradesmen of the time who wanted a greater say in the affairs of the church.

In time David went further and became a leading light in the 'Old Scots Independents', a group of churches who anticipated by many decades the sort of churches who came to form the Congregational Union. He built his own church and learned Greek and Hebrew to equip himself as a preacher. His sermons filled his church Sunday by Sunday.

The last point of his life was completely taken up by church life for he handed over the mills to the husband of one of his daughters, a man called Robert Owen. Owen was a Utopian who, because of his compassionate social vision rather than any Christian faith, took New Lanark into directions David Dale could never have imagined.

If you visit the restored New Lanark, it is clear that the Puritan work ethic of David Dale had an enduring influence and that the Christian faith retained a significance in the whole project. David Dale did not live at the mill, so he was not there to enforce religion but rather to ensure children got all the information and experience they needed and the opportunity to journey in their faith. The Puritan work ethic guided his own life, and the aim of his preaching would be that others too would find success like he did by turning to God.

Mechie, S: *The Church and Scottish Social Development 1780-1870* (1960).
Escott, H: *History of Scottish Congregationalism* (1960).

66

LADY GLENORCHY
Lady Bountiful?

PERHAPS no one in the history of the Kirk in Scotland has so clearly deserved the title 'Lady Bountiful' as Lady Glenorchy (1741-86). She was born Willielma Maxwell at Preston, near Kirkcudbright in the south-west of Scotland. Her father was a doctor of medicine. She not only was well-born and well educated but she married well. It seemed to run in the family, for her sister married the Earl of Sutherland.

Willielma married John Lord Viscount Glenorchy, heir to the Earl of Breadalbane. On marriage, she went to an estate at Taymouth but spent part of the year in fashionable shows such as Bath and Bristol. Part of the year she spent in London. This brought her to mingle with people very much caught up in the evangelical movement then termed 'Methodism.' She knew John Wesley personally and particularly spent time with those who were the followers of George Whitefield, the evangelical preacher who had several successful visits to Scotland.

All this was the setting for Lady Glenorchy's personal conversion at the age of 25. She had been and indeed remained after this new start a loyal supporter of the Church of Scotland. She couldn't at the end of the day share John Wesley's convictions but in any case the centrality of Jesus was more important to her than the denomination one belonged to.

It is unclear whether her husband shared her new religious convictions but he certainly supported her as she began to devote her wealth to supporting evangelical work. In any case he died within ten years of their marriage. Her remaining 15 years as a widow were dedicated to schemes: in so doing, she spent most of the money she inherited.

Before her husband's death, they had purchased a lot of property in the Barnton area of Edinburgh. She built a chapel and acquired a chaplain for it. The city centre beckoned to her and there her first project was in a former Catholic chapel, St Mary's, in Niddrie Wynd. There she irritated her friends in the Church of Scotland by inviting a stream of visiting preachers from England.

In the 1770s, Lady Glenorchy decided to take advantage of the Church of Scotland's need for more churches. She informed Edinburgh presbytery of her plans to build a kirk in the under-churched and very poor Leith Walk area: they registered no objections. Lady Glenorchy's chapel resulted, a beautiful building with 2000 seats. It was only when it came to appointing a minister that for seven long years Lady Glenorchy and the presbytery couldn't come to an agreement. Eventually they agreed to a Welshman Thomas Jones who had been ordained by Presbyterian ministers in London. Despite this agreement, however, the chapel was never fully incorporated into the Church of Scotland but remained an evangelical centre. As such it had a powerful influence, both in his formative years and then in his time as assistant minister, on Greville Ewing whose work was so important in forming the Congregational Union.

Lady Glenorchy travelled a lot, partly for her health and wherever she went was always anxious to find out if there was an evangelical church in the locality. She purchased a church in Carlisle and funded a minister. She did the same at Buxton in Derbyshire and founded the Hope Chapel in Bristol in her dying years. She was approached and helped with the building of a chapel at Killin in Perthshire. It is safe to say that when she died, most of her money had been spent on churches and on providing ministers for them. From the little that was left, she ensured a £5000 legacy to fund training for the ministry in both Scotland and England for those who came from poor and humble origins.

Lady Bountiful then. In common with many Christians of her time, she believed that if the gospel were preached with feeling, it would lead to a general uplifting of the population. It might be naive but with her it was beautifully sensitive and caring.

Jones, T S: *A Life of Willielma, Viscountess Glenorchy* (1824).
Thompson, D P: *Lady Glenorchy and her Church* (c 1960).

67

HENRY MONCRIEFF WELLWOOD
'A Force to be reckoned with'

HENRY Moncreiff Wellwood (1750-1827), a prominent figure in Scotland in the late eighteenth and early nineteenth centuries, illustrates very clearly how an evangelical kirk minister could combine partisanship with a representative role. After all, why should deep conviction lead to narrowness?

The Moncreiffs were a distinguished line of kirk ministers, so it was not surprising that Henry Moncreiff Wellwood (as we now know him) was destined for the ministry from birth at the manse in Blackford, Perthshire in 1750. Glasgow University at 13 led to Edinburgh University where he was still studying for the ministry when his father died. So loved was his father, and so promising was Henry, that the parishioners kept the parish vacant for four years until he finished his studies. It was very much the tradition of St Augustine that the pastor was 'wedded to the parish.'

His outstanding qualities, his high social standing (he inherited a baronetcy), and the effects of crown patronage, ensured that Henry stayed only four years in Blackford. He was called to St Cuthbert's in Edinburgh and there served the cream of Edinburgh society from 1775 to 1827. His sermons were evangelically based, beautifully constructed: and it was all prepared for and followed up by assiduous visiting of his people: a remarkable combination of the dignity of his blue blood with a kindly nature which earned him continued respect like his father.

Just a parish minister? He would have rejected the implication that the parish is unimportant. In fact his ministry became a power base. He was an outstanding evangelical party leader in the Kirk. In 1785, by the age of 35, he became Moderator of the General Assembly, and then chaplain to George III in 1793.

It was not, however, all a success story. Overseas missions had begun in Protestantism but not in Scotland. In 1796, Moncreiff Wellwood petitioned the General Assembly for official backing for an Auxiliary Missionary Society. It failed, but advanced the cause of missions behind the scenes.

Again in ecclesiastical politics, his was to be a prophetic but unsuccessful voice. He was active in the Popular Party, campaigning for the congregation to have the right to veto the patron's appointment of ministers. He was prominent in the failed campaign of the 1780s. It wasn't that he was so far ahead of his time as to maintain every member of the congregation should get a vote. It was only the heritors and elders—but it would have been a start!

In the 80s too, he was allied with the radical Whigs, the followers of Fox, who opposed the accepted 'Dundas connection.' In politics, therefore, his associates were decidedly 'out': this is significant for the understanding of how radical thought can combine with evangelical insistence on the fundamentals of the faith.

Henry Moncreiff Wellwood's legacy emerged from his campaigning interests. His biography of the evangelical John Erskine is a monument of Enlightenment historiography with its elegant style, clear content and attention to detail. He published his own sermons and the respect they earned facilitated his work in the Society in Scotland for Propagating Christian Knowledge. Its work, spreading both knowledge of the faith and literacy, has been accused of suppressing Gaelic but from when he was involved (1769) the official line was that the language should be used in the Highlands. He collected money and preached for the three aims of re-Christianising the Highlands; converting Catholics to Protestantism; and spreading literacy.

There is no doubt that in his day Moncreiff Wellwood rose to become the leading minister of the Church of Scotland. He was known as an evangelical and the evangelicals were not the dominant party in the Kirk. Yet he was recognised as the man who stood for the clergy, launching funds to help their sons and widows. He was said to have the standing of a bishop. Although he did not always succeed, he was a force to be reckoned with.

Moncreiff, Sir H M: *Sermons*, with preface by Sir J W Moncreiff (Edinburgh: 1831), volume 3.
Bebbington, D W: *Evangelicalism in Modern Britain* (Unwin Hyman: 1989).

68

ROBERT BURNS
Saint or Sinner?

ROBERT Burns (1759-96) has been projected as saint and as sinner in almost equal measure. Biographers such as Currie thought they were doing him a service by producing a 'genteelised life' of Burns with all the wild oats forgotten: and so it was not until the first decade of the nineteenth century that his memory was severely criticised as a man who was just far too much of a sinner to be held up in public esteem.

ROBERT BURNS

Today the picture we have is less black and white. Robert grew up in bitter poverty in Ayrshire, his father a labourer in everything from gardens to farms, who stands out for the sacrifice he made to educate at least Robert and Gilbert in his family. In fact the excessive hours of work as a youth on the farm and his later job as an exciseman contributed to the early death of Robert Burns. But in his relatively short life, a great deal of time and effort was spent developing his fluency not only in colloquial English, but also colloquial Scots. He was also capable of writing comfortably in French and lists among his favourite reading Addison, Shakespeare, Milton and Henry Mackenzie.

Burns had a cultured and sophisticated mind. While claiming to be tone-deaf, he could take down a fiddle tune, writing the notes as well as the words. He had a masterly ability to take and reshape a song's words and match them to another tune. On the broad themes of love and the dignity of labour and liberty, he produced words and ideas which were easy to translate into other languages.

Jean Armour was the great love of his life and with her he had seven children. He also had as many other children outside marriage. It seems that he enjoyed a number of romantic liaisons in his native Ayrshire. No doubt this popular reputation continued when he was adopted by Edinburgh society. In this, however, not only was his love real, but also his remorse.

And thus we face a most challenging paradox for Robert Burns' rightful place in the story of God's people in Scotland: his love poetry is so focussed and communicates so directly to the modern age because it is so real—yet its inspiration contradicts both the Christian ideal and the Calvinist embodiment of that ideal in moral standards. People have looked at this dichotomy and at Burns' savage criticism in his 'Holy Willie's Prayer' and wondered whether he had moved away completely from Christian faith.

To even begin to believe this would be to misunderstand the man. His appetite for life makes him a great poet, but he is clear (see his poem 'Address to a young friend') that an 'atheist's laugh is a poor exchange for Deity offended.' He enjoyed himself in Edinburgh but was more at home in hard-drinking Ayrshire (note the nightmare of Tam o' Shanter's wild but fearful ride into the meeting point of known and unknown).

Burns' father stands for the norm and there we find a deeply religious man cast in the mould of 'The Cotter's Saturday Night.' It was a settled, secure life of piety centred on the Bible, with prayers in the home and high standards of private and social life, in an atmosphere coloured by such fears as daughter Jenny falling into the hands of a malicious rake. Holy Willie is the opposite, for he is seen as a *deviant from* the Kirk—and a hypocrite—rather than a representative of the Kirk. The Cotter is a decent Christian who minds his own business, whereas Holy Willie's concern is to tell other people what to do and, like many a minister, take himself far too seriously.

Burns took the old values and helped the Kirk towards being

a more tolerant and balanced church. His was the last generation to experience public condemnation of sin from the pulpit: although he chafed at it, he endured it when it was his turn.

In terms of morality it should also be remembered that in an eighteenth century Ayrshire background, extra-marital affairs were not seen as so destructive of public and personal morality as in other more precisely defined situations.

Burns appears as an intensely human, mixed-up sort of person who today, as in his own day, would have been noted for his contributions to fashion and the political dialogues of the day. He sadly died in poverty in Dumfries, suspected of being a radical. Typically his worries were more focussed on the fortunes of his beloved Jean Armour. The sinner seems somehow saintly?

Kinsley, J.(ed): *Burns: Poems* (Oxford University Press).
Roy, Ross (ed): *Letters* (Oxford University Press).
Craig, Cairns (gen ed): *History of Scottish Literature* (Aberdeen University Press).

BURNS' MONUMENT on CALTON HILL, EDINBURGH

69

THE HALDANE BROTHERS
From the Deep Sea to Evangelism

ROBERT Haldane (1764-1842) and his brother James (1768-1851) were born into a wealthy family with land in Stirlingshire. They went to Edinburgh High School and although Robert went to Edinburgh University for a while, they each had separate careers at sea. Robert was in the Royal Navy at the Relief of Gibraltar and James was a captain in the East India company. Both experienced strong religious conversions in mid life and both were indebted for their religious education to an expatriate Scot, David Bogue, who had a ministerial academy and church at Gosport near their home port of Southampton

The 1790s brought for them the coincidence of their personal conversion to Christ and the receipt of inherited money which gave them a base for a new phase of life (Robert got £60,000). Robert was at the forefront of promoting in Scotland the missionary activity which was all the rage in England. David Bogue himself had been involved in the founding of the London Missionary Society in 1795. Robert himself served with Bogue as a London Missionary Society director from 1796-1806.

Encouraged by the Baptist missionary, William Carey, Robert volunteered to go to Bengal, but the East India Company blocked the venture. Fired partly by the ideals of the French Revolution and the fears of the death to religion it threatened, he became a proposer of Sunday schools and in 1797 established the Society for the Propagation of the Gospel at Home, an aggressive organisation committed to travelling to rural areas with no churches, and industrial areas. The Sunday schools evolved into preaching stations and the preaching stations into independent churches. Robert used his wealth to found short courses for ministers at Glasgow, Edinburgh, Dundee, Montrose and Elgin. The Church of Scotland and seceding Presbyterians saw this as infringing upon the parish system, or even as seedbeds of revolution. In turn, the Haldanes said the Church of Scotland was not truly preaching the gospel in whole regions.

In 1799 James began long years as minister of a congregation meeting in a building called 'the circus.' In 1801 the brothers opened 'The Tabernacle' at the top of Leith Walk in Edinburgh which, with its 3000 seats, was then the largest place of worship in Scotland.

The story wasn't over, however, for in 1808 the Haldanes both submitted to rebaptism as they had come to hold the view that Baptism is only appropriate for consenting adults making a decision for Christ. The next years were difficult with constant wrangles, for Robert had built so many of the independent churches and still held the deeds to them. The pressure led to the independent churches bonding together in the Congregational Union in 1812. The Baptist Union of Scotland only became a reality in mid-century, but the work of the Haldanes made growth possible for that movement in the same way as it had done so with the origins of the Congregational Union.

There remained one last chapter to the story of the Haldane Brothers. James continued in his long ministry in Edinburgh. Robert, however, was to achieve even wider influence for the evangelism which fired all his different phases. After peace was established at the end of the Napoleonic Wars, he ventured to Europe searching for new missionary opportunities.

From 1816-19, he spent six months at Geneva and a much longer spell at Montauban in the south of France. From these bases, he was able to inspire a new generation of European ministers with his evangelical convictions.

The Haldane Brothers may not impress us as the easiest of people to get on with, but no one can doubt their energy and their inspiration to two of the independent church traditions which have enriched Scottish church life.

Escott, H: *History of Congregationalism* (1960).
Haldane, A: *Lives of Robert and James A Haldane* (Banner of Truth: 1991).

70

GREVILLE EWING
Congregational Man of Peace

IN an age when Christian disagreements were sorted out with passion—or made worse—Greville Ewing (1767-1841) emerges as a man of conviction who yet preferred the path of compromise when that was possible.

Born and educated in Edinburgh, Greville Ewing was apprenticed as an engraver and worked as such until he was encouraged by his minister to study for the ministry. This he did at the University of Edinburgh and began as an assistant minister in Lady Glenorchy's Chapel. This was an interesting beginning because this chapel was founded and run by Lady Glenorchy's generosity. It was connected to the Church of Scotland but not under its jurisdiction: a shortage of churches had made the Kirk open to such arrangements for church extension.

Like the Haldane Brothers, he was drawn to the new missionary interest which had come to Scotland from England. As editor of *Missionary Magazine*, Ewing mirrored for a Scottish audience the content and even the style of London's *Evangelical Magazine* and *Evangelical Chronicle*. The material shaped many of his attitudes.

Bengal beckoned when the Haldane brothers were intending to go to establish a Scottish mission, but when the East India Company blocked the project Greville Ewing turned his attention to the home front. From his base within the Church of Scotland, he co-operated with the itinerant missionaries being sent throughout Scotland. By 1798 this brought confrontation because the Church of Scotland wished to defend the parish system and so condemned the poorly educated itinerant missionaries. In the end he resigned to join the Haldanes. Here his own educated background enabled him to move swiftly to a position where the Haldanes relied on him to tutor the missionaries before they set out on their journeys throughout Scotland.

This connection with the Haldanes weakened in 1802 when they parted ways on the issue of their search for Christianity as it existed in the Apostolic Church. The Haldanes' desire to model their services on the New Testament led to the introduction of practices which Greville Ewing wanted no part of. One problem was the lack of order caused when everyone was invited to stand up and say their piece in the service. Greville Ewing opposed the confusion and lack of dignity.

In 1808 another crisis loomed when the Haldanes decided to adopt the Baptist view over the question of whether infants could be baptised. Greville Ewing was left to consolidate the Congregational movement as it built up to form the Congregational Union. From a base in Glasgow Theological College he spent his life teaching, preaching and writing books. In clear contrast to the Haldanes, he wished the Congregational movement to maintain continuity with the Church of Scotland in terms of both doctrine and the way services were organised.

One incident clearly illustrates how different Grenville Ewing was from the fiery combative Haldane Brothers. In the 1820s there was a bitter controversy within the British and Foreign Bible Societies as to whether they could print the Apocryphal books with the Bible in their foreign editions. Since it was against the constitution of the British and Foreign Bible Societies, the Haldanes withdrew their support in protest. Greville Ewing objected but made no ultimatums and, working from within, saw the Societies reverse their policy at a later date.

The Congregational Union of Scotland owes much to the qualities and stability of Greville Ewing.

Matheson, J J: *Memoir of Greville Ewing* (1842).
Escott, H: *History of Scottish Congregationalism.*

71

JAMES HOGG
The Shepherd Sinner

STARING out across St Mary's Loch in the Scottish Borders is a bronze statue of the Ettrick Shepherd, James Hogg (1770-1835). Hogg looked after sheep like his father did before him. Hogg's own sons were also to follow this tradition. He loved the beauty

of hills and loch; but his earliest education came from his mother, learning by heart the psalms, folk songs and stories of the past. This gave him a clarity and strength of vision which enabled him to paint from inner reflection a description of his environment *and* the haunting fears and mystery of life close to nature.

At the end of his teens he was able to turn his 'folk' education into something more formal. Learning to read and write did not, however, destroy his aural and oral sensitivity. Failure in 1801 to make a success of the printing of *Scottish Pas-*

JAMES HOGG

torals, Poems, Songs etc led Walter Scott, then Sheriff of Selkirkshire, adopting Hogg. This patronage led to some success (although less successful dabbling in farming), a time in Edinburgh, and finally marriage in 1820 when a bequest of a farm at Altrive Lake (now Eldinhope) from the Duchess of Buccleugh gave him the secure base he needed for a rapid succession of poetry and prose.

Poems such as 'Kilmeny' and 'The Witch of Fife' swept the board for they avoided gothic elaboration, concentrating on the subtleties of the ballad style in which he excelled. He ended his days as a well-known figure of Edinburgh society, describing himself as 'The King of the Mountain and Fairy School.' It was paradoxical that he was laughed at as a shepherd, for his outrageous teeth and wild unkempt hair were symbolic at first of his unique 'otherness'; but in the long run nothing spoiled the appreciation of his wide-ranging literary achievements.

James Hogg was well read and enjoyed life. He ate and drank well and spent what he earned. All of this gave colour to his unique grasp of the supernatural as embodied in the rich folk tradition which stretched back into the middle ages. It also stemmed from a rigorously Calvinist conviction about the Bible as the sole interpreter of life. This last was central. Before he could read the Bible, he listened to it and learned large tracts of it by heart. Certainly it was dramatically effective with Hogg. He continued as a church-goer and read the Bible as well as a wide range of contemporary authors, thus developing a specific biblical skill: for one of the most powerful literary forms in the Bible speaks of the present in the light of the ancient prophetic messages of God, challenging us to look beneath the surface of the present. Hogg makes us re-read books in the light of the Bible and learn to recognise good religion when we see it.

Note his remarkable *Private Memoirs and Confessions of a Justified Sinner* (1824). His publisher was reluctant to touch it and the reviewers were hostile. It was in fact only after the book was republished in 1947, with an introduction by Andre Gide, that real appreciation emerged. Hogg's novel is as relevant today as it was in his own time, for it puts bits of the Bible together in a ridiculously but seemingly wonderfully reasonable way to parody empty religious observance. Hogg presents the most worrying devil of all: not as the traditional black creature with the three-cornered tail, but as a smartly dressed minister mouthing sweet reasonable words. Such 'sweet reason' is as unreal today as it was to the wild yet sophisticated shepherd: Amos reborn to challenge any 'easy' religion, ushering in an era where religion remained central in literature but in a much more self-questioning way.

Groves, D: *James Hogg: Growth of a Writer* (Scottish Academic Press: 1988).

Hogg, J: *Private Memoirs and Confessions of a Justified Sinner* (Cresset Press: 1947)

Wright, D F (ed): *The Bible in Scottish Life and Literature* (Saint Andrew Press: 1989).

72
THOMAS McCRIE
Light from the 'Auld Lichts'

THE sect knows as the 'Auld Lichts' appears in history as some-what narrow and withdrawn, but the fact that it produced char-acters like Thomas McCrie (1772-1835) would suggest it had an inner dynamism which betrays the outward appearances. Thomas McCrie's writings were to shape succeeding generations of pres-byterians in Scotland and John Jamieson, another member, pro-duced in Edinburgh the first *Etymological Dictionary of the Scots Language* in 1808. All this is quite far removed from the way James Barrie patronisingly described them in his native village of Kirriemuir: *The Little Minister* (1891: dramatised 1897) described the rigid pettiness which could ensue, but also clearly described the strengths.

Thomas McCrie was born at Denny and became an Anti-Burgher minister in 1796. This was the more extreme part of the Secession Church which took the insistence on the independence of the church to the point of refusing the Burgher Oath. In 1806, when a further split took place, Thomas joined the 'Auld Lichts', the hardest line group of the Anti-Burghers. From then on, he preached in a little church on the south side of Edinburgh, on the corner of Davie Street off West Richmond Street. As editor of the *Christian Magazine* he had a platform for spreading his ideas to a wider audience, but with its wide coverage it also pointed to McCrie's wider interests.

These interests came to a peak with the publication of the lives of *John Knox* in 1811 and *Andrew Melville* in 1819. He advanced them as the pioneers of the church he belonged to, the church he ardently believed other churches had backslided from. It is sig-nificant that he highlighted the importance of Andrew Melville, an importance in the development of the Church of Scotland which modern historians have reaffirmed. As a result of his books, two generations took inspiration from the image of John Knox giving

Mary Queen of Scots a row and Andrew Melville calling James VI 'God's sillie vassal.' It has been argued that people were prepared for the Free Church at the Disruption by these works, which were described 'as the *Iliad* and the *Odyssey* of the Church of Scotland.'

Thomas McCrie's effectiveness as a historian stems partly from his commitment to re-finding the roots of a church he thought had lost its way, but also because his meticulous care ensured that his history broke out of the confines of his own vision and prejudices. In the eight years after publishing *John Knox* he worked relentlessly at the story of Andrew Melville. It is said that for all eight years 'he never picked up his newspaper.'

Wider interests still are evidenced by his publication in 1829 of his *History of the Reformation in Spain*. Again too he clearly made history attractive, for his son Thomas (1798-1875) was to become a professor at the Presbyterian college in London. He published a life of his father in 1840, some five years after his death, and went on to write several books including *Sketches of Scottish Church History.*

Article on 'T McCrie' in the *Dictionary of National Biography.*

73

ANDREW SCOTT
Building for the Future or Exploiting the Poor?

BORN in the Enzie in Banffshire at Chapelford farm in 1772, Andrew Scott was to become somewhat of a colossus in the redevelopment of the Roman Catholic Church in the West of Scotland. He stubbornly clung to the idea of becoming a priest from as early as five years old, even though this took him to spartan training at Scalan at the age of twelve, then to Douai on the continent, and finally back to the chapel house in Aberdeen when the French Revolution brought danger and the closure of the college. He was finally ordained and worked at Dee Castle, the poorest parish in Scotland, and then Huntly, before being moved to where his lifetime's work would take place (Glasgow) and later the whole Western District of Scotland.

A challenge faced him as resident priest in Glasgow. The massive immigration of Irish workers had made the numbers of Catholics rise dramatically, with the one church becoming proportionately far too small. It had also imported sectarian prejudice from Northern Ireland and increased fears of unemployment in the established working community. Bishop Alexander Cameron had brought Scott in from the north-east of Scotland precisely because an Irish priest would not be acceptable to Protestants such as David Dale the mill owner who, in 1792, helped to build a Catholic chapel to attract Highland workers to the cotton industry. The other side of that coin was that the Irish workers resented having in Scott a Scottish priest and, later, bishop. It seemed Cameron couldn't win.

Andrew Scott's congregation rose from 450 communicants in 1805 to 3000 in 1814. A new church was critical but the new members were the poorest of the poor and Bishop Cameron had made things worse by commissioning Gillespie Graham as architect. Buoyed up by his successful St Mary's Cathedral in Edinburgh he produced a grandiose scheme for Glasgow which was beyond all possible resources. But Scott divided Glasgow into 50 districts and collectors with every working man expected to contribute one shilling, and every working woman a sum ranging from one penny to a shilling. The scheme was aimed at raising £100 a year, but mass unemployment the next year ended any chance of the scheme succeeding. Some of the Irish community saw their chance. A certain Mr McGavin accused the priest of 'milking the Irish to build a grandiose church and a chapel house for several more priests to be able to milk them more'. The matter was brought to a head by the specific accusation that Scott had refused baptism to a mother who had not paid her dues. Scott sued for libel and, represented by Francis Jeffrey and Henry Cockburn, he won. The donations of £4000 to his cause were put to the church building fund and transformed it.

Another landmark came in 1817 when Kirkman Findlay's work enabled a Catholic school to be built, provided it used a Protestant Bible. Here again, Scott was either hailed for his openness and vision, or accused of betraying the faith by accepting this.

In 1828 Scott became co-adjutor bishop for the Western District with his main work then being in the Clyde valley: but when he became bishop in 1832 he left the central belt to his new co-adjutor bishop John Murdoch, and Scott worked in the West Highlands and the South West. Despite the Highlanders resenting him for not being a Gaelic speaker, he built them proper chapels and they had much cause to be grateful.

When he died in 1846, Andrew Scott had proved himself to be a skillful administrator, but for many he was loved as the bishop who gave them churches and who belied his patronising dominant manner by also being the priest who walked fearlessly among the cholera victims. Christ's commitment to people rather than buildings or self-advancement, would seem to have clearly triumphed.

Scott, A: *Letters* (Scottish Catholic Archives).
Johnson, C: *Developments in the Roman Catholic Church in Scotland 1789-1829* (John Donald: 1983).

74

JOHN PHILIP

The Kirkcaldy Weaver who fought for the Blacks

JOHN Philip (1777-1851) was born in Kirkcaldy of weaver stock. He died in the Cape Colony of South Africa, depressed that his struggle for justice for the black community was doomed to failure. His example, however, has continued to inspire and is still a constructive factor in the dialogue that is giving hope to South Africa.

The Haldane Revival in Scotland was the spark which led Philip to the ministry. After training in England he became minister of the first Congregational church in Aberdeen (1799) and a continuing supporter of the London Missionary Society. He was a popular and successful minister with 20 years experience behind him, happily married with a family. Such experience led the London Missionary Society in South Africa to send Philip and his family (along with John Campbell) to reorganise the mission during a crisis. Philip became resident director in a confrontational situation between the LMS and the South African government, as well as with some of the Society's own ministers, over the treatment of blacks. In fact four ministers left the Society to join the Dutch Reformed Church, but John Philip very rapidly sided with the blacks, concluding that the structure of the colony was fundamentally unjust.

Twentieth century assessments of John Philip either see him as an unfair liberal critic of a system he did not understand or as a founder of the liberal movement in South Africa. But modern categories of attitude do not apply. He was an aggressive passionate man, dedicated to the truth. He trod on toes: he might have achieved more by being conciliatory. But Philip thought that too many had been silent in the face of oppression. But insistence on human equality blinded him to the values in *traditional* African society, as did the fact that the Khoi people within the colony, whom he knew best and who warmly responded to Christianity, had already lost their traditional culture, destroyed by the gun and serfdom on white farms. To see the need for Africanisation would have required a leap of imagination probably impossible for anyone at that time, and certainly impossible to a man like John Philip.

Philip was very evangelical and saw humanity as sinful. What was significant was his uncluttered conviction that when redeemed by the love of Christ and given education, every human is equal. Philip might have used the term 'savages' at times about Africans, but he also used it of whites. For him it was not a racial epithet but a moral one. In that light he believed the system of law was unjust. In this he was able, until it faded in the 1840s, to enlist the support of the Anti-Slavery organisation in Britain in demanding 'equal civil rights for all the King's subjects in South Africa.' Through that he advanced the argument that there was no point freeing blacks from slavery if there are no rights. He was able to win the 'Ordinance 50' in 1828 which forbade discrimination by colour.

Sadly he did not live to see many of his Cape coloured receive the vote in the new constitution of 1852. Because of Ordinance 50, the franchise was granted not on the basis of *race* but on *property* and *education:* some blacks got the vote and some whites did not. There was a white majority, but many constituencies could not be won without black support. Left alone this constitution would have led to the evolution of a black majority. The Afrikaner people of the Cape went for 60 years without any alarm. But everything changed when in 1910 the Cape was unwillingly forced into the union of South Africa with the Orange Free State, the Transvaal and Natal (British, but just as racist as the other two). All white males got the vote and the number of black voters was frozen at the 1910 level, some to be removed in 1924, the rest in 1948.

Why was John Philip such an outstanding advocate of racial equality, perhaps the forerunner of Father Huddleston, Desmond Tutu and Allan Boesak? The answer lies in the particular form of evangelical faith of the period which produced the powerful Anti-Slavery movements both in America and Britain. It also lies in his Scottish experience which declared that Christianity and education brought equality and the chance to fulfil all talents.

Ross, A: *J Philip* (Aberdeen University Press: 1986).
McMillan, W M: *The Cape Colour Question* (1960).

75

JOHN LEE
In the Tradition of St Luke

IT may be significant that John Lee (1779-1859) was trained as a doctor before becoming one of the most influential ministers of the nineteenth century. On one hand he preserved the ordered structures of the 'Auld Kirk' after the breakaway of the Free Kirk at the Disruption; but he also drew attention to the desperate plight of

JOHN LEE

the poor of his day much to the annoyance of the evangelising Free Kirker, Thomas Chalmers. Lee stood against the view that only the 'deserving poor' should be helped: the concept that Christian commitment frees a person from the chains of poverty. Lee was like St Luke, the gospel writer. Luke was thought to be a doctor and certainly applied a very ordered mind to the writing of his gospel which was centred on the fact that Christ came to those very same poor who were despised by the rich. He stressed that very often the only thing the rich and poor had in common was that both were *undeserving of* and *equally dependent on* God's love. In this respect, Luke's conviction certainly parallels John Lee.

John Lee was born in Stow in 1779. He had the best Latin scholar in Europe as a schoolteacher before going on to the Seceder College at Selkirk. After a spell as a tutor to a Borders family, he became a minister under the patronage of the famous 'Jupiter Carlyle.' (Carlyle's father, as minister of Inveresk, inspired his minister son to respect established church peace from the time when, as a child in the manse garden at Inveresk, Carlyle's father had witnessed the butchery of war during the '45 rebellion.)

John Lee's career as minister took him first of all to London and then back to Peebles. This led to a post as professor of Church History in St Mary's College, St Andrews with a lecturing spell in Aberdeen, and then to three ministries in Edinburgh: at the Canongate, Lady Yesters church and the Old church (part of St Giles). Then from 1840 to 1859 he was Principal of the University of Edinburgh.

These are the bare facts, but the reality of Lee and his influence lie somewhat deeper. He was Moderator of the General Assembly 1840, but even more important he was the guardian of good church order as clerk to the General Assembly all through the years of the Disruption when church order could easily have disintegrated.

For the greatest bibliophile of his day, it is ironic that he was involved in a major tragedy for historical sources. He worked with Laing to restore the minutes of the early General Assemblies from where they turned up at Zion College on the banks of the River Thames. With the help of the Archbishop of Canterbury he got them as far as Parliament, but there they were destroyed in the fire which destroyed the Commons building and made way for the building of today. Nonetheless, his work is important for the history of Glasgow and Edinburgh in different ways.

It was, however, in the mundane matter of giving evidence to Royal Commissions that his character shines out. To the intense annoyance of Dr Thomas Chalmers, who wished to portray the caring Christian community in a favourable light, he ruthlessly catalogued the desperate poverty of those who were forced to work for fourpence a week and had to walk out into the country to gather birch twigs to make into 'besoms' for sale to the better off. He forced people to look at the reality of the city slums of Scotland: three or four families in a room and others huddled down under the building works and street arches, a family in one corner and a dog in the other.

Engels quoted Lee's material: St Luke would have been proud of his witness. Although undoubtedly an ambitious man, by the end of his days he was certainly appreciated throughout Scotland.

Lee, J: *Correspondence* (National Library of Scotland).

76
ANDREW THOMSON
Evangelical but Enlightened

ALL too often in Scottish church history it seemed that to be evangelical meant to be *against* the 'enlightened' values of being involved in intellectual development and social change. Andrew Thomson (1779-1851) brought both together.

Like so many others in the history of God's people in Scotland, he was a son of the manse in Sanquhar in Dumfriesshire. It was real covenanting country and father John Thomson was Moderator of the Kirk's General Assembly in 1785.

Andrew was educated at the University of Edinburgh and became minister of Sprouston in 1802. In this rural parish alongside the Tweed, he involved himself with every area of community life and as a result published in 1807 a *Sacramental Catechism*, mainly for the young. It ran to thirty editions with 130,000 copies, one of the most successful books of the century.

In 1808 Andrew Thomson was to be found in the East church of Perth: in 1810 New Greyfriars in Edinburgh: and finally 1814 brought him at the age of 35 appointment as the first minister of the glorious new St George's church in Edinburgh's West End. The building—which is new West Register House in Charlotte Square—reflects the prestigious parish church it was for Edinburgh's New Town.

Despite the upper class setting, Andrew Thomson was a Whig: a liberal in politics and committed to improving the condition of the common man. His faith was evangelical and this he preached to the urban élite to motivate their interest in social concerns: his preaching he then extended to membership of countless philanthropic ventures and societies. Journalism was another tool and here too he became extremely successful. From 1810 to 1830 he edited *The Christian Instructor*, an evangelical Edinburgh review covering politics, science and the arts: in other words it took the old moderate ideal of social engagement and integrated it into the evangelical thrust of having a personal faith in Christ. The journal was one of the many means in which Thomson became leader of the whole evangelical revival; taking the tradition of the old Calvinist party and drawing vigour from the growing evangelical movement in England. Being an evangelical had become respectable.

Music was another field of the mission of Andrew Thomson. He revived church praise and congregational involvement. This took courage and planning: to help him he attracted R A Smith as precentor, from Paisley where he had made his name. Publications followed: *Sacred Harmony* (sermons) in 1820, *Sacred Music* in 1825, to which he contributed 13 tunes, as for example 'St George's Edinburgh' for Psalm 24.

In the courts of the church, Thomson was an effective debater: in politics a power to be reckoned with: and in preaching and philanthropic societies a man of considerable persuasion. He had, however, his blind spots. He helped to found, and was active in, the British and Foreign Bible Society but in the controversy over whether Bibles for abroad should contain the Apocrypha, his vehement arguments against their inclusion brought final victory but greatly weakened the Society.

In one particular social issue, Thomson's name deserves an honoured place. He was a champion of the Anti-Slavery movement. He saw slavery as completely un-Christian and was a leading preacher and speaker against the practice, demanding that it should be brought to an end immediately, even if to do so involved violence. He spurred the middle classes of Edinburgh into action on the issue.

From 1827-31 Andrew Thomson was the undisputed leader of the evangelical party as pressures built up towards the Disruption. Many feel he might have been able to avert it because of his connections with the Whig party and his political instincts. We'll never know if that is true but what we do know is that Andrew Thomson proved you could be both evangelical and 'enlightened.' It was a very real breakthrough.

77

THOMAS CHALMERS
Together or Apart?

THOMAS Chalmers (1780-1847) gave the Scottish Kirk an enduring vision of how the parish could be a force for community, but also led one third of the Kirk and ministers—and over half of the parishioners into the split known as the Disruption. Despite that divide, he is still respected in the Free Church tradition which he formed and the establishment kirk which he left.

THOMAS CHALMERS

A son of the manse in Anstruther, Thomas went to St Andrews University, matriculating at the age of 13. Post-graduate study at the University of Edinburgh followed his arts and divinity studies at St Andrews, but he returned to lecture there in mathematics and write a treatise on Political Economy. Before that, however, he had accepted a presentation by the patrons to the parish of Kilmany in Fife in 1802, but found no contradiction in his lecturing, convinced that a minister need only work on a Saturday and Sunday to fulfil his role.

Then crisis came. He came down with prolonged and life-threatening consumption, suffered the break-up of a romantic attachment and experienced a deep sense of failure about both his academic career and the ministry. Out of the crisis came evangelical conversion in 1811-12. He threw himself into preaching and became almost an itinerant preacher throughout Fife and Angus. He also got deeply involved also in raising money for mission for the British and Foreign Bible Society.

In 1813 he rediscovered the parish and started regular house to house visiting and making poor relief effective: school on Saturday and a bible society helped him to build his 800 parishioners into a very real community. Success brought him a call in 1814 to the Tron in Glasgow where, from 1815 onwards, he tried to replicate the Kilmany parish community in a parish of 12,000. He set out visiting but soon realised that the clear breakdown of community in the pressures of a growing commercial and industrial society needed new remedies. He recruited visiting elders, deacons and schoolteachers for each block of 400 in his parish. It was effective. It also gave him the tool for a wider vision in which the institutionalism of poor relief would be abandoned for a system in which the rich would provide for those in genuine need, while the poor would be enabled to improve their own situation rather than be pauperised by hand-outs. In 1819 Chalmers persuaded the council to establish a new parish, St John's, where his ideal became a reality.

He believed sincerely it was a success. Kilmany had come to Glasgow. Critics, however, felt that the suffering of the poor on their way to changing their condition could not be justified.

Pastoral success brought the academic preferment that had eluded Chalmers in the early days. In 1823 he was given a chair at St Andrews and in 1827 a chair at the University of Edinburgh: a generation of students came to share his vision. Applause at his lectures was commonplace.

Further influence opened up, for he became in 1831 leader of the evangelical party in the Kirk which achieved majority power in 1834. He used it to advance his dream of establishing a network of parishes (no bigger than 2000) and schools throughout Scotland. For this he successfully preached for voluntary contributions from rich and poor alike with the pledge that he would then get the government to endow the new parishes. Two hundred and twenty-two new churches were opened, but in 1838 the Whig government refused to fund them and in 1839 challenged their very existence as a threat to the established order of things.

Chalmers' rage at this was accompanied by rage at the 1834 Veto Act of the General Assembly—which restricted patron's rights to impose ministers on parishes—being declared illegal in the courts in 1838. Thomas Chalmers saw the independence of the Kirk being undermined with the right to expand and the right for people to choose their own ministers being taken away. In May 1843 he led the Disruption which split the Kirk and formed the Free Church as a free national establishment. His energy helped to ensure 700-800 new churches and schools. He himself was professor of Divinity and principal of the new Divinity College. In 1846-50 New College itself was built.

The measure of Thomas Chalmers' greatness is perhaps that in his last years he remained committed to his vision of the parish as community. He devoted a great deal of time to a final community experiment in the West Port of Edinburgh and left it as a pattern for the church to follow; a working-class church, school, savings bank, clothing store and laundry facilities. He even tried to involve all the churches ecumenically in building his vision. In that at least he speaks to us today.

Hanna, Dr: *Memoirs* (1849-52), in 4 volumes.
Correspondence (1853).
Brown, S J: *Thomas Chalmers and the Godly Commonwealth in Scotland* (1982).

THOMAS CHALMERS
IN LATER YEARS

78

CHRISTOPHER ANDERSON
Charlotte Baptist Chapel and more!

THE irony of the story of Christopher Anderson (1782-1852) is that he founded and was identified with Charlotte Baptist chapel in Edinburgh and in so doing brought the more liberal English Baptist tradition to Scotland. Yet was summarily ejected from the same chapel with his friends by a young minister, Alfred Thomas, in the very year Anderson died.

Christopher was the youngest son of William Anderson, an ironmonger in Edinburgh. His grandfather was brought up in Dunfermline and trained for the ministry of the Church of Scotland before becoming convinced of the unscriptural constitution of the church and resigning. He moved to Edinburgh and joined the old Scotch Independent meeting in Candlemakers Hall where David Dale of New Lanark used to preach sometimes.

Christopher's poor health as a child led him to be sent to Polton near Lasswade before being apprenticed to John Muir, an Edinburgh ironmonger. Finding the Candlemakers Hall service boring, he moved to the Scotch Baptist meeting house. He wasn't converted at first because he wanted to enjoy life (*ie* music and dancing). At 18 he made friends with some English Baptist students at the university and was baptised by one of them in March 1801. His father was happy that he had at least become a Christian.

Anderson went to London and Bristol Baptist church to deepen his knowledge of the faith. He wanted to go to India with the famous Baptist missionary William Carey but was refused on account of his poor health. Back in Edinburgh he gathered people to Richmond Court by his attractive preaching, but he also tended to put them off by his rigorous moral teaching so they soon left. In 1818 he went with his flock to Charlotte chapel which he bought from the Scottish Episcopal church (now St John's). This was a single storey building. The present chapel is on the same site and was built in 1912. From the beginning, Charlotte chapel was the base for work which opened out in all sorts of directions.

English students at Edinburgh University found a natural home with him and some went on to become famous ministers in England. He took a personal interest in his converts: they were his substitute family (his own child died young of tuberculosis). He was quite firm in his distinction from the Scotch Baptists and their 'lay elders who discussed the service for those within rather than how to go out to those around.' He was much more directly evangelistic and aggressive, but did not allow his congregation to get involved in what he regarded as petty disputes, even about baptism. He encouraged them to be Christians first and if they wanted to be Baptists, fine!

Anderson was an open-minded man who worked well with other ministers, as in the Bible Society of Edinburgh. He had quite early on gone on missionary journeys to the Highlands and Islands and then to Ireland. In his diary of 1810 he tells how he 'preached at Macduff to nearly 1,000 people at the old kirk. Walked back to Banff and preached to 2,000 or more.' After basing himself in Edinburgh he raised money for itinerant preachers and the Gaelic School Society to promote education in the Highlands. He supported one successful ministry in Aberdeen and a failed one in Falkirk. In Ireland, even some of the priests encouraged children to go to his schools.

Another example of Anderson's wider vision was his membership of the Edinburgh Anti-Slave Trade Association. He also had a range of publications about Ireland, and here at home he published *Animals of the English Bible* and *Domestic Constitution*, a book of family ethics which he published shortly after the early death of his wife Esther. She died from tuberculosis,

Anderson was a man of contrasts, a pre-Victorian in so many ways, but strangely modern in the openness of his missionary instincts.

Anderson, H: *Life and Letters of Christopher Anderson* (Edinburgh: 1858).
Whyte, W: *Revival in Rose Street* (Charlotte Chapel).

79

DONALD SAGE
Man of the People in Sutherland

DONALD Sage (1789-1869) earned the description 'Man of the People' during the Sutherland Clearances. That identification gave him, despite coming himself from the ranks of the established clergy, an unease about the Kirk which in 1843 led him to join those who, with great solemnity and reluctance, walked out of the General Assembly to form the Free Kirk.

Donald's grandfather was the famous 'Aeneas Sage' who brought presbyterianism to the episcopalian Gaels of Lochcarron who deeply resented what was seen as a mission to a rude, pagan state. Aeneas was a physical giant who won people over by his presence and teaching. Donald's father was Alexander Sage. Aeneas was 70 when Alexander, his sixth son, was born.

School at Cromarty led Donald to King's College, Aberdeen (following family tradition). A post as schoolmaster was followed by the charge of minister at Kildonan in Sutherland. His first appointment was to Achness while his father was still at Kildonan. From then we have Donald's *Memorabilia Domestica*, a voluminous book of memoirs, to illustrate events in his life. It is of great value as a social commentary on the time and as an insight into the world of ministers, although Sage does not have the self-analysis characteristic of many of the evangelical Christians of the time.

During the Sutherland Clearances, lairds and landowners, in particular the dukes of Sutherland, tried to implement current economic thinking to make the land more productive. This was to be achieved by replacing people with sheep: they justified this with moral and quasi-scientific arguments about proper stewardship of the land.

Donald's memoirs recount in detail his first encounters with the simple firm faith of the evangelicals who came into Sutherland, like the pious M'Kay family from Rea country. Donald Sage visited these 'heroes of faith', revering them for their innocent piety.

The vast majority of ministers, who were, after all, dependent on the patronage of the Duke of Sutherland, either acquiesced or sought to justify the clearances. Not so Donald Sage. In his memoirs he speaks clearly of the sudden clearance of Strathaven by Patrick Sellar (factor) and James Loch. It is not a romanticised account. He stayed with his parish as the deadline approached. News had reached them on that wild night that the glen would be cleared forthwith. Sage preached his last sermon out of doors and rode through the glen while the houses were still smoking, the tenants' effects stacked outside, the people thrown out into the cold. A sense of anger and bafflement burns through the narrative.

Donald went at first to Kildonan. He received a call to Rothesay in the Isle of Bute, marrying at this time a girl who herself came from a long line of ministers. This was the beginning of a line of Sage ministers within almost a 'caste' of presbyterian ministers. His heart, however, was in the north and so he gladly accepted a call to the parish of Resolis in Sutherland in 1822 and stayed there until his death in 1869. It was a fruitful ministry despite the continuing distress of the clearances all around.

There was another crisis. The great divide over patronage between evangelicals and moderates continued. When the crisis came in 1843, Sage did not take part in the public debates as to how the church should react to the increased patronage which had been put in place. Although in Edinburgh, he stayed in his lodgings, praying for guidance before taking his decision to join the Free Church, with all the uncertainty it meant for his ministry.

To the end Donald Sage represented the strengths of the Free Church tradition, quite independent from externally imposed forms of service or prayer. There was never any question of him trotting out the same old sermon or being confined to what was in a prayer book. His Christian faith meant that he could never be beholden to a patron, but instead was free to preach the Word of God 'in season and out of season, welcome or unwelcome.'

Sage, D: *Memorabilia Domestica* (Wick: 1889).
McInnes, J: *The Evangelical Movement in the Highlands of Scotland* (Aberdeen University Press: 1951).

80

EDWARD IRVING
'The Spirit moves ...'

WHEN a nineteenth century Scots preacher attracts new attention today from such diverse thinkers as a Catholic theologian,
an Anglican vicar and the populist charismatic movement, he
certainly demands a second look. Edward Irving only lived from
1792-1834 but he made an impact
both in London and Scotland which
is now being reassessed.

EDWARD IRVING

Early days in Haddington led
Edward to the University of Edinburgh before returning to Haddington as a schoolteacher. At his
second teaching job in Kirkcaldy
he met Thomas Carlyle and, like
so many others, found the meeting
a challenging one. Challenging also
was his first post as a minister, as
assistant to Thomas Chalmers in
Glasgow. This was the very same
Chalmers who in the future was to lead the Disruption, but meantime was engaged in a major experiment in bringing the gospel to
the poor.

In 1822 Irving was called to be minister of the Caledonian
church in London. His brilliant preaching attracted large crowds
and all the leading intellectuals of the day. Parliamentarians came
to listen. So did the great literary characters of the day, like Charles
Lamb, Samuel Taylor Coleridge, Thomas Carlyle and many others. A church in Regent Square had to be built to accommodate the
numbers.

Irving was the preacher or theologian of Romanticism. His
evangelical commitment led him to a fundamental protest against
the rigid orthodoxy of the past in favour of a teaching of univer-

sal love. That journey, which mirrored McLeod Campbell, Erskine and A J Scott, brought a new exciting understanding of how Christ is head of the whole human race and therefore of how all nations find salvation and freedom in Christ. All were thrown out of ministry in the Kirk.

Irving preached a series on the Incarnation which was then published. He maintained that Christ assumed our frail fallen humanity to sanctify it. Christ was anointed by the Holy Spirit and so did mighty works and miracles of healing. In 1830, filled with this vision, Irving's assistant A J Scott went to Dunbartonshire, the territory of McLeod Campbell. There he met Mary and Isabella Campbell. The theme was 'greater things you do when you receive the Holy Spirit.' Mary Campbell spoke in tongues, the first recorded happening of the kind in Scotland. Next came the gift of healing, for Mary was dying of tuberculosis and was miraculously healed. When A J Scott returned to London, Irving preached Christ's Baptism by the Spirit and our possibility of being similarly baptised in the Spirit and subsequently doing wonderful things in our frail fallen humanity. Speaking in tongues began in the congregation.

The excitement gave way to the chill of a heresy trial on the grounds that Irving was preaching that Christ was a sinner. This he strenuously denied and appealed to the Fathers of the church with their dictum that what in human nature is unassumed by Christ remains unredeemed. He challenged the authority of the London presbytery and so the case was referred to the presbytery of Arran, which in 1832 took up the charge and deposed him from the ministry.

The elders of Regent Square went on to charge him because women, by definition not ordained, were speaking in tongues. The London presbytery deposed him, but 90-95 per cent of his congregation followed him into what was to become the Catholic Apostolic Church. Edward Irving was the first angel: he never spoke in tongues himself but refused to deny it to others: 'who am I to forbid the Holy Spirit?' A year later he was dead, but not only did his work reverberate with people like Coleridge but went on to influence much subsequent church life. The remarkable minister of St Giles, Harry Whitley, was brought up in the Catholic Apostolic Church.

It has become clear that Edward Irving was not only an exciting preacher, but also a brilliant theologian: the Anglican Tom Smail has urged the re-publishing of his writings. The Orthodox Colin Gunton of London University has shown Irving's roots in Athanasius and the Cappadocian Fathers. The presbyterian, Gordon Strachan, with his 'New Age' interests, has refound many of Irving's insights for today. Perhaps the charismatic movement today could well benefit from his practical theology of Christ's humanity and find the parallels between Paul's arguments to the Corinthians and Irving. Irving could well become a man for today.

Carlyle, T: *Miscellaneous Essays* (1837), fourth edition.
Strachan, G: *The Pentecostal Theology of Edward Irving* (Darton, Longman & Todd: 1973).

THOMAS AND JANE CARLYLE
Twin Pillars of the New Faith?

MARRIAGE as a creative partnership has rarely been so vividly illustrated as with Jane and Thomas Carlyle (Thomas 1795-1881: Jane 1801-66). It was an unlikely alliance. Jane came from a middle class family in Haddington and Thomas from a working class family in Ecclefechan. They met when she was 20 and he 25 and only married after six years of correspondence.

THOMAS CARLYLE

Thomas benefited from the Scottish educational opportunities open to the poor and made the most of his years at Edinburgh University. His parents were members of the Burgher Seceders, an intensely committed breakaway group from the Kirk, with his mother bringing the wider Church of Scotland tradition to his background. They intended him to become a minister but he went instead into science, then into the translation of European literature, finally emerging as the main exponent of German literature first in Scotland and then in Britain.

Married life for the Carlyles began in Comely Bank, Edinburgh and was then followed by six years on an inherited farm, Craigenputtoch. The solitude spurred Thomas to creative energy, but it eventually became an intolerable burden to both sociable, brilliant talkers. With no income from a steady job, like the schoolmastering he could not stand, finances were precarious. They decided to go to Chelsea as a one year gamble. As Jane put it: 'let's burn our boats.'

More strength of character was soon required in those early

days in London when John Stuart Mill accidentally burned the first volume of Carlyle's *French Revolution*: a year's work. Soon, however, hard work and their interactive creativity brought success. Recent studies of Jane's independent lifestyle and her wide circle of friends show her to have been not only a feminist before her time, but also the keenest of literary critics, a brilliant letter writer and the most accomplished woman of her day. Questions have been raised about the independent lifestyles of Thomas and Jane, but perspective is given by Jane's early death. The effect on Thomas was devastating: to quote her gravestone at Haddington, 'it was as if the light of his life had gone out.' It was the end of his imaginatively creative writing, though it led him to write the greatest autobiography of the nineteenth century—*Reminiscences* —which charts the story of their life together.

Carlyle's letters continue to challenge and inspire. The University of Edinburgh is publishing all the surviving Carlyle letters in an edition which will run to well over 40 volumes. In fact there are 11,000 in all: to ministers, bishops, rationalists, poets and atheists alike. They represent the cutting edge of a fundamental moral challenge to society which has its parallels today, but is embodied in a more integrated Victorian way in Carlyle's major works. His work thus influenced the whole development of the Victorian era.

Two books in particular illustrate a religious dimension: the masterpiece *Frederick the Great;* and *Sartor Sartorus* (1831-2) which draws on Goethe and on the religion of Carlyle's parents to produce what can be described as a new religious synthesis. It is rounded off in 1866 when, as rector of the University of Edinburgh, he gave his address: in it he embodied his own moral experiences as advice to the younger members of his audience.

Although they had close minister friends such as John Sterling, Thomas and Jane rarely went to church, but yet they spoke to a generation at the end of the era of simplistic faith, when people realised only too well the limitations of human knowledge and took refuge in a private faith which can easily be misunderstood as hypocrisy. Thomas warned the Victorians that they had lost their spiritual life in gaining mechanistic life. With his wife he worried that values could easily be lost sight of, and in this they sowed the seeds of the whole Victorian movement of Social Conscience as developed by the great Victorian novelists and critics.

When Thomas Carlyle died, he was given the treatment normally reserved for royalty: there were black edges to the newspapers. Westminster Abbey was offered for the funeral, but it was typical of him, and symbolic, that his wishes were to be buried in his family grave in Hoddam kirkyard. (Jane had been buried in Haddington.)

Both independently and together the Carlyles had stood for a new class consciousness, but they had stood back from that society sufficiently to tell a faithless age very vividly what it was too busy engaged in doing to understand properly for itself.

The Collected Letters of Thomas and Jane Welsh Carlyle (Duke University Press: 1970), Duke of Edinburgh edition.

Campbell, I: *Thomas Carlyle* (Hamish Hamilton: 1974).

Carlyle, T: *Reminiscences* (Dent: 1972) (Oxford University Press: 1984).

82

JOHN McLEOD CAMPBELL
'Atonement and Assurance for all'

VIEWED by many as the greatest theologian Scotland ever produced, John McLeod Campbell (1800-72) was condemned by the Kirk of his own day. But it is arguable that because of McLeod Campbell, today's Kirk has preserved the breadth of John Calvin's vision instead of concentrating on the narrowness of Calvin's teaching on predestination: the latter would surely have lead to the Kirk's self-destruction as the national church.

He was born a minister's son at Kilninver near Oban, went to Glasgow University at eleven and then on to divinity at Edinburgh. In 1825 he became minister of Row near Helensburgh. Six years devoted work endeared him to his congregation: Campbell was yet another in a long line of great Scottish kirk theologians who hammered out their theology in a pastoral situation. It was that theology which brought condemnation in presbytery, synod and assembly, despite the pleading of his godly passionate minister father.

To find out why John McLeod Campbell was condemned takes us to the heart of a contradiction he experienced working in the Kirk with his parishioners. He found himself asking why there was no joyful assurance in his people, but instead an introspective guilt-ridden conscience. He concluded this was due to the Calvinist stress on examining yourself for evidence of a conversion experience before you could be admitted to the communion table. This in turn derived not so much from Calvin himself but from the line of thought beginning with Calvin's successor Beza, and continuing through Perkins, Cartwright and the Puritans into the *Westminster Confession of Faith*. The *Confession* maintained that the atonement of Christ was only for some—the elect. Although an English document, the *Confession* became the secondary standard of the Kirk and engendered an atmosphere of fear in Scotland. Ministers like Samuel Rutherford and Thomas Gillespie took the thought to its logical conclusion. People asked themselves how they could know whether Christ died for them? Subsequent ministers like the famous Thomas Hogg of Kiltearn, Easter Ross began 'fencing the table' of the Lord's supper to keep it for the elect alone. He reduced the communion roll from 600 to 25. Thus in the Highlands the vast majority of adherents did not feel that they belonged to the Kirk.

McLeod Campbell could not accept this sort of attitude. He was a saintly man who would not accept compromise to his belief that (see Calvin's *Institutes*, book IV) Christ was sent to save all: that atonement for sin was the manifestation of the nature of Christ and God, which is love. This is what McLeod Campbell taught and he was condemned for his faith in the universal atonement and in the work of the Holy Spirit, taking the Christian from a narcissistic preoccupation with self to love of God and others. This brings about an assurance of salvation—and joy!

Dismissed from the ministry in 1831, he worked without bitterness for two years as a missionary in the Highlands before becoming in 1833 minister of an independent church in Glasgow. There he worked without remuneration for 26 years before retiring to die peacefully in Roseneath, once again rehabilitated in the Kirk he loved. His personal stand was to serve that Kirk well, for it led ultimately to the declaratory acts later in the nineteenth century which continue to allow ministers of the Kirk a liberty of conscience with regard to the *Westminster Confession of Faith* without which most could not function.

As another legacy to the Kirk, McLeod Campbell left three beautifully written masterpieces: *Thought on Revelation* (1862); *Christ the Bread of Life* (1851); and *The Nature of the Atonement*. This last is the classic summary of his thought and witness which places him firmly in a select band of theologians in the Kirk who felt the need to break out of classic Calvinism, yet still communicate its inner strength to succeeding generations. Glasgow University in later years gave him an honourary DD, a symbol of the influence he had in English theology and then in Scotland.

Memorials written by Campbell's son 1877.
Tuttle, G: *So rich a soul—John McLeod Campbell on Christian Atonement* (Scottish Academic Press: 1986).

83

HUGH MILLER
The Mass Media hits the Kirk

IF the era of the penny newspaper heralded the era of the mass media, then Hugh Miller (1802-56) heralded the era of the mass media for the Kirk. His origins in no way suggested what was to follow. His father was a seaman from Easter Ross who died at sea when Hugh was three. His mother was a fey, superstitious woman from a Gaelic-speaking background. Theirs was a conventional presbyterian family. Hugh was a sensitive child who saw the ghost of his great grandfather John Fiddes in the cottage at Cromarty. He had vivid memories too of seeing a severed hand floating in front of his face on the day his father died at sea.

HUGH MILLER

The young Hugh Miller went to Dame school in the village of Cromarty, but was thrown out after a fight with the schoolmaster. He worked as a storeman in the quarries of Easter Ross and then went to Edinburgh. There he was shocked at the living conditions of the poor. The experience remained with him when he returned to the north and began work in the Commercial Bank. He began writing with much success for the local papers in Inverness.

In 1839 Miller published his *Letter from the Scotch People to Lord Broom*, a biting attack on the practice of landlords imposing their choice of minister on parishes—'patronage'—which had recently been reaffirmed by the House of Lords. This led to Hugh being adopted by evangelicals in the Kirk and so he was invited to Edinburgh to edit *The Witness*. This also gave him scope for his other great interests, paleontology and geology, where his careful work brought original discoveries. In three or four years *The Witness* became the second best selling paper in Edinburgh. He ran the paper initially single-handed and brought it out without fail twice a week. After 1843 it became the paper of the Free Church. His description of what happened at the split in St Andrew's church (now St Andrew and St George's in Edinburgh's George Street) was vivid, one of the best ever written.

The paper's success was not, however, just because of its reporting of church events. Miller wrote incisively of the working conditions of workers both in south-west Scotland and the Highlands, the coming of the railways and the latest political developments. He created a public by his writings, within which evangelicals and then the Free Church itself flourished. In doing so, he attacked the theory that faith can never be squared with science. And he anticipated much of Darwin's thought and integrated it into the newspaper's vision of the whole of life. It was almost instinctive for him to see the biblical account of Creation as a metaphor and as such perfectly compatible with changing scientific views of the world. His *Testimony of the Rocks*—the last volume of essays —is quite magnificent in this regard. It was at least partly to his credit that the Free Church was packed with scientists: Chalmers in 1805 is noted for having pipes installed in his house against the day when gas would be used for heating and lighting.

Hugh Miller married Lydia Fraser, the daughter of an Inverness merchant. Lydia revered her father as a saint, but others thought him a bit of a crook who conned old ladies out of their savings. The Millers lived in the Meadows area of Edinburgh, but as finances improved, thanks to the artifacts Hugh catalogued, they moved to Shrub House in Portobello. It was there that Hugh shot himself. The theory in the late nineteenth century was that Hugh Miller ended his life in despair because he could not reconcile his faith with the findings of science. Not so. His friend, Professor Miller, carried out the post-mortem, finding clear evidence of a brain tumour. There was also evidence of silicosis of the lung.

A final note of tragedy: when professor Miller took the 'suicide' revolver to the famous gunsmith Leslie at the top of Leith Walk, Leslie accidentally shot himself testing the gun. Miller and Leslie were buried in the same cemetery on the same day.

Tragedy apart, Hugh Miller is remembered as a polemicist and social journalist: his scientific work on the sudden bursts of evolution is presently being reassessed as being of real significance; and his witness in and through the emerging media to the cause of independence for the Kirk could scarcely be overestimated.

84

THOMAS GUTHRIE
Preacher of the Ragged School

STATUES of two of the great founders of the Free Church face one another in the centre of Edinburgh. Thomas Chalmers has the open book in his hand—the Bible presumably, but perhaps a hand-book of self-help social welfare.

Thomas Guthrie (1803-1873), however, is represented with an arm around a ragged orphan, illus-trating clearly the practical social campaign which Guthrie led for the poor. He was not content to say, as Chalmers did, that preach-ing the gospel alone would im-prove the lot of the poor.

Thomas Guthrie was the son of a Brechin merchant who later became Provost. Guthrie studied science and divinity at the Uni-versity of Edinburgh and then at

THOMAS GUTHRIE

Paris. He then began as a minister of the Kirk at Arbirlot, but in 1837 he moved to Old Greyfriars, and then to St John's in 1840 (both Edinburgh). He was happily married: in fact, his sons edited his *Autobiography* in the two years after his death.

In 1843 he joined Thomas Chalmers in the great walk-out of the established church which created the Free Church: all the talents he had been quietly nourishing then came to fruition. He founded Free St John's at Castlehill, where the Free Church Assembly still gathers each year. In eleven months of an amazing campaign (1845-46) he raised £116,000 for the building of Free Church manses. His gifts of oratory were outstanding and he used them to great effect campaigning against landowners who did not allow Free Church congregations to worship on their land. Part of his response was to organise rather rickety floating churches moored at the edge of the lochs: thus the church not only survived but thrived!

Guthrie's *Plea for Ragged Schools* in 1847 began a process which ended in his recognition throughout Britain as an expert in dealing with the crime and destitution which resulted from approximately a thousand young people living rough on the streets of Edinburgh alone. Compulsory and effective education *for all* was his ideal, but the founding of 'ragged schools' was for him a first step.

The ragged schools were remarkably ecumenical in concept despite the bitterness of the divisions which had just ripped the Kirk apart. This ecumenism extended to everyone in theory, but in practice Guthrie was not able to extend it to Roman Catholics. This was illustrated very clearly by the controversial establishment of the United Industrial School in Edinburgh (1847-1900). *The Scotsman* at the time recorded Guthrie's speeches which made it clear that no Catholics were on the committees of the ragged schools. Guthrie attacked the Catholic view that the Bible 'was not to be read but through the eyes of the priest.' Any such restriction on the use of the Bible would make his schools 'Popish schools.' In one of the court cases the advocate James Simpson asked Guthrie, 'does the fact Roman Catholics make no complaint give you the right to pounce on them and make them Protestants?' Guthrie in turn accused the Catholics of trying 'to blow out the candle of ragged schools.' 'I shall,' he said, 'bind the bible to the Ragged Schools.'

The United Industrial School had separate religious education for Catholics and Protestants, but Guthrie could not contemplate such for his own school. That apart, however, the work of Thomas Guthrie was of value for improving the lot of every child caught in the poverty trap. It was a very vital part of what proved to be an even wider vision of the challenge to Christians of the problems of the city. This he expressed very forcefully in 1857 in *The city: its aims and sorrows,* and it was a recurring theme in his editorship of *The Sunday Magazine* from 1864 onwards.

Another campaign which may have reflected his Calvinist

narrowness and evangelical insights on man's sinfulness was his role in the pressure which built up to the Forbes McKenzie Act with its severe restrictions on the sale of liquor and Sunday opening of pubs. Closer examination of the extent to which drink aggravated the problems of industrial Scotland at that time would suggest that his fervour was not just moral rigor but real Christian caring.

Autobiography (1874-75), edited by his sons.
Smeaton: *Life of Thomas Guthrie* (1900).

EDINBURGH UNITED INDUSTRIAL SCHOOL

85

ALEXANDER DUFF
The First Kirk Missionary

ALEXANDER Duff (1806-78) was the first official missionary of the Church of Scotland. From when the Kirk in 1796 decided not to support the Missionary Societies, Scots had gone to the mission field with voluntary societies such as the Scottish and the Glasgow Missionary Societies, or with the larger English organisation, the London Missionary Society. Eventually, the moderates and the evangelicals sorted out their differences in the established church and decided to look outwards to foreign missions. A group of seven had arisen as the St Andrews University Missionary Society in Duff's student days due to the dynamic vision and lectures of their professor of Moral Philosophy, Thomas Chalmers. Duff was inspired to offer himself as a missionary by another student who died when still young and thus Duff became the

The YOUNG ALEXANDER DUFF

first missionary to go abroad. The country of India was the call.

He was been born of Gaelic-speaking farming stock at Moulin near Pitlochry in Perthshire. His parents were deeply influenced by Charles Simeon, the Anglican preacher, who on coming to Scotland had grave doubts as to whether he could in all conscience preach in a presbyterian church. Simeon resolved his doubts with the thought that the monarch, on coming to Scotland, would have to worship there.

A 'lad o' pairts', Duff went to study for the ministry at St Andrews where his future work was shaped by Chalmers' view that the centre of the Arts syllabus was the unity of truth. And that this was demonstrated in science, literature and the social sciences, all deriving from God's revelation of Himself in the Bible. Knowing God's teaching would free a person for other knowledge.

Duff's journey to India was eventful. He took a whole library with him, but was shipwrecked—he eventually landed with only two books. The brash young Scot with supreme confidence in his own ideas was resented by many of the missionaries established there, but he impressed the most senior English missionary, William Carey, the father of Indian missions. Duff felt that the vernacular preaching in the bazaars was only attracting a few converts from the bottom or outside of the caste system. He talked of 'planting a mine under the whole citadel of Hinduism' rather than chipping away at the edges. Though he learned Bengali and Sanskrit, he decided to operate by offering a broad-based Chalmers-style education in English. In some ways his approach was negative and patronising to the great faiths such as Hinduism, but in a real sense he took them seriously for the first time.

Duff was remarkably successful because Arabic and Persian had been abandoned by the colonial administration in favour of English. This created a demand for learning English. In addition, there was a group of Hindus unhappy with the burning of widows and other aspects of the traditional faith. Here Duff was able to engage in a dialogue with Ram-mohun Roy. Roy was influenced by the reading of the Koran to see the polytheism of Hinduism as a corruption, and then from the reading of the Gospels to see 'the precepts of Jesus as the guide to happiness.' Through him, Duff was able to get access to Hindu families and fifty high class converts transformed the whole missionary scene. This group produced a number of important Christian leaders, ministers and scholars. In 1843 Duff cast his lot in with the Free Church and so had to start all over again. In 1844 he helped to found the *Calcutta Review* and is honoured still as one of the founders of the University of Calcutta. He was Moderator of the Free Church in 1851 and 1873 and made Doctor of Law at New York University and Doctor of Divinity at Aberdeen. In 1863, however, he had to return to Scotland when his health collapsed. The £11,000 he received as a parting gift he gave to create a fund for invalided Free Church missionaries.

Coming home meant a new beginning. Duff raised £10,000 to endow a chair of 'Evangelistic Theology' at New College, which in itself was a major achievement. He became the first professor and set out to make the chair into the beginning of a new institute for the encounter of Christianity with the other religions of the world. He was not a good professor, however, and rather sadly his vision did not last much beyond his own day. It is only in New College, now within the University of Edinburgh, that his vision is being re-created in a new more radical form.

As for the man himself, he was the best and worst sort of archetypal Scottish scholar, painstaking and dedicated. The most tragic aspect of his achievement, however, was the cost to his family. He was away from home for long, long stretches.

ALEXANDER DUFF in LATER YEARS

Particularly sad was the story of the son meeting the father on his return and being ignored in the railway carriage while his father read the newspaper. Greatness sometimes has too great a cost.

Paton, W: *Alexander Duff, Pioneer of Missionary Education*.

Laird, M A: *Missionaries and education in Bengal* (Oxford University Press: 1972).

Piggin, F S and W J Roxborogh: *The St Andrews Seven* (Banner of Truth: 1986).

86

JAMES BEGG
Happy Homes for Working Men

JAMES Begg (1808-83) was born at New Monkland and made a normal progression to minister of the Church of Scotland in Paisley and then Liberton. After he walked out of the established church in the Disruption of 1843 he gradually rose to prominence in the Free Church, being tipped as a likely successor to Thomas Chalmers as leader of the movement. What is remarkable about Begg is his combination of evangelical zeal typical of the Free Church with commitment to social issues, such as housing, more associated with 'moderate' churchmen and enlightenment values.

By this time Begg was based at Newington in Edinburgh. He was a political radical who supported the Chartists in their belief that democratic reforms were necessary, but he was forthright in telling them that he could give them a better charter. This came directly from his Calvinist convictions. It also came from taking up the mantle of Chalmers, as the Free Kirk itself moved away from social community building to emphasise individual morality and responsibility. His charter stated that self-improvement was the key to a better future and the working class should be helped to do that by education. Here Begg advocated a national system to make the existing state system more coherent and efficient. Working people themselves could contribute to their development by temperance and success at their daily work. Begg's temperance campaign had at least some significant effects on people's attitudes.

It was in advocating municipal and philanthropic housing improvement from 1858 onwards that Begg established his reputation and did his most significant work. In 1861 he helped to set up the Edinburgh Co-operative Building Company whose aim was to build better housing for working people. It built 2800 such houses over 50 years, but eventually lost sight of the original ideal and became a scheme of houses for the middle class instead. A pamphlet in 1866, intriguingly entitled *Happy Homes for Work-*

ing Men and how to get them sums up Begg's: 'The eighth commandment requireth the lawful procuring and furthering of the wealth and outward estate of ourselves and others: thus placing, in effect, our obligation to promote sanitary and social reform on the strongest foundation on which they rest *viz* the direct commandment of God.'

Again in pursuit of God's commonwealth in Scotland, Begg was very much in the vanguard of the National Society for the Vindication of Scottish Rights, being prominent both in debate and pamphlets. One of the aims of the movement was to have a separate Scottish Secretary of State, which of course we still have.

As Begg attained greater prominence, other sides of his character dominated: so much so that his biographer said: 'had he died in 1865 [when he was nearly killed in a railway accident] he would have been remembered well today.' It was partly Begg's outspokenness, and the fact that some of his ideas came to be seen as retrogressive, that led such men as Principal Rainy to describe him as 'the evil genius of the Free Kirk' who did more harm to unity than any other man. This referred to bitter campaigns in which Begg built an alliance with the *Highland Host* newspaper to promote traditional attitudes and resist change. He led bitter attacks on Roman Catholics, publishing a *Handbook of Popery*, campaigning relentlessly. Within his own church he opposed the singing of hymns and the introduction of organs and kneeling at prayer. In church affairs he resisted the moves towards union with the United Presbyterian Church. In this he insisted on the fact that Chalmers had left the established church on the establishment principle. The Free Church saw itself as a shadow established kirk: the true national community kirk. The movement in the Free Church to the voluntarist principle was blocked by Begg and only came about (with union to the Free Presbyterians) after his death. Whatever the judgment on his resistance to religious change, Begg is remembered for his very real achievements.

Smith, T: *Life of James Begg*
Drummond, J and J Bulloch: *The Church in Late Victorian Scotland 1843-1897* (Saint Andrew Press: 1978).

87

NORMAN MACLEOD
'Whole Salvation not Soul Salvation'

THIS famous dictum from the late Lord George MacLeod of Fuinary, which summed up his pioneering work in the Iona Community in more recent times, sums up also the aim of one of his distinguished predecessors in the ministry, Norman Macleod of the Barony in Glasgow.

Norman MacLeod (1812-72) was born into a long line of ministers in Argyllshire. The dynasty of ministers stayed loyal to the Church of Scotland through all the years of disruption. Norman himself, however, was close to and sympathetic to one of the great leaders of the Disruption, Thomas Chalmers. In fact Norman Macleod began his studies for the ministry at Glasgow University, but moved to Old College in Edinburgh to sit at the feet of the exciting Chalmers.

Macleod's first charge in 1836 took him to Loudoun (Newmills) in Ayrshire. Here his instinctive care for the poor did not take him as far as the Chartists and radicals he encountered, for he was a conservative both in church affairs and politics. But that was balanced by real identification with the needy. Amid the drama of the Disruption in 1843, he moved to Dalkeith, still very much with the established church.

In 1857 he took up the charge at Barony in Glasgow where he worked until his sudden and much lamented early death. Not only did his heart go out to the unemployed and poor—with food and entertainment—in this densely populated parish in Glasgow's East End, near the cathedral, but his care extended to the crowds of destitute lying in cellars and under the bridges. He preached day in and day out that you cannot care for the souls of the poor without caring first for their bodies. He visited tirelessly himself and called on the wealthier members of his congregation, particularly the elders, to raise money and visit the poor. He was loved by people from near and far. One story goes that the United Presbyterian minister was called to a poor family when illness struck them. When he ascertained which parish they were in, he asked why they had not sent for Norman MacLeod. 'Oh no,' they said 'he's too precious to invite: he might catch the infection.'

Macleod became Queen's Chaplain in 1857 and later travelled to India to see how they tackled the whole question of mission. He instituted a magazine to be read on Sundays so that the Sabbath would not just be a day for church alone for the poor. From 1860 until his death, he tirelessly edited and contributed to *Good Words* and wrote several books in addition.

It was his care for the poor and the way they spent their Sundays which led to his intervention in the Sabbath Wars. In 1865 the bitter debates about the nature of the Sunday came to a head with the decision of the railways to run trains on Sundays. Street protests led to a dramatic debate in Glasgow Presbytery on a motion to denounce what was happening. Norman Macleod rose to his feet and for three hours spoke eloquently and incisively on the danger of the church confusing the Lord's Day with the Jewish Sabbath. The principles of the Jewish Sabbath could not be transferred lock, stock and barrel to the Christian Sunday. He won the day and they failed to have him condemned the next year at the General Assembly for his stance. Far from being condemned, his stature remained undiminished. Three years later (1869) he was elected Moderator of the General Assembly. He had successfully stood for 'whole salvation' for his poor, rather than a narrow 'soul salvation' which he was convinced was wrong, and which would in any case have left them untouched.

Macleod, N: *Memoir* (1876).

88

DAVID LIVINGSTONE
' ... I presume'

THE greeting used by the American journalist Stanley to greet David Livingstone when he finally located him in the depths of Africa (only to be told 'I didn't know I was lost'!), is somewhat symbolic of the entire story of David Livingstone (1813-1873), the great Scottish missionary to Africa. Wrong presumptions about everything from his marriage ('he could not have loved his wife and left her alone for so much of his life') to his missionary motivation ('he was just a patronising white religious coloniser') have consistently undermined our true understanding of this great Scot.

DAVID LIVINGSTONE

David Livingstone was born of a Gaelic-speaking and skilled working-class family in Blantyre. It is stated on record that he read the Gaelic Bible to his grandmother. David's father left the Church of Scotland to join an independent chapel (later to become a part of the Congregational Church). The young David worked in the weaving sheds, but went to the factory school at night, finishing the day by studying until midnight. Work began at 7 a.m. Such determination enabled him to attend Anderson's College (later Strathclyde University), where the degree course was organised as seven months of intensive study, so that poorer students like David could work the other five months at the mill. Having completed his degree in Chemistry, he then went to London for missionary training and experience at a teaching hospital before returning to Glasgow to sit the Royal College examinations to become a doctor.

The Christian faith came naturally to Livingstone all his days. China beckoned, but listening to the great Scots missionary, Robert Moffat, attracted him to Africa in 1840. A modern presumption has been that he only began to move north in his remarkable journeys because he was a failure in the south. Careful study of an early letter shows, however, that he was immediately attracted by life in the bush. He went by cattle wagon from South Africa into Southern Botswana. He intended only to stay long enough at an established missionary station to learn the language and then head for the bush. At his first base in Botswana he met Robert Moffat and his daughter Mary, whom David was to marry later on. Mary shared David's conviction about the importance of his mission. To the modern observer this may give credence to the view that he was totally inconsiderate to his wife. This was not the case. They loved one another but he had a larger vision. In the pursuit of that vision he stayed for nearly twelve years in what is now southern Botswana and the northern Cape. During this time, however, he made several long exploratory journeys northwards. There he found a dense African population in contrast to sparsely populated Botswana. It was also an area free from the threat of whites stealing the land—the constant threat in the south.

Here Livingstone could try to work out his conviction that missionaries and honest traders together could help the African people develop their country, free from the threat of white conquest. But they would need a way in and the route from Cape Town was far too long. So he spent from 1853 to 1856 seeking a new route in. He went by cattle wagon to northern Botswana and western Zambia (where his cattle died). He continued by foot to the Makololo people on the Zambesi river. From there he travelled to the Portuguese coast of what is now Angola, but Portuguese slave-raiding led him to reject this as a missionary route. Rejecting the offer of a ship back home, he walked back to try the opposite direction. Another 1800 miles took him down the Zambesi and Victoria Falls to Mozambique. A ship gave him passage home where he was presented with a Royal Geographical gold medal, the freedom of Liverpool and Glasgow, and gave the Cambridge University lecture which inspired their famous Missionary Society.

The London Missionary Society had neither the funds nor the other resources to develop the Zambesi valley, so Livingstone accepted government aid and became the leader of the disastrous Zambesi Expedition of 1858-63. He was such a failure as a leader of a white official expedition that it has been asserted that he could not get on with people. He did get on with Africans, however, but his white companions were English, middle-class, mid-Victorians new to Africa. Livingstone was an evangelical working-class Scot who had last lived in Britain in the 1830s. Indeed, as recently as 1851 he had publicly supported Khoi rebels against the Cape Colonial government. His simple belief in the equality of all, irrespective of colour, was a pre-Victorian idea. When in his last years of wandering, trying to find the source of the Nile and report on Arab and Portuguese slaving, he became again a hero in Britain. But it was the Victorian writers' Livingstone that was the hero, not the man himself. It is only recently that the real Livingstone has begun to emerge.

It was individuals like Paraffin Young in West Lothian who were so convinced of the value of his work that they enabled Livingstone to return in 1866 on an expedition to try to find the source of the Nile. He died there with his faithful attendants in 1873.

Livingstone's writings inspired missionaries and geographers: and exposed the trade of the Portuguese slave-traders. His life today is a continuing Christian challenge to the presumptions which still hold back the equality of black and white.

Livingstone, D: *Private Journals 1851-53* (1960).

ALEXANDER PENROSE FORBES
'Slumming it in Dundee'

IT was a long journey from the portals of Edinburgh society to the remarkable scene of 6000 working people filing past the mitred, robed corpse of a Scottish episcopal bishop in the tenements of Dundee. This is the story of Alexander Penrose Forbes (1817-75).

Alexander was born of an aristocratic family who lived in York Place and Ainslie Place in Edinburgh. His father was a judge in the Court of Session in a city in which the legal profession dominated. He was one of the first pupils of Edinburgh Academy and despite his hankering to be a priest, was sent by his father to what promised to be a lucrative career in the East India Company. A year tutoring, followed by studies at a college for Indian civil servants, led to an India posting. But then his health broke down.

The priesthood now beckoned. Four years at Oxford University (1840-44) led to ordination by the Bishop of Oxford, a curacy outside Oxford, and then the slum area of Oxford itself. After a few months in Stonehaven in the north-east of Scotland (his first charge) he went to the radical Anglo-Catholic ritualist parish of St Saviour's, Leeds. Then the influence of the future prime minister, William Gladstone, brought him election as bishop by the seven priests of the Brechin diocese.

DUNDEE'S FAMOUS LANDMARK, the ORIGINAL TAY BRIDGE, which was DESTROYED on 28 DECEMBER 1879 by a FURIOUS STORM

Dundee, with the jute mills taking over from the flax industry, was second only to Glasgow as an industrialised city. Irish immigrants packed the city centre's tenements, mingling with the native labourers. Sanitation was hopelessly inadequate. The wealthy had moved out to Broughty Ferry. By deciding to stay in Dundee city centre rather than in the old medieval See of Brechin, Alexander Penrose Forbes made an unusual decision for a man with such a retiring disposition: it was difficult, but the natural consequence of his faith. Although his aristocratic and Tory background could have been an obstacle to his identification with the poor, they were in fact what made it possible. Instinctively he involved himself far beyond his own Episcopal congregation. He set to work establishing the Agricultural College in Drumlithie for working men, a college for schoolmistresses and became involved with the Free Library Service. Above all, he was the only minister to visit all the patients in the Royal Infirmary no matter their denomination. In 1871 one of his curates was carefully instructed not to go to the fever patients. That risk Forbes took himself, taking ginger biscuits 'to eradicate the scent of infection.'

The popularity this identification brought was to stand Forbes in good stead in the next significant area of his life: a charge of heresy. Forbes was celibate in the tradition of the Anglo-Catholic renewal he encountered at Oxford University. His doctrine was 'high church'. But in ritual he conformed to the prevailing 'low church' practice, warning one priest to leave candlesticks aside until people were ready for them. His conviction that Christian doctrine was the means to bring Dundee's poor back to Christ led to a charge to the clergy about the 'real presence' of Christ in the Eucharist: this led in 1860 to a charge of heresy, ironically brought by a priest who had rivalled him in his election as bishop all those years before. He was tried by other Episcopalian bishops in the Freemasons Hall in Edinburgh's George Street. The papers blazed the word of his possible condemnation for heresy, but in the end the bishops merely admonished him. A petition of 5000 working men of Dundee was one factor of many which insured he remained in office.

Looking back it is clear that Forbes divided the Scottish Episcopal Church, mirroring the divisions in the Anglican Church in England, but he worked for a greater unity with Roman Catholics on the continent. When a group of Roman Catholics split after the 1871 Vatican Council definition of Papal Infallibility within prescribed circumstances, he was active in supporting the establishment of the Old Catholic Church. On his deathbed he learned with deep satisfaction that his diocesan synod had supported those moves.

For an aesthetic man, who read Dante in the original Italian for recreation, and for the aristocrat who shuddered at his 'dark, gloomy house', the legacy of Alexander Penrose Forbes was to point his church back to the poor Christ come to serve.

90

JOHN TULLOCH
Moderately Depressed

JOHN Tulloch (1823-86) is an outstanding example of a deeply religious man who had to struggle with increasing depression all his life, but still bestrode his century as an outstanding broad church theologian and a witness for moderation in both religion and political life.

Born at Dron in Perthshire, he was a son of the manse. His father was a Church of Scotland minister at Tibbermore and he himself, after studies at St Andrews and Edinburgh, became a minister. His first charge was briefly in Dundee just after the Disruption in 1845. This and his next charge (1849) at Kettins in Angus were in the established church, because he was somewhat estranged from the fierce evangelicalism of some of the leaders of what was to be the Free Church, and more attracted to 'moderate' theology, convinced of the value of a close connection between church and state in ensuring Scotland stayed a Christian country.

John's five year rural ministry in Coupar Angus was marked by conscientious and caring pastoral work, but his heart was drawn to academic work. In 1864 he went to St Mary's College, St Andrew's as professor of Theology and principal of St Mary's. In due course he became, by seniority, principal of the whole University giving leadership at a time when it was small and threatened.

The smallness of the University was something he turned to advantage. He taught for six months in the year and studied for the other six months. He wrote a very fine history of theology, specialising in the work of the Divines of the seventeenth century and the Latitudinarians in England. From his studies he rejected the extremism of Anglo-Catholics, traditionalists, evangelical and rationalist unbelievers alike. Fundamentally he believed that Christianity could be defended by reason, and that theology was composed by creatures of time and therefore had to be continually up-dated. In 1876 he was involved in the early days of the Scottish Church Liberal party, but as early as 1862 the same attitudes are clear in his *Address to young men, beginning life.*

A particular area of sensitivity was his desire to convince people that the *Westminster Confession of Faith*—the subordinate standard of faith for the Church of Scotland—was made by men immersed in the conflicts and attitudes of the seventeenth century and therefore was not unchangeable. It would amaze him to learn that the same issue still divides Protestants in Scotland today.

John Tulloch was drawn to Germany and German scholarship, and this formed much of his witness and breadth of knowledge. His Scottish roots remained just as deep, however. This showed itself in his passionate defence of the established Church of Scotland and the principle of establishment. He attacked the views of the voluntaries who maintained that the state connection undermined the independence of the Kirk. His eloquence on this issue at the General Assembly characterised his later years. It looked as if the Liberals (with Gladstone equivocal) were about to disestablish the Kirk, though in fact they did not. Tulloch therefore won his battle, but perhaps his arguments rose above even the issue itself, because they were the reflection of theological balance about faith being both traditional and reasonable.

No article on John Tulloch should conclude without paying tribute to his wife. He was devoted to her and their relationship was a happy one. (One of his sons, Willie Tulloch, became a well-known minister in the west of Scotland). John Tulloch's achievements are in large part due to his wife's support, for the fact is that she kept him going despite his depression. And his extreme sensitivity, which made him desperately upset if he got something wrong, never disturbed his convinced moderation. In that he may well still be an encouragement for those who struggle against similar problems today.

Tulloch, J: *Address to young men, beginning life* (1862).
Oliphant, M: *Memoir* (1888).

91

ROBERT RAINY
'Principal Rainy'

IT is a tribute to Robert Rainy (1826-1906) that he is remembered by his university title, but there is in fact a great deal more to him than his remarkable academic career, bringing intellectual credibility to the newly established Free Church.

Robert was the son of an eminent Scottish physician and went to the University of Glasgow to become a doctor. The Disruption, however, with its immediate demand for a new generation of ministers, attracted him to the Free Church ministry. His first charge was Strathbogie, near Huntly, but he moved in 1854 to the Free High church of Edinburgh. Then from 1862 until 1900 he held the chair of Church History at New College, with the distinction of becoming principal in 1874.

Both in the parish and academic life, Robert Rainy tried to realise Thomas Chalmers' ideal of a 'godly commonwealth.' Here there are divided opinions. Many admire him, but some see him as a sort of 'evil genius' of the nineteenth century, separating the church from the social problems of the time. It was not that he lacked caring and commitment. On the contrary: on occasions like the Rail Strike in 1891, he intervened on behalf of the Railway Union. The problem was that he saw society as a group of individuals, each pursuing self interest and individual salvation. In that sense he adopted a Thatcherite position which found echoes in Britain in the 1980s.

On the positive side, Principal Rainy was dedicated to building up a tradition of academic respectability for the Free Church. He defended Darwin's ideas and their consequences in evolutionary biology. He stood for a scholar's freedom of enquiry into the teaching and study of the Bible. In this regard, he defended William Robertson Smith when the case for his dismissal from his academic chair was brought to the General Assembly, but found him so impossible as a person that he left him to his fate.

In politics, Rainy was a liberal (and indeed a relative of Gladstone). He worked accordingly for the franchise to be increased. The Liberal connection was, however, to be a disappointment. The problem was that in 1872 he became convinced of the need for the Kirk to be disestablished. By 1874 he had achieved an alliance with the United Presbyterian Church for the purpose. The Free Church, he believed, should come to terms with a pluralist society: in that society the church would be most effective if totally free. And disestablishment would enable the church to be at its most effective because it would then be totally free. In addition the way would be clearer to a union of all the Presbyterian churches in Scotland. So Rainy organised a national campaign, tried to get individual Liberal MPs to back it, and used his influence with Gladstone to try to enlist his commitment. Sadly for Rainy, Gladstone decided that Scotland was divided on the issue, so there would be an electoral cost. Thus in 1885 Gladstone pulled back from supporting Rainy's campaign and in 1886 the split in the Liberal Party on the question of Irish Home Rule ended what had been a very close run thing.

In a quite different sphere, major achievement lay ahead. In 1900 Principal Rainy was instrumental in bringing the Free Church and the United Presbyterian Church together to form the United Free Church on the twin pillars of spiritual independence and disestablishment. At the finish, however, this major achievement was marred by the refusal to join in of a minority, mainly in the Highlands. Now known as the 'Wee Frees', this group argued that the Free Church of Thomas Chalmers was based by him on the establishment principle (the 'Godly commonwealth'). On this basis, they gained all the former Free Church property in a House of Lords decision in 1904. Even though there was a more equitable share of property decreed in 1905 by Act of Parliament, Rainy died an exhausted and fairly disillusioned man. He would be pleasantly surprised to know how many still look to him for inspiration.

Simpson, P C: *Life of Robert Rainy* (1909).

92

MARGARET OLIPHANT
A Scots Victorian Feminist

MARGARET Oliphant (1828-97) spent her early days in Haddington, Wallyford and Musselburgh, but most of the rest of her life in
England or Italy. Despite that, it is notable that she stands out in
the nineteenth century, both in person and writing, for her reflection of Scottish values. She was part of a literary tradition which
on the one hand stood back critically against an untidy acceptance of the old Calvinist tradition; but on the other hand, 'by
cocking a snoot against it', stressed the fact that Kirk and minister
—both country and town ministers—represented stability and
security in a time of rapid change.

Margaret's husband was an artist in stained-glass. Although
he remained a somewhat middle of the road craftsman, they did go
together to Italy as part of his career before his early death. From
that time onwards, Margaret emerged as far more than the pious,
good, hard-working, grieving widow she appeared to be at first
sight. In many ways she was the strongest, most brave, most
respected woman of her time: the epitome of the professional
woman long before the modern age. By her hard work as an author
she supported not only her children, but also her brother, a vast
range of in-laws and a remarkable range of lost causes in the
process. Her *Passages in the Life of Margaret Maitland* in 1849
made her reputation, but to keep the wolf from the door (as is
seen in her letters to her publishers, Blackwood), she wrote 99
books slowly and painfully in longhand in the midst of all her
domestic work.

She was of middle height, middling looks and perhaps limited
talent but Margaret Oliphant had great reserves of energy and
application. Her books have certain recurrent themes which reflect
the challenges and achievements of her own life: the lot of women
alone in a society dominated by men; the question of women finding their identity inside and outside marriage; the issue of whether

marriage itself is necessary or the only possibility for women. In other words, can a doctor's daughter or a minister's wife escape the roles society imposes on them?

The Chronicles of Carlingford was set in the Oxford area, where Margaret had gone to ease her family's progression through Eton and Oxford. But the book is packed with Scots men and women and their intrinsic values. Most things in her life—and her novels —fell apart, but Margaret Oliphant persevered. In life and art, men did the talking, but the strength somehow always seemed to lie in the quiet little woman in the background. In Margaret's case it was not, however, a case of grim Calvinist endurance, as it has been sometimes caricatured. Margaret enjoyed her life to the full and spent her hard-earned money accordingly. In fact, it was finances (or lack of it) which took her back to her writing again and again.

One fascinating encounter in Margaret Oliphant's life was with the independent-thinking, independent-living Jane Carlyle in Chelsea. Both women came from Haddington and their common journey together through past and future is surely the subject for a good play.

Margaret wrote to the end of her days and gained universal respect. Her achievements are in history, biography (such as that of Edward Irving) and in seeing Scotland 'from a distance.' She is now recognised, however, for her *Autobiography and Letters*, 1899. The *Autobiography* is a must for anyone interested either in the literature or history of her century. It illustrates her feminism as not just an attitude or a pose, but as a way of life. She was a church-goer who wrote of the inner strength she drew from her faith, but it is the interaction between her own strength of character and the enduring faith of her ancestors which provide the intriguing enigma which has rekindled Margaret Oliphant in present day studies.

Autobiography and Letters (1899).
Williams, M: *Margaret Oliphant* (Macmillan).

93

DONALD MACFARLANE
The Timid Giant

DONALD Macfarlane (1834-1926) was one of those quiet timid men in history who do not seek greatness, but have greatness thrust upon them, responding with a power that had previously been unsuspected. His story lies behind the spiritual tradition which gave birth to Lord McKay of Clashfern's celebrated resignation from the Free Presbyterian Church at the end of the 1980s and the split between those who supported his official attendance as Lord Chancellor at Roman Catholic funeral masses and those who condemned him. The clash of principle was typical of the origins and history of the Free Presbyterian Church —and of Donald Macfarlane.

Macfarlane was born in 1834 in North Uist, receiving most of his education from his farm-manager father and a brother who had trained as a schoolteacher. At the age of 16, he went to the 'ladies school' on the island to study Greek, Latin, Scripture and Catechism in the tradition of the lowland ladies who founded these schools. Donald McDonald was his teacher there, but after Macfarlane experienced religious conversion at the age of 22, he became close friends with McDonald and other like-minded religious people.

Education was his first interest. He became assistant to a man called Donald McDonald as a teacher in the same ladies school. But he eventually decided that his call was to the ministry. For someone with little formal education, this was a long road and a tribute to his commitment. It took ten years for him to qualify, working out his time at the school and then Glasgow University, followed by the Free Church divinity college. In 1876 he was inducted to Strathconan and this was followed by other charges.

More and more Macfarlane became concerned by the changes in the Free Church which seemed to stem more from the pressures of society and not from how things should be. The church was in fact split between those who believed the church should stand still and refuse to change its doctrine or creed (the constitutional party), and those who believed the church had to adapt its doctrines and practices to changing circumstances.

The crunch came in the late 1880s when an attempt was begun to adapt the *Westminster Confession of Faith*, the secondary standard of faith for the church. Macfarlane sat in the background as others shouted out against this. In 1892 a Declaratory Act was brought to the assembly in line with similar acts in the United States of America, Scotland, England, Australia and New Zealand. Macfarlane saw it as an attack on the Calvinist nature of the church and so, in 1983, when the leading opponents stayed silent, the 'quiet timid man' stood up in the hostile assembly and tabled his protest, effectively severing his connection with the church. It was an act of incredible courage for such a man. Donald McDonald and ten of the brightest divinity students followed him. Both ministers were cast out of their churches and had to preach in the open air until a meeting place could be found. Macfarlane was sent to Skye and for five years had to be rowed back to Raasey each weekend to conduct the services.

The numbers who joined the new Free Presbyterian Church is open to debate, but certainly there were many thousands in its power base in the western Highlands and Islands. It was another example of how—for a range of reasons—the Highlands reacted to what they saw as southern liberals interfering with the traditional faith. Donald Beaton observes that 'had they had more ministers, they would have had more congregations.' Some of the ten divinity students went to Assembly College in Belfast with the distinguished Professor Watts, where they scored highly in the examinations. The Highland exile communities in Edinburgh, Glasgow and Greenock also provided power bases. The congregation of Jonathan Rankine Anderson, who had earlier been thrown out by the Free Church, joined the Free Presbyterian Church early on and so also did a whole congregation at Kaimes in Argyllshire where Macfarlane stopped on his way back from the Assembly to Raasey.

In 1903 Macfarlane was called to Dingwall which was, and still is, one of the great congregations in the church. The quiet timid man had given way completely to a public figure whose letters in the press and interventions in the issues of the day made this new Macfarlane a force to be reckoned with. The problems of the Free Church from 1900-1904 in the split and property wrangle over union, gave Macfarlane a very real sense of vindication. It was not just *his* struggle!

Beaton, D: *Memoir, Diary and Remains of the Reverend Donald McFarlane* (Dingwall, Inverness: 1929).

McPherson, A(ed): *History of the Free Presbyterian Church of Scotland* (Free Presbyterian Publication, Inverness: 1973).

94

LORD OVERTOUN
Capitalist Monster or Christian Gentleman?

LORD Overtoun (1843-1908) was born John White of a prosperous upper class industrial family and became Lord because of his services to the Liberal party under Gladstone. He is revered as a pillar of the Free Church of Scotland tradition, but labelled as a murdering monster by Keir Hardie, the Labour party pioneer.

The future Lord Overtoun's father was a senior partner in a chemical factory at Shawfield in Lanarkshire and had been prominent in support for the Free Church at the Disruption in 1843. This support was both in adherence and financially in the massive building operation the Disruption involved.

Overtoun went to Glasgow University, attained an honours degree in chemistry and worked there for a spell with Lord Kelvin before returning to the family factory. In 1884 he succeeded his father in running the business and about the same time succeeded him as convener of the Livingstone Committee which—after David Livingstone's death in 1875—was established to find and support the Livingstonia missions in Malawi. This was one of the best provided mission areas in Africa as a result. Lord Overtoun's role is marked still by Overtoun Institution, one of the best known High Schools in Malawi. At home Lord Overtoun supported the Moodie and Sankey mission to Scotland and built the building in Glasgow to house the Young Men's Christian Association and the Bible Training Institute. He also taught Sunday school right up to his death.

At the union of the Free Church and the United Presbyterian Church in 1900, when the remaining element of the Free Church—despite the overwhelming majority of members going to the United Free Church—won court possession of New College, Trinity College and indeed all the previous Free Church property, Lord Overtoun paid for the lawyers who fought the case and made an immediate donation of £10,000 to the United Free Church.

All this massive commitment fuelled Keir Hardie's attack on Lord Overtoun as a prominent Christian and Liberal politician who could yet appear to condone the fact that 'men are poisoned as they work in his mills.' Everyone conceded that if any employee had a personal problem, Overtoun was only too willing to be approached and to help. His Christianity and his compassion were genuine, but he believed there was an iron law of economics which demanded that in the face of his competitors he could not interfere in working practices to pay for them to be safer without in the process destroying the wealth which everyone needed. Despite Keir Hardie's appeals and the pressure of the growing Trade Union movement, Overtoun refused to bring in the preventive measures which would have stopped poisonous gases getting to the workers and inflicting long-term damage.

Keir Hardie's protest and highlighting of the contradiction were right, but the story of Lord Overtoun is not the story of a wicked exploiting factory owner, of whom there were all too many. It is the tragedy of a genuine Liberal and a genuine Christian who was nonetheless blind to what Christian faith should have made obvious. He died a respected old man, but a symbol of all that was wrong with Edwardian Scotland.

95

WILLIAM ROBERTSON SMITH
Intellectual Colossus who paid the price

ONE of the most intriguing questions in history is how great intellectuals emerge to prominence. With William Robertson Smith (1846-96) the answer lay in his early family background. He was born a son of the manse of Keig in the uplands of West Aberdeenshire. His father was a schoolmaster who gave up his school in 1843 to become a minister of the Free Church in Keig; a dedicated and scholarly man who not only made a name for himself, but raised and tutored his family in an outstandingly scholarly home.

At a very early age William went to Aberdeen University. A brilliant academic career followed in Edinburgh (Chalmers' New College), Bonn and Gottingen. He was offered chairs in mathematics and science in various parts of the world but refused them because as an evangelical Christian there was no worthier career than the ministry. By the age of 25, Smith was professor of Hebrew and Old Testament Exegesis in the Free Church college at Aberdeen with glittering references from leading scholars like Wellhausen and sponsored by A B Davidson.

From the start the new professor applied the critical methods he had learned to his studies of the Bible. Within five years (by 1875) an article of his in the *Encyclopedia Britannica* (under the heading 'Bible') horrified traditionalist evangelicals with suggestions that Genesis was not the oldest book in the Bible and that David had not written all the psalms. A case against him was started in presbytery and slowly rose through synod to the General Assembly. His enemies were a mixture of real hard-liners and devout Christians who felt his news undermined the fact that the Bible was the Word of God. A nationwide debate was instigated on the reliability of the scriptural narratives. The deeply devout and enthusiastically evangelical Smith urged people to 'take off your dogmatic specs and look at the Bible through the eyes of those who wrote it!' He would make the same appeal today.

In the 1880 General Assembly Smith was narrowly acquitted in a case argued out over the book of Deuteronomy, but had a severe warning to behave from the Moderator. The coincidental publication of a new article in the *Encyclopedia Britannica* (under 'Hebrew language and literature') seemed like deliberate defiance, and so in 1881 he was deposed from his chair (although allowed to continue as a minister as long as he did not teach). His departure was partly due to the way he stood up for his principles (Principle Rainy described him as an impossible man) and was ruthless with what he described as 'pious bumblers.' Nevertheless most would see it as a tragedy for the Church of Scotland to lose in this way one of the most outstanding scholars it ever produced.

William Robertson Smith went on to produce such brilliant works as *The Old Testament in the Jewish Church* (1881) and *The Religion of the Semites* (1889). He continued to work as co-editor of the *Encyclopedia Britannica* and was chief editor of what is regarded as its greatest edition in 1887. Meantime he was appointed Lord Almoner's professor of Arabic at Cambridge and in 1886 University Librarian and Adams professor of Arabic.

Smith remains an up-to-date and relevant challenge to attitudes to the Bible in the Kirk today. He was a pioneer of the discipline of 'Religious Studies', an important factor in education today. And yet he remained an evangelical until his death. 'In the Bible,' he said, 'I find God coming to men and speaking to them.' That faith is still the meeting-point of evangelical faith and modern biblical studies.

Balck, J S and G Chrystal: *Life of William Robertson Smith* (1902)

96

MARY SLESSOR
The Red-haired Firebrand

THE Nigerian civil war of the 1960s and 70s brought back into focus the Dundee mill girl Mary Slessor (1848-1915), for the break-away state still held memories of the red-haired white woman who not only brought them Christianity, but identified with their *whole way of life*, becoming for them a living legend. The ultimate compliment was that her memory became encrusted with superstition as well as being inextricably linked with the beginnings of Christianity in that region.

MARY SLESSOR

A Victorian jute mill was not the most uplifting working environment. Mary worked there from an early age at a weaving machine. She came from the sort of broken home which is supposed to erode personality, but with her it contributed to a strength of character which nothing could undermine.

Mary's commitment was not typical of many Victorian missionaries to Africa. It was not an escape from the church here, but rather an opening out of a commitment which was already very real in Dundee. Her characteristic leadership qualities were already evident: she led (at the age of 20) a Bible class for teenage boys in the most run down areas of central Dundee. She was no genteel Christian visiting the world of the poor with the good news of the Gospel: *she came from that world.* It is a remarkable tribute to her minister that he allowed the Bible class to take place at all: Victorian society would have been horrified at the thought of a young working class girl alone with 'all those young lads.'

It was just as well she went to Africa. Her unconventional ways it took her many years to realise her ambition. She was after all a woman: only a few professionally qualified female teachers and doctors had been allowed to work on the missions. Worse still, she had no academic qualifications. Only the sheer force of her personality won the day in 1876 when she was accepted at last by the United Presbyterian Church to work in Nigeria.

After some time in the main mission in Calabar, Mary Slessor went into the bush. Just as she had gone to the poor in Dundee to enable them to achieve respect and a sense of worth, and only then Christian faith, so she went to the poorest villages in Nigeria. There twin babies were seen as a curse from 'God' so she adopted abandoned babies and raised them as her own family. The psychologist—in the light of her early family background—might analyse how readily she took to this sort of motherhood rather than marriage, but that is largely irrelevant in the context of the Christian and human love and courage which enabled her to build such a family out of the rejects of African society, yet still find acceptance herself in that same African society. She clashed with the chiefs but got away with those confrontations in exactly the same way as she got away with her regular clashes with those in the official church structures who oversaw her mission and let her work in such an unconventional way.

On visits home Mary Slessor enthralled the popular missionary meetings which kept support for the missions alive. She died in southern Nigeria on 12 January 1915 while Europe was locked in the throes of the Great War. Biographies afterwards gave her an unreal pious gloss. The challenge today is to get back to her radical enculturalisation and Africanisation of Christian Mission, the qualities she instinctively acquired but which must now become the theory of any conceivable Christian mission. It is best summed up by the petty Government official and the shocked missionaries who held up their hands in horror at the red-haired white woman in bare feet and loose shift, with one of her many black babies on her hip, who emerged from the bush to meet the hooped, booted ladies in stays who stood for the values of an unenlightened era.

Livingstone, W P: *Mary Slessor* (1931).

97

HENRY DRUMMOND
Free Kirker or Free Thinker?

IN 46 short but hectic years (1851-97), when, it has been said, he had no time to get married, Henry Drummond was one of the most outstanding evangelists ever in the Free Kirk of Scotland. He was also a brilliant intellectual builder of somewhat controversial ramparts against Darwin's view that learning about evolution out-dated belief in God.

The city of Stirling retains pride in being Drummond's birth-place, with the Drummond Trust and the prestigious biennial Drummond Lectures continuing to pay tribute to his memory. Henry made his own personal commitment to Christ at an early age with his remarkable uncle Peter Drummond (who sent religious tracts with packets of seed around the world) as his inspiration and encourager. The University of Edinburgh brought him a parallel love of geology and botany, leading to a love of science. Divinity studies were balanced by visits to the back streets and slums of Edinburgh. This resulted in the conviction that 'when Christian-ity shall take upon itself in full responsibility the burden and care of cities, the Kingdom of God will openly come on earth.' Drum-mond looked at Luke 4:16-21 and saw in it Christ's programme for 'the city and the hospital and the dungeon and the graveyard, of the sweating shop and the pawn shop and the drink-shops: think of the cold, the cruelty, the fear, the famine, the ugliness, the loneliness, the pain.'

Moody and Sankey's great mission came to Scotland in November 1873 and Henry interrupted his studies at New College to work with them. Moody became a lifelong admirer and friend.

Crucial decisions had to be made at this time which formed the immense influence he was to have on his own and succeeding generations. Full-time evangelist or back to New College? Then a little later, parish minister, scientist or evangelist? In 1877 the answer came with a post lecturing at the Free Church College,

Glasgow in Natural Science and being ordained as an elder. In 1884 he became professor of the new chair of Natural Science and an ordained minister. In all this he was responding to the crisis of faith which Darwin's *Origin of the Species* (1859) had brought to so many: Drummond's book *Natural Law in the Spiritual World* began rather typically with lectures to working men in the Possil Park mission station which was his charge in Glasgow.

At other stages of his life we find him ministering to a group of miners in Polmont, instigating the Associated Workers' League in London, associated with the Canal Boatmen's institute at Port Dundas in Glasgow and supporting the Boys Brigade and its founder Sir William Smith.

It has been said that Drummond never had the time to marry. His love of children and family was evident, as well as his influence on the intellectual, artistic and political leaders of his day, people like Lord and Lady Aberdeen and Mr and Mrs Gladstone. A sense of duty took him into their circle: his legendary ability to relate with people enabled him to be effective there. His immense status in Scotland spilled over into journeys, at the crossroads of science and religion, to the United States, Canada, Africa, Japan and Australia. When he died in 1897 he was mourned in services throughout the world. Like any pioneer and imaginative thinker he was viciously attacked in his own church but loved by many more.

Henry Drummond is a continuing inspiration for work on the meeting point of science and religion, but also a lesson in the listening which should mark both Christian caring and evangelism. In *The Greatest Thing in the World,* he spoke of love: 'Lavish it on the poor where it is very easy: especially upon the rich, who often need it most: most of all, upon our equals, where it is very difficult and for whom perhaps we do least of all.'

Smith, G A: *The Life of Henry Drummond* (Hodder & Stoughton: 1899).
Stewart, Revd and Mrs F J: *Henry Drummond* (Macdonald: 1985).

98

SIR GEORGE ADAM SMITH
The Historical Geographer of the Bible

SIR George Adam Smith (1856-1942) is most remembered as a historical geographer of Palestine, but he has place equally as a dramatically successful parish minister, a critical or liberal evangelist and the father of a family of distinguished and influential Scots.

Missionary work in India had given his own family a breadth and depth which balanced traditional Free Church evangelical commitment and piety. The quality of his own education and background became apparent with his dynamically successful period of ministry at Queens Cross in Aberdeen (1882-92). But that was not all. During that period he became professor of Hebrew in the Free Church College in Glasgow. Very quickly it became clear that he was an advocate of the same principles as William Robertson Smith in the previous century. He was a critical or liberal evan-

SIR GEORGE ADAM SMITH

gelical, committed to using modern scientific criticism of the literary forms used in the Bible to illuminate the message of the Bible as the Word of God for today as yesterday. He was not, however, as contentious as Robertson Smith, and so when he and another Free Church scholar were attacked, the persecution fell at the last fence (General Assembly) when it tried to destroy him on the basis of his book on criticism and preaching of the Old Testament.

Attention to detail has made his historical geography of Palestine a book to remember. It was used by Allenby in the Great War, and the distinguished historian Professor A Cheyne recalls how he sat on the top of the mountains of Central Palestine and used the same book to identify the biblical locations. It made the Bible come alive.

In personal terms, Smith was a small, not particularly impressive man to meet. However, far from being a remote academic, he was a very practical and efficient administrator and a man who loved his family. One son came to teach in the University of Edinburgh and is better known now as Lord Balerno. Another is Alec Buchanan Smith, the well known Member of Parliament, and two grandsons were to become ministers of the Church of Scotland.

Many of his former students were to remember his lectures with gratitude. The cloud of official suspicion did not affect them, for his liberal use of modern insights had become very much the accepted way to deepen biblical appreciation and understanding. It was only after World War II that American influence and imported literature—and the pressures of an uncertain world—led to a resurgence of what are loosely described as fundamentalist or conservative biblical views. This would sadden and surprise George Adam Smith a great deal.

The later phase of his life was a series of important recognitions of both his scholarship and biblical commitment. From 1901, he was principal of Aberdeen University. During the Great War, he emerged as something of a 'sabre-rattler', an eloquent propagandist for the justice of the cause of the Allies against Germany.

George Adam Smith was knighted in 1916 and was elected Moderator of the General Assembly of his church. Among his books too, the commentary on the book of Isaiah was a classic of his time and has since been used by generations of scholars and preachers. Quality endures.

Smith, L A: *Life* (1943).

99

GEORGE JACKSON
'For the Making of Good Men and Women'

GEORGE Jackson (1868-1914) had a simple and direct approach to his main years of Methodist ministry in Edinburgh. He was there 'for the making of good men and women.' John Wesley's octagonal chapel, built in the Low Calton in 1766, had been pulled down when the General Post Office was erected. The Nicholson Square church was opened in 1815. However, in 1888 George Jackson was called straight from his native Yorkshire and theological college to open a mission right from scratch in the new villas and tenements of the West End of Edinburgh. He was only 23 years old.

At first his discussions with the small committee from Nicholson Square pointed in the direction of opening a church in a couple of rooms in a tenement. Realising that this might be small-minded and limiting, they thought bigger and managed to hire a crude building called the Albert Hall in Shandwick Place. The invitation in November 1888 was revealing. It meant all seats were free: that cut through the system of pew rents in the established churches where others had to queue for the few free seats. Second, there were free hymnbooks, a competent chorus and a soloist. Third, and most importantly, it introduced a regular evening service to Edinburgh for just about the first time. This was designed to meet the opportunity presented by the increasing practice of girls in domestic service leisurely promenading along Princes Street on their Sunday afternoons off. One of the older members of Methodist Central Hall recalls how some of the parents only allowed them to join in this practice on condition they were going to listen to Jackson, and related: 'I remember how in later years, when "the little one" had become a thousand, older members would lament the loss of the "happy family" feeling that marked those first days.'

Numbers rapidly built up for what Jackson was offering. He

made it clear that he was not trying to steal people from other denominations: 'Christ's army is none the stronger merely because a hundred of his soldiers are persuaded to change their regiments.' And so in 1890 George Jackson's series of sermons on Judas Iscariot were crowded out. The next step was to rent out the United Presbyterian Synod hall with accommodation for 2000 people. It was well and truly filled.

The turn of the century saw the establishment throughout Britain of Central Methodist halls as dual-purpose centres of mission for the city centres. The building at Tollcross fitted in to that pattern, but was a massive act of faith on the part of George Jackson. He felt crushed by the initial difficulties of raising the necessary £52,000 and finding a site: 'The years were slipping by, and if all the doors remained closed against us, I could only regard this as an indication that my work in Edinburgh was done.' He had to travel the country appealing week after week. Eventually, with the help of St John's Episcopal church school and a generous baker, a large enough site was found. The success of the enterprise was regarded as being due to the sheer preaching force of George Jackson.

The dual-purpose building opened with only half the money raised, but it built up a membership of 1700. He had a cinema before they became common in the city: feature films were shown, and when J Arthur Rank started producing religious films, these too were shown. It was a centre for a largely artisan and lower middle class congregation along with the working people of the Tollcross area. The building throbbed with every sort of conceivable activity.

George Jackson never enjoyed robust health and in the autumn of 1905 he suffered a major breakdown. He resigned in 1906 and worked for seven years in a Toronto city centre pulpit. Here a problem came to a head that had been rumbling on in Edinburgh. Jackson had taken advantage of being in Edinburgh to familiarise himself with new scholarship about the Bible (which he often set side by side with the local newspaper!) and to integrate this into his preaching. In Toronto he spoke at the Young Men's Christian Association about Genesis and Creation and was publicly opposed by the fundamentalists. Undeterred, however, he carried on.

But when he came to England to teach in the Didsbury Theological College in Manchester, Jackson was charged with heresy. Brought before Conference for not teaching the true doctrines about Jesus Christ, he was exonerated from the main charges, although it was said that he had not expressed himself wisely and judiciously. However, the stigma hung over him. It is certainly a tribute to his strength of will that he continued teaching nonetheless. At the end of his time, his legacy to Edinburgh was not just a building, but a preaching style and a courageous commitment to both the Bible and to the people.

Hill, M: *For the Making of Good Men and Women* (Edinburgh Council of Social Service: 1988).

100

MARGARET SINCLAIR
'The Scaffie's Daughter'

IT is said that you can tell a lot about an era if you know about its heroes or heroines. Therein lies the significance of Margaret Sinclair, a scaffie's daughter from Blackfriars Street, the Cowgate, Edinburgh. Born at the turn of the century, she worked at french polishing and then in a biscuit factory before becoming, at the age of 23, an extern nun with the Poor Clares in London. The Poor Clares in Liberton, Edinburgh did not have a place for her at the time.

The last nine months of her life with the Poor Clares was spent in a sanatorium at Warley, dying slowly and painfully from tuberculosis of the throat. Her life seems perhaps undistinguished until we consider that soon after her death, Margaret Sinclair became acclaimed as a saint by Roman Catholics in England, Japan, Canada, the Netherlands, and the United States, as well as in her native Scotland. She was declared 'Venerable' (which means that her candidature as a saint has been officially recognised) after a painstaking investigation which began officially in 1952 with a long interrogation of witnesses to the nature of her life in the city of Edinburgh.

It would be easy to dismiss this as saying more about the 'saint-oriented' spirituality of twentieth century Roman Catholicism as it struggled to establish its credentials in both social and religious terms in Scotland. But to do so would be to miss many small but significant aspects of the short life and character of Margaret Sinclair, aspects which have made her both attractive and which have contributed to her significance.

She stands at the crossroads of a Roman Catholic spirituality which could only see its high points in religious life or in the priesthood. Thus her case was not pushed by the Poor Clare order which she entered so briefly, but by a series of priests who found in her what they preached about to their congregations: and these 'heroic virtues' were *lay* rather than *religious*. The Jesuit priest Father Agius, who was her spiritual director during the period when she agonised over breaking her engagement and entering the convent, advocated that she be declared a saint on the basis of what he knew of her life *before* entering the Poor Clares as an extern sister.

What all the witnesses testified to was a personality of immense kindness, sensitivity and the ability to enjoy life. Margaret Sinclair emerged triumphantly over the sort of social and family pressures which cause the 'cycle of deprivation', with all its crushing effects on the human spirit.

Margaret's mother, for instance, turned to drink under the pressures of poverty, eight children and a husband and son fighting in the Great War. She routinely battered Margaret who stood up to the beating, saying: 'Hit me if you must but dinna gie in tae the drink.'

Margaret confided her own nightmare fears of being made redundant to her father, who in turn learned from his daughter how to listen to the heartbreak of one of his own workmates.

A neighbour spoke of Margaret promising to pray for her at morning mass and lunchtime prayers in the church nearest the factory: the neighbour recalled Margaret Sinclair's shining eyes, her lovely hair and her warmth.

Margaret nursed a schoolfriend with tuberculosis until the girl died. The night before, in an act of selflessness, Margaret quietly slipped the girl's mother her own Christmas present money.

Margaret's sister told how Margaret, in an age when daily communion was only beginning, explained to her that 'you don't go to Communion because you're good but *to get the help to be good.*'

The arrogant Mother Superior of the Poor Clares tried to crush Margaret's Scottish spirit by deliberate cruelty. She mocked her 'coarse speech and manners'. She complained when Margaret was frightened to sing before the whole community. She raged unreasonably at the girl when Margaret thought it impossibly funny to be asked, as a test of obedience, to plant cabbages upside down. And, perhaps worst of all, she condemned Margaret for 'dozing' at prayer at the very time when Margaret's illness had finally been revealed to the Mother Superior.

And finally we have the priests, sister, nurses and scullery girls all inspired by the courage of Margaret's nine month ordeal, dying in agony from the tuberculosis. (Another story is told how during those months a bee stung her at the back of the throat. The pain must have been almost unbearable.)

Margaret Sinclair nailed once and for all the lie that twentieth century social deprivation inevitably limits the development of human potential. The acknowledgment of this 'incarnated grace of Christ' by modern Scottish Roman Catholicism, witnesses probably both to the strength and to the struggle of the whole community.

Sacred Congregation for the Causes of Saints (Rome: 1965).
O'Brien, F: *The Cheerful Giver* (St Paul Publications: 1989).

101
ERIC LIDDELL
Running for God

ERIC Liddell (1902-45) could have been described as having been running for God all his adult life. He holds the unmatched distinction of having won the Crabbe Cup as the outstanding athlete of the Scottish Amateur Athletic Games in 1921, 1922, 1923 *and* 1924: and of course he won the gold medal and fame in the Olympics (the inspiration for the film *Chariots of Fire*) when he stood down from the 100 yards, his strongest event, because he would not run on a Sunday for his own glory or even his country's. What is not so well known is that this 'running for God', to borrow St Paul's metaphor, took Liddell away from his Scottish evangelical work to an amazing life of mission work in Northern China.

ERIC LIDDELL

Eric's father was a London Missionary Society missionary in China. It was round about the age of ten that Eric and his older brother came here to Scotland and were educated at Eltham College, an English non-conformist public school originally established by the London Missionary Society. In the year above him at school was another outstanding athlete L G Gracey. Both played together in the rugby team and continued their partnership for Scotland no fewer than seven times, although of course it was in athletics that Eric became the sort of cult figure who attracted massive crowds wherever he went. Despite that, he remained genuinely modest and unassuming, and got on well with the other athletes.

He had a dead-pan sense of humour which was only part of a remarkable personality which had people falling in love with him, even starting fan clubs.

Side by side with his athletic career he gained a Chemistry degree at the University of Edinburgh. It was also the beginning of his missionary work. The famous evangelist D P Thomson came from Drymen, as did Liddell's father, so he approached Eric to preach at evangelistic meetings. The first was in 1923 at Armadale's Miners Institute. Despite the fact that he was not a particularly good speaker, Liddell's popularity went from strength to strength at such meetings.

It should be remembered that he needed all the strength of his Christian convictions in that famous decision not to run in the Olympic hundred yards. Newspaper headlines described him as a traitor to his country: the Prince of Wales tried to blackmail him into changing his mind. But that sort of pressure eventually gave way to adulation when he won the gold for an event he was given no chance in.

Only a few days afterwards Liddell graduated and went on from there to a year's study at the Scottish Congregational college before heading for China to teach in a college in the town of his birth.

He continued, when he had the time, with his running but refused to train at the expense of his work. Despite that, he was told he could win the 800 yards in the next Olympics. He was tempted but he did not go in the end because it would interfere with his work.

Liddell was ordained in 1932 and, despite the Japanese invasion of China and the pleadings of his colleagues, he began work as a District Missionary out there. The study of those days is a film in itself for Liddell showed incredible courage crossing backwards and forwards across no-man's land to visit the Christian enclaves.

Pearl Harbour brought the Allies into the War with the Japanese, but in the period between the attack and internment, Eric ensured that his wife and children were able to leave for the safety of Canada (the country where his wife originally came from). He, in the meantime, stayed with his people and was interned.

There he was one of the few missionaries to escape the criticism of even the most cynical. For, from both the perspectives of Christian teaching and as an incredible inspiration and organiser of young people, Eric was again a winner. While he had resisted all pressure to run on a Sunday for glory, during his interment he at first refused to organise the games on a Sunday, but set aside his principles when some of the young people were hurt fighting during the unsupervised games.

And when everyone was shunning a White Russian prostitute, Eric was the one who treated her no differently from anyone else, even putting up shelves for her and ignoring what people might say.

A brain tumour brought his death shortly before liberation, crucifying him in his last days with distress, depression and self-doubt which had been foreign to his nature. Even then, however, he never allowed it to affect others. He held on 'to win the prize.' A memorial in China today is only a small testimony, but still a quite remarkable one, to his continuing inspiration.

Magnusson, S: *The Flying Scot* (Quartet).

102

JOHN WHEATLEY
Irish—and what's worse, a Catholic!

JOHN Wheatley (1869-1930) learned to smile at the abuse that he was Irish—and what's worse, a *Catholic*! Many felt that it was the memory of Keir Hardie's attitude to John Wheatley being a Catholic which led to Wheatley's rejection as the successor to Ramsay McDonald as leader of the Labour party, when other factors seemed to point to him as the natural choice: and it was also an issue which was to destroy Wheatley in court. The irony was that he needed greater endurance a lot nearer home, in the fifth pew of his own Catholic church in Shettleston to be exact, where a certain Father Andrew J O' Brien ranted and raved about him before every election for betraying his faith by being a Socialist.

Wheatley was only Irish by birthright: he was born in a small village in Waterford in southern Ireland. Soon after, his father moved to become a miner in Bailleston, an area of high unemployment and poverty near Glasgow. His childhood memories of living in a single-end cottage with seven brothers and sisters—and a lodger to make ends meet—etched themselves into his character. The lavatory, shared with other families, was forty yards away and became a symbol for him of his commitment to better housing conditions for the poor.

At school Wheatley's bright intelligence responded to an amazing Dutch missionary priest, Father Terkin, but survival meant going down the pit at the age of twelve. He continued to educate himself, however, walking the ten miles to Glasgow and back for classes two evenings a week after work. He worked in a shop in his spare time, then started a greengrocer's business, became a reporter and then advertising agent for the *Glasgow Observer* and *Catholic Herald* before finally starting a publishing and advertising company and publishing the *Glasgow Eastern Standard*.

Political involvement began with his roots in the United Irish League, but his remarkable uniqueness stemmed from a twin visionary outlook. He founded the Catholic Socialist Society in 1906 in a lifetime commitment to convince the sceptics in the Roman Catholic Church that socialism was not the enemy of Christianity, but the logical conclusion. Parallel with this insight, he saw clearly that a immigrant community could not find acceptance in Scotland by staying in a self-interested ghetto: it could only do so by taking the risk of standing side by side with all those who were committed to making society more just. To that end he moved from the United Irish League into the Independent Labour party, despite becoming in the process the victim of vicious campaigns by certain of the clergy. At the end of the day they failed to get the hierarchy to condemn him and his arguments won the day. In doing so he not only inspired public figures, like his nephew and namesake Lord Wheatley, to rise to the very pinnacle of Scottish society, but also gave hope to the ordinary men and women he fought for all his life.

At first, however, it was a lonely road. Though he was a quiet, shy man who cared about every single employee, and began on the streets selling pamphlets for a penny on subjects like *How the miners were robbed*, Wheatley was drawn into public life. He became a Lanarkshire county councillor, and then represented Shettleston on Glasgow city council from 1912 onwards, even though Father O'Brien so inflamed his congregation that they marched as a mob on Wheatley's house, burning an effigy of him and howling hatred. John Wheatley brushed aside those who feared for him, saying, 'I know those people, they are my people.' He quietly walked to the bottom of the garden and said, 'Don't be daft, go home.' They did. In the *Forward* he appealed, 'If I am an enemy, am I your only one?' He spoke of God's gifts of good housing, food and living standards: 'These gifts of God have been stolen from you.' He went from strength to strength, becoming a folk hero during World War I by fighting the evictions of the families of serving soldiers. He was elected to Parliament and became Minister of Health in the first Labour government, where he took his housing expertise onto the wider scene. His 1924 Housing legislation established the whole pattern of local authority housing which so transformed the housing of the poor this century.

His enemies had their last fling by trapping him into a libel action. It was part of a vicious anti-Catholic campaign fuelled very directly at that time by the Church of Scotland. It was some six months after the crushing loss of this libel action that he learned from a woman juror what had happened. The foreman of the jury addressed them, saying that Wheatley had a good case, but 'Don't forget that he's an Irishman, a Catholic and an Socialist: and our King and Queen are in Edinburgh this week.'

Wheatley died of influenza, a broken man, his illness contracted while waiting for a train at Crewe Junction. His greatness endures to this day but it could have been so much greater. When he was going to quit in 1927, it was Ramsay McDonald who persuaded him to stay on, and many close to the action felt that but for the Irish Catholic prejudice Wheatley would have become leader.

The veteran Red Clydesider and atheist Harry McShane went on record in the early 1980s, saying that John Wheatley alone could have averted the split in 1931 which finished the Independent Labour party and damaged the Labour movement for a generation. Nonetheless, in many Roman Catholics, like his nephew Lord Wheatley, John Wheatley's life and work bore an immense harvest as the century went on.

Wood, I S: *John Wheatley* (Innes Review 31: 1980).

103

JAMES BARR

Home Rule, Pacifism and Socialism in the Kirk

JAMES Barr (1862-1949) stands firmly in the Free Church tradition, but stands also at the crossroads of many of the major movements in Scottish society in the twentieth century. Home rule, pacifism and socialism in secular life are balanced by the central Kirk argument as to whether its alignment with the state or its independence is the more effective in making Scotland Christian.

James was born on a farm near Fenwick in Ayrshire and progressed from being dux at his local school to first-class honours at the University of Glasgow and a subsequent Bachelor of Divinity. That scholarship must have continued, for he wrote a very interesting *History of the Scottish Covenanters* in later years.

His first parish charge was in 1889 at Johnstone and Wamphrey Free church, followed by Denniston Free church, and finally in 1907 the parish of St Mary's in Govan with which his name is most associated.

Barr began as a very serious young man, very typical of those who joined the Young Scots Society, a Liberal party ginger group highlighting issues such as pacifism, a Scottish parliament and social reform legislation: as well as temperance and the moral and spiritual improvement of the working class.

He was bitterly opposed to the Boer War and this led to a completely pacifist stance by the time of World War I. He was not an active campaigner against the war like John MacLean, but he was a conscientious objector who did not hesitate to defend his stance as a Christian one. He was never picked on for his stance, but allowed to continue his work for the community by his parish duties, his involvement in the school board and his membership of a Royal Commission on Housing.

James Barr's time in Govan made him a social radical. Even before World War I shook everyone's ideas, he can be found inter-

245

vening in an industrial dispute and making representations to the management on behalf of the workers. It was an age when the minister's social prominence led to a natural involvement in politics. Working in Govan led Barr very naturally to a deep sympathy with working people. It is important to appreciate, however, that Christian faith shaped all his Socialist ideas. Theoretically he has been associated with the group known as the 'Red Clydesiders': James Moxton, Thomas Johnston, Mannie Shinwell and George Buchanan in particular—but his socialism was a matter of bringing heaven closer to earth so that the improved social conditions would make Christianity more attractive.

This complex motivation led Barr into the Independent Labour party after the War. He was elected MP for Motherwell in 1924 and stayed there until he lost his seat in 1931. He made—not the done thing—the longest maiden speech ever in parliament, 80 minutes worth, 18 columns in the parliamentary record of proceedings, *Hansard*. It was mainly an attack on the established church of Scotland over the Properties and Endowment bill which was intended to enable the union of the Church of Scotland and the United Free Church of Scotland. This he opposed, being pledged to the voluntarist point of view which said that the church should not be aligned with the state but remain an independent or voluntary coming-together of Christians. He lost out in this political struggle, as he did in 1927 when his Home Rule bill was talked out.

After leaving parliament, James Barr remained politically involved despite all he had suffered. He was in fact chairman of the parliamentary Labour party when it split in 1931 (as a result of McDonald's stance on the national insurance issue) and chaired the final meeting before the split; so there were many disappointments.

Disappointment too surrounded his Free Church connection. Despite his stand, both inside and outside parliament, the union went through between the United Free Church and the Church of Scotland. He stayed outside in the rump that was left behind—the United Free Church Continuing—their first Moderator, and Moderator again in 1943 before retiring from active church and political involvement in 1945. In some ways his is a sad story, but his influence was in many ways much greater than his achievements.

104

JOHN WHITE
A Man of Contradictions

JOHN White (1867-1951) stands out among twentieth century Scottish churchmen as a man of contradictions. It is the case either of a man who got out of touch with the church he served, or a man whose church abandoned the values he stood for.

John's father was a flour miller in Kilwinning in Ayrshire who died young. John was supported by his mother during his studies at the University of Glasgow. There he benefited from the Neo-Hegelian ideas of Edward Caird before taking up his first charge as parish minister of rural Shettleston in 1893. In 1904 he was in south Leith, but he returned to Glasgow and the prestigious Barony church in 1911. In all these parishes he was committed to Thomas Chalmers' ideal of a caring community which looked after people in every sense of the word. In south Leith he involved himself in parish visitation, bible club, poor relief, cycling club, boy's brigade, literary society, unofficial employment exchange and Christmas breakfasts for the poor. He had afternoon services for working people and a keen concern for urban deprivation.

That same vision of Chalmers gave White the impetus to become involved in the movement to reunite the Presbyterian Churches of Scotland. The United Presbyterian Church and the Free Church had been united to form the United Free Church in 1900. Then in 1906 negotiations were begun for the purpose of uniting the Church of Scotland and the new United Free Church. White became a leading member of the Church of Scotland committee assigned in 1908 to conduct the union negotiations that were to continue for over two decades. Because the Church of Scotland was an established church, parliamentary acts were required to pave the way to the church union. White proved a consummate ecclesiastical politician, able to manoeuvre the corridors of power in London to gain the necessary cross-party support.

Although a staunch Tory, White gained the respect and co-operation of Liberal and Labour politicians. The high point of his career was the union of 1929 between the United Free Church and the Church of Scotland, an event which he saw as undoing the damage of the Disruption of 1843. Much of his stature had come from his fiercely patriotic stance in World War I. He preached the justice of the war cause and then spent a year as chaplain to the Cameronians in the trenches on the Western Front (August 1915 to September 1916). Men remembered him as a man of great courage, not just conducting burials at the front but, though a man of nearly fifty, carrying the wounded back to safety on his broad shoulders. He was active too on the Church of Scotland commission assigned to consider the 'spiritual and moral meaning of the war' and to help plan post war 'reconstruction' so that the sacrifices of the war would not be in vain.

After the war, White was bitterly disappointed in the 'new world', with its industrial stagnation and party divisions of social class and political confrontation. It was far from Chalmers' ideal of community. As a church leader he tried to mediate between the social classes until the General Strike of 1926 showed this to be unrealistic. Even though he had been one of the leaders in establishing the Church and Nation committee in the Kirk in 1919, White now said it should leave aside social issues and argued against John Baillie and George MacLeod, saying that it should confine its interests to issues of personal morality such as temperance, censorship and sabbatarianism.

However, other aspects of his bitterness were more

JOHN WHITE

damaging. During World War II he argued with George MacLeod on the issue of pacifism and accused the Iona community of being 'a refuge of pacifists.' More sustained, and at first sight contradictory to his work to end divisions, was the way he led the Church of Scotland in the 1920s to attack the Irish immigrant Catholic community as the reason for unemployment and low wages: they were 'taking the jobs of Scots Protestants.' But perhaps it is not all that contradictory, for one way to unite a group is to foster and direct its hatred towards an enemy that can be defined as 'outside the covenant' and made into a scapegoat for all the ills affecting the group. So he launched a vitriolic campaign, arguing to Sir John Gilmour in 1926 that 'the superior Scottish race was being supplanted by the Irish inferior race.' Then after World War II, White turned his attention to a bitter crusade against communism which some believed was a bit extreme.

On the positive side, however, John White's commitment to church extension remained all his days. After the 1929 union and through the 1930s he translated the Chalmers ideal into the building of hundreds of churches in new housing areas, each aimed at being the centre of the new communities. Again in the 1940s, he fought for resources both for bomb-damaged churches and for new ones, despite the difficult financial pressures of those days of hardship and rationing. Here at least there were no contradictions.

105

ANDREW JOSEPH McDONALD
'The Archbishop who relished a Fight'

TYPICAL of Archbishop Andrew Joseph McDonald was his regular presence at the back of a parish church, checking that the local
priest was punctual and competent at preaching and celebrating
mass! Many say that he was also a ruthless but significant influence on major developments in Roman Catholicism in this century.

He was born Andrew *Thomas* McDonald on 12 February 1871
near Fort William, the son of a laird. From the Abbey school and
the Royal High in Edinburgh, he entered the monastery at Fort
Augustus, taking the name *Joseph* as a novice on 23 January 1889.
Studies at Fort Augustus and Bonn University led to ordination as
a priest in 1896. After various monastic jobs in the Fort Augustus
community, he worked in a Benedictine parish and also temporary
postings in secular parishes in Scotland and Liverpool before
returning to Fort Augustus as abbot. There he shook up the abbey,
refounded the school and established three other houses: the two
in America are now abbeys. He was physically very strong. Just
for exercise he swam the mile across the bitter cold waters of
Loch Ness. And, to see if it could be done, he followed—half
running—the 40 mile route taken by Montrose's army along the
mountain terrain parallel to the Great Glen, the route which took
the enemy by surprise and won the famous victory at Inverlochy.

On 24 September 1929 McDonald became Archbishop of St
Andrews and Edinburgh, and immediately shook up the administration after ten years of neglect. It was a critical time. The
1930s saw not just depression but the rise of the Protestant local
government political party in Edinburgh, and the anti-Catholic
riots which caused terrible fear and violent reprisals among
Catholics reacting against the taunts and the hatred. When Protestant orators were calling for blood, McDonald refused to be out-
wardly provoked. Many historians credit him for preventing a
cauldron of bloodshed. Others accuse him, despite letters he sent

to the English papers, of lacking positive leadership qualities necessary to expose the attackers as anachronistic and un-Christian.

Another significant period was his anti-communist invective. He preached with increasing commitment about it being the greatest anti-religious force in the twentieth century. For this he was decried in the House of Commons and threatened with prosecution: nothing came of it. It has to be asked, however, whether his principled stand in this matter, as in others, did more to preserve the social implications of Christ's message or to alienate many miners and unemployed workers from the Church at a time when communism seemed the only means of practical political protest. Might dialogue, instead of proclamation at the pit and picket line, have given the Church a more constructive teaching role?

McDonald's relationship with his clergy is another area of positives and negatives. He was resented as an outsider and for his rigid attempts to discipline 'from above', but admired for the courage and insight which enabled him to send many of his priests to Oxford and Cambridge Universities when this was a brave step from both Catholic and secular points of view. In this he did much to make Catholic clergy both intellectually respectable and equipped for social change. However, again it was left to his successor Cardinal Gray to produce a practical proposal for a national Scottish seminary; and, when this was refused by the West, to provide Scottish training at an East of Scotland seminary at Drygrange. This achieved a cultural identification of the clergy in the East, balancing the input from the continent and south of the border.

In the end it can be said, provisionally, that McDonald achieved much both by his spirituality and by his leading of the Roman Catholic Church in the East of Scotland into intellectual respectability with all the values and dangers of that advance. In administration, his was a strong and intrusive presence, but may have lacked the practicality which comes from partnership. He prepared the way internally for the Catholic Church to come of age and to be equipped for inter-Church dialogue, but it was his successor Cardinal Gray who would cautiously build the real advances. Archbishop McDonald remains somewhat of an enigma, or even in some senses a man of contradictions.

106

WALTER MURRAY
The Kirk and Scottish Home Rule

WALTER Murray (1877-1936) is one of the unsung heroes of the interface between religious faith and political development in Scotland. Both his religious stories and his political stories are challenging.

Murray was born in Glasgow on 9 September 1877 and went to Allan Glen school and then the University of Glasgow. Then he went to Manchester Unitarian college, the University of Manchester and gained a Bachelor of Divinity degree from London. He was ordained to the ministry of the Unitarian Church in Cross Street church in Manchester (1919), and then Chesham Unitarian church, Bury in Lancashire (1921). This was not the end of his spiritual journey, however, for he was next admitted to the United Free Church as a student on trials for licence, and then in 1921 licensed by the United Free Presbytery of Glasgow before taking up a charge at Deerness. The journey comes full circle when he moved first to Olrig in Orkney in 1927, and finally to Torrance United Free Church on 26 September 1929 just before the union of 1929. The union took him into the Church of Scotland until his death on 10 November 1936.

Parallel with this rather intriguing and unusual spiritual journey is a political journey which stemmed clearly from his religious, and then directly Christian, convictions. Murray started in the Liberal party in the Young Scots Society, where the issues were Scottish home rule and a solution to the Irish question. After World War I, however, he joined the Independent Labour party and continued to campaign for home rule. His classic statement of belief can be found in the pamphlet *Scottish Home Rule: the case in sixty points* (Glasgow: 1922). It became the handbook of many in the movement from that point on. Then in 1928 he was a founder member of the National Party of Scotland which was later to become the Scottish National Party. His love of Scottish culture and history became more and more evident at this time: he made no bones about being a keen admirer of Burns. All of this led him during the 1930s to edit the *Scots Independent*, the newspaper of the National party, and to work within the Church for the cause of Scottish independence.

Like James Barr in the Labour party, Murray's faith shows through his political writings in the conviction that people should be treated fairly. His nationalism stemmed from that conviction too, but also from a cultural sensitivity and identification. It was a matter of proper dignity and respect for being Scottish. As late as April 1931 we can see this in a letter to *Life and Work* replying to Sir Robert Bruce, editor of the *Glasgow Herald*.

Another conviction which marked him out from many at the time was the amount of work he put into preventing sectarianism in the National party. Many felt that the concept of a Protestant nation would appeal to the Protestant masses. This was particularly attractive because of the tide of anti-Catholic sentiment which took over the General Assembly at this time. Murray stood against the tide and gave a categorical assurance to Catholics that a separate Scotland would not be sectarian. Murray's deep involvement in nationalist politics had a mixed reaction in the Church of Scotland. It was an age in which ministers had a great deal of choice of political affiliation, and an age in which their position of leadership moved easily into political leadership. The Church of Scotland support today for the 'Claim of Right'—as expressed in the Scottish Convention—is the reflection of the ideas of Walter Murray. He believed in a separate nation balanced by a separate Kirk; but he retained a deep liberal conviction that the Kirk's role in society is not to dominate and govern, but to help and influence. His spiritual journey through the Unitarian Church to the United Free Church and into the Church of Scotland was a journey which retained that conviction.

Murray, W: *Home Rule for Scotland* (Glasgow: 1922).

107

THOMAS TAYLOR
The Builder of a 'Scottish Lourdes'

ALTHOUGH no doubt an exaggeration, a story still exists about the remarkable Lanarkshire priest who built a grotto of saints. It was to these saints that he attributed all the seeming miracles which he himself performed in his daily pastoral work. A generation saw the quiet unassuming, yet dynamic, Monsignor Thomas W Taylor of Carfin (1874-1963) as more of a saint than the saints whose honour he advocated.

Thomas Taylor studied for the priesthood at the legendary rigorous San Sulpice in Paris. While there he was one of the first Scots to visit the shrine at Lourdes, where many Roman Catholics believe Mary the mother of Jesus appeared to the peasant girl Bernadette with a message of biblical simplicity, prayer, fasting and repentance for sin. That message, which came from the French connection, was the great inspiration for the young girl known now as the 'Little Flower'—Therese of Lisieux. She was born in Alencon on 2 January 1873 (the year before Taylor) and died in the Carmelite convent at Lisieux on 4 October 1897 (while Taylor was studying for the priesthood in Paris). Taylor was to become a minor, but significant, actor in the process which led to her speedy declaration as a saint.

The next critical factor in the making of Thomas Taylor was his appointment as a priest to the Lanarkshire mining village of Carfin. It is situated on the long railway route from Glasgow to Edinburgh, deep in the part of Scotland which bears the worst scars of the industrial revolution. His congregation was made up of one of the most deprived sections of the population. In 1920 he went with a group of his parishioners to Lourdes, an experience which in some ways is similar to George MacLeod's experience at Fingleton Mill in 1935 and Iona from 1938 on. Taylor felt that many in Scotland could not afford to journey to Lourdes, so he was determined to build a shrine in Scotland to encourage prayer for the sick, and to give that honour to Mary and the saints which he believed could strengthen the faith of his people. Like George MacLeod,* Taylor also grasped the vision of the basic dignity and self-respect which working on a project like his shrine could give to unemployed working men. The miners' strike of 1921 enabled countless numbers of miners to give their time freely to transform a one acre site of waste ground into a grotto with statues of Mary and Bernadette.

When Father Taylor arrived back from the beatification of Therese of Lisieux in 1923, he was convinced by a spirituality he felt was simple and straightforward enough to help the people he worked with to have lives of prayer. Volunteers from neighbouring parishes, such as Cleland, excavated Our Lady's Lake in the lower grotto: more statues provided more simple stories to illustrate his processions and sermons. He went on to achieve international recognition, writing about a Scots priest preaching seven times in a day in a crowded church in New York and five times in an afternoon to packed congregations in Chicago! Crowds thronged to Carfin, 30,000 for the celebration of the canonisation of St Theresa in 1925. A whole new impetus for the Roman Catholic Church's missionary work abroad came through the papal declaration of St Theresa as patron of the missions, not because she had gone there, but because she had attuned herself in prayer with lonely missionaries abroad. Father Taylor saw that by prayer and money in the Holy Childhood society, his people could learn to be missionary minded—even the young and the sick. Yet another spiritual revolution among Roman Catholics in the twentieth century was symbolised by the 35,000 Scots schoolchildren and teachers who gathered on 9 June 1951 to honour Blessed Pius X, the Pope who made it clear that communion was not a reward for being good but a daily path to goodness which even children could embark on.

Monsignor Taylor—as he was then—led his last procession at his beloved Carfin Grotto on 8 December 1962, celebrated his last mass on 11 December of that year and died at the age of 90 on 1 December 1963. As a symbol that his work goes on beyond the thousands who were transformed by meeting him at the Grotto which became his life's focus, the chapel of the Glasgow Garden Festival of 1989 was moved to Carfin. It was to be called 'Star of the Sea', but as it was being built the 'Maid of the Sea' jet was tragically blown up over Lockerbie. The chapel was renamed 'Maid of the Sea', yet another in so many symbolic calls to prayer in Thomas Taylor's legacy to the Scottish Church.

McGhee, S: *Monsignor Taylor of Carfin* (Burns & Oates: 1972).

* *Lord George MacLeod of Fuinary was alive and active when* GOD'S PEOPLE? *was finalised. Otherwise his outstanding contributions to Iona, the Iona Community, and the cause of world justice and peace would have been included. Ronald Ferguson's biography* GEORGE MACLEOD: FOUNDER OF IONA COMMUNITY *makes that clear.*

108

JOE HOLDSWORTH OLDHAM
Christians together to change the World

JOE Holdsworth Oldham (1874-1969) has been described by Dr Andrew Ross of New College, Edinburgh as the 'most influential Scottish Christian in the twentieth century.' He pioneered new attitudes to black Africans, helped lay the foundations of the Ecumenical movement, and galvanised influential groups of Christian lay people to take their faith out from the church into world affairs.

He was born in Bombay, his father a colonel in the Indian Army. When his father retired early to Scotland, Joe was educated at Edinburgh Academy before taking a degree at Oxford. He intended to enter the Indian civil service, but experienced conversion at university which sent him to India with the YMCA (1897-1901). There he lived in Lahore—an Indian among Indians on an Indian level of salary. This marked him for life. Illness forced him back to Scotland where he completed ministerial training at New College for the United Free Church. Although not ordained, after being licensed to preach he served as assistant at St George's West, Edinburgh.

Out of the blue he was asked in 1908 to be organising secretary of the International Missionary Conference at Edinburgh in 1910. This, the most international and ecumenical Protestant gathering thus far, propelled Oldham onto the international stage where he remained for his entire life. It was the first such conference where Christians from Africa and Asia were present in a significant way.

The next platform for his work was his editorship of the *International Review of Mission* (1912-27). This was started by the 1910 Conference which also planned the creation of a permanent International Missionary Council. The Great War intervened, delaying the inauguration of the Council which did not emerge until 1921. This Council, with its international conferences, played an important role in forming modern ecumenism, finally merging with the World Council of Churches in 1961.

As secretary of the International Missionary Council and also of the British Council of Missionary Societies, Oldham became the central figure in attempts to affect the British government's colonial policies. An early achievement was the ending of forced labour in Kenya in 1921. Oldham had an important role in shaping the era's most important statements on African policy: the Devonshire declaration of 1923. This stated that in any territory north of the Zambezi, the British government should always put the interests of the indigenous African people first. Another vitally important intervention was over the call by white settlers for the merging of Northern Rhodesia, Nyasaland, Tanganyika and Kenya in a new 'white' Dominion. Oldham played a key role in the Hilton Young commission's finding against the idea and the ensuing controversy in parliament which was not resolved until 1930.

Another important year in the story of Joe Oldham was 1934, for he became and remained secretary of the Life and Work movement right up to its merger into the World Council of Churches in 1948. Its inter-Church and international work, to do with the areas of Christian concern about justice, economic development, opposition to Fascism and the challenge of Communism, was matched by his foundation of the Christian Frontier Council, an organisation of expert lay Christians who met regularly to discuss how their professional tasks and their Christian faith were related.

Oldham was also a popular, effective writer. In 1916 his book *The World and the Gospel* ran to 100,000 copies. It contained profound material for thought, presenting this challenge to a world shocked by the Great War: 'The greatest problem facing civilisation is whether the African people will find a way of life that is theirs or end up being the servants and tools of others.' In 1924 his best-selling *Christianity and the Race Problem* described race as the major problem facing the world.

His ideas appear moderate and at times commonplace today, but in their time they were profoundly challenging. In so many areas of social thought, when we look for the origins of its development, we find Joe Oldham.

Article on 'J H Oldham' in the *Dictionary of National Biography*.
Oldham, J H: *Christianity and the Race Problem* (1924).

109

THE BAILLIE BROTHERS
'Brotherly Inspiration'

ONE of the most fascinating things to speculate about in twentieth century Scottish life is the intellectual interaction between the brothers John and Donald Baillie (John 1886-1960: Donald 1887-1954). Between them they have shaped many of the great ministers still living and working today.

They were born of Gaelic-speaking parents in the Free Church manse of Gareloch, but their father died when they were small and the Gaelic influence waned when they all moved to Inverness. Both grew up to become distinguished graduates in Edinburgh's well-known philosophy faculty and then in New College, the United Free Church divinity college. At this stage their paths diverged, but the relationship must have remained active.

After a spell with the Young Men's Christian Association in France, John went to lecture at Auburn College in New York (1919-27); Emmanuel in Toronto (1927-30); and Union Seminary in New York (1930-34) where he joined a galaxy of stars including Reinhold Niebuhr and Harry Emerson Fosdick. By the time John Baillie came to the chair of Divinity at New College in 1934, and right up until his retirement in 1956, he had earned the reputation of being one of the finest theologians in the English speaking world. He was able to place his students in key positions in theology faculties around the world, and in 1954 he was one of the presidents of the World Council of Churches at Evanston.

By strange coincidence Donald Baillie also moved to a chair of Theology in 1934. This was at St Andrews University and it was to be Donald's task for most of his life. His route to the chair of Theology was quite different from John's. This was partly due to his indifferent health. Regardless, his previous pastoral involvement undoubtedly made his academic work more practical. It also must have influenced his brother. Donald was a minister in the United Free church in Kincardineshire from 1919 to 1923: St

John's in Cupar (1923-30) and St Columba's, Kilmacolm (1930-34)

Both Donald and John wrote beautifully and stylishly in clear lucid language. John wrote much more than Donald, however, with standard books such as *And the Life Everlasting*, *Our Knowledge of God*, and *Sense of the Presence of God* (his best book, taken from the Gifford Lectures). He was a liberal theologian who was deeply influenced by the continental theologians, Karl Barth and Emil Brunner, but left aside the rigid restricting categories to adapt a position which could be described as liberal orthodox. It could be summarised as making him a fairly commonsense thinker who never lost sight of the personal relationship with Christ which all Christians are trying to speak about. This he outlined in his *Diary of Private Prayer* which has been translated into a number of languages (including Japanese) and is still used for ministers as a manual of Spiritual Life. With his brother, he believed that the insights of Bultmann, Tillich and Bonhoeffer had to be integrated into a synthesis which would balance out the 'liberal' theological movement.

Donald wrote less, but produced one of the most important books of the century in 1948—*God was in Christ*. It attempts to balance those who overstress the divinity of Christ and those who undervalue it at the expense of the humanity of Christ. His particular theme uses the paradox of grace (God's bit and our bit!) to parallel and illustrate the person of Christ. This led him into prominence in the Faith and Order aspect of the World Council of Churches.

Both Donald and John therefore found in their own theology the motivation for pioneering work in the movement towards Christian Unity. John was one of the signatories of the ill-fated Assembly report on 'Bishop's in the Kirk' in 1957, and both, while sad today about the collapse of the proposed bringing-together of Anglicans and Presbyterians, would be convinced that Churches, being true to the Lord Jesus, will bring eventual unity.

Macquarrie, J: *Twentieth Century Religious Thought* (SCM: 1971).

110

ARCHIE CRAIG

'The Prophet is never appreciated in his own Country'

Dr Archie Craig (1889-1985) was for many years the prophet and pioneer of Christian unity in Scotland. Born at Kelso, he was first inspired by the vision of Christian unity when studying for the ministry at Edinburgh University. His time as a student coincided with the famous 1910 World Missionary Conference which is reckoned to be the beginning of the modern ecumenical movement. A close connection with Joe Oldham, one of the founding fathers of the British Council of Missionary Societies (which was to lead to the British Council of Churches), continued through Craig's experience of World War I (where he won the Military Cross) and during his first parish ministry at Galston, Ayrshire and his post as the first full-time chaplain of Glasgow University.

Craig's most significant formative impact on British ecumenical life began with his appointment as the first general secretary of the BCC in 1942. Stories abound about his pioneer work in England and Wales from his London base. Personally Craig was saddened that the Church of Scotland was less committed to local ecumenical ventures, and was sometimes quite resistant to his vision of organic unity among the British Churches.

At one point he narrowly missed being killed by a flying bomb and did so only because he was late for a meeting. Mainly, however, the excitement was of a less dramatic nature, but *excitement* is probably the right word to describe what people were experiencing in the 1930s and 40s along the road to Christian unity.

A major achievement from 1939-1946 was the series of 'Religion and Life' weeks organised over the country, which became the basis of many local ecumenical ventures. The central theme was the relationship of the Church with the modern world; in that context, the differences between the Churches seemed to Craig less important. But again the Kirk's home board stood apart, claiming that the work was not appropriate in the Scottish context.

In the two decades after World War II, Craig became more deeply disappointed with Scottish attitudes to Christian unity, but never gave up hope or energetic involvement. He began with a year as associate leader of the Iona Community, showing evidence of his deep respect and admiration for Lord George MacLeod. The next appointment went one stage further: he became lecturer in Biblical Studies at Glasgow, not in the divinity department, but in the arts faculty. It confirmed his conviction that the Christian faith should be moved out from the constricting confines of the institutional churches. Although at times Craig saw the Kirk as a 'repulsive institution', he always he cared for it passionately.

In the 1950s Craig worked with immense conviction as convener of the Inter-Church Relations Committee of the Church of Scotland. The proposals for new more open-ended structures in what came to be caricatured as the 'Bishops Report', were thrown out, both in principle and actual formulation. He resigned.

Retiring in 1957, Archie Craig went to live in Doune, Perthshire, partly to be near Churches' House, Dunblane to carry on his work for Christian unity. Despite the fact that many were disturbed by his committed pacifism from the 1920s onwards, and irritated by his anti-clericalism and scathing condemnation of ministerial cant, Craig became more and more appreciated for the outstanding Christian he was. At 6' 2" he towered over gatherings, but came across as a warm caring person who interested himself totally in other people, be they 'important people' or 'little people.'

As Moderator of the General Assembly in 1961 he had a spectacular year in office, making historic visits to Pope John XXIII in Rome and Eastern Patriarchs in Jerusalem. In his later years, more and more people journeyed to seek his advice. They found a man with a deep sense of humour who attacked any suggestion that Christian faith and real life are not compatible. He was open in dialogue to everything in the world and sensitive to the riches of art, literature and music. A man for all seasons?

Templeton, E: *God's February* (British Council of Churches: 1991).
Small, M: *Growing Together* (Scottish Churches House).